Froissart Across the Genres

Froissart Across the Genres

Edited by
Donald Maddox and Sara Sturm-Maddox

University Press of Florida
Gainesville · Tallahassee · Tampa · Boca Raton
Pensacola · Orlando · Miami · Jacksonville

Copyright 1998 by the Board of Regents of the State of Florida
Printed in the United States of America on acid-free paper.
All rights reserved

03 02 01 00 99 98   6 5 4 3 2 1

Library of Congress Cataloguing in Publication Data:
Froissart across the genres / edited by Donald Maddox and Sara
Sturm-Maddox.
p. cm.
Includes bibliographical references and index.
ISBN 0-8130-1619-3 (alk. paper)
1. Froissart, Jean. 1338?–1410—Criticism and interpretation. I.
Maddox, Donald. II. Sturm-Maddox, Sara.
PQ1061.F8Z666 1998
841'.1—dc21   98-301-30124

The University Press of Florida is the scholarly publishing agency
for the State University System of Florida, comprised of Florida
A & M University, Florida Atlantic University, Florida International University, Florida State University, University of Central
Florida, University of Florida, University of North Florida,
University of South Florida, and University of West Florida.

University Press of Florida
15 Northwest 15th Street
Gainesville, FL 32611
http://nervm.nerdc.ufl.edu/~upf

CONTENTS

Introduction. Writing: History, Fiction, and the Self
    Sara Sturm-Maddox and Donald Maddox 1

Part I. Testimony and Textuality in the *Chroniques*

1. Configuring Transience: Patterns of Transmission and Transmissibility in the *Chroniques* (1395–1995)
Peter F. Ainsworth 15

2. Froissart, Personal Testimony, and the Peasants' Revolt of 1381
Charles T. Wood 40

3. Froissart's 1389 Travel to Béarn: A Voyage Narration to the Center of the *Chroniques*
George T. Diller 50

Part II. Framing Selfhood in Froissart's Poetry

4. *Le joli buisson de Jonece:* Froissart's Midlife Crisis
William W. Kibler 63

5. Froissart's Poetic Prison: Enclosure as Image and Structure in the Narrative Poetry
Keith Busby 81

6. Imitation, Metamorphosis, and Froissart's Use of the Exemplary *Modus tractandi*
Douglas Kelly 101

7. History and Narration in Froissart's *Dits:* The Case of the *Bleu chevalier*
Rupert T. Pickens 119

Part III. Verse Romance and Poetic Renewal

8. *Meliador* and the Inception of a New Poetic Sensibility
Michel Zink 155

Part IV. Froissart and His Contemporaries

9. Theory and Practice: The Portrayal of Chivalry in the Prose *Lancelot*, Geoffroy de Charny, and Froissart
Elspeth Kennedy   179

10. Froissart and Chaucer
John M. Fyler   195

Part V. Image and Reception

11. Image and Propaganda: The Illustration of Book 1 of Froissart's *Chroniques*
Laurence Harf-Lancner   221

Contributors   251

Index   253

Introduction
Writing:
History, Fiction, and the Self

SARA STURM-MADDOX AND DONALD MADDOX

In Jean Froissart we encounter one of the great synthesizing minds of the fourteenth century and one of the most engaging writers of his age. To that age, he was a privileged witness: Born in Hainaut in 1337, he entered as a young man into the service of Queen Philippa of England, the wife of Edward III, and his eight-year period as *clerc de chambre* acquainted him with the English and French nobility and afforded occasions to travel widely in Scotland, France, and Italy; after Philippa's death he enjoyed the favor and protection of a series of nobles in Hainaut and elsewhere, before and after taking holy orders. His literary production covers his entire adult life, while the *Chroniques*, a vast work frequently revised, recast, and expanded, ends with the death of Richard II, four years before Froissart's own death in 1404. Chronicler, lyric poet, and narrative artist, he was renowned in his own time as a leading cultural figure, one whose influence readily transcended national boundaries; "up until quite recent times," one critic observed, he was "the best known and the most widely read French writer in England."[1] To posterity, upon which he often mused, he left an extraordinarily rich assortment of writings. His works offer us an unusually diverse and vivid array of perspectives on this frequently turbulent, always dramatic period, which witnessed not only devastating political upheavals and the ravages of warfare and pestilence but also a vigorous renewal on several fronts in the arts and humanities.

The critical reception of Jean Froissart *écrivain*, however, has long presented something of a paradox. While he has been widely acclaimed as France's greatest chronicler, as author of "the last Arthurian romance," and as a lyric and narrative poet of considerable range, his works themselves have often been judged with severity, occasionally with condescension. A notably different orientation emerged from the Amherst Froissart

Colloquium in 1995, at which most of the essays assembled here were first presented.[2] The participants—among them recent and current editors of the *Chroniques*, a number of the scholars who have in recent years provoked new interest in the Froissartian corpus by initiating a reassessment of its individual works, and Froissart's English-language translator—came together to join their insights in a new project: to address the achievements of Froissart *écrivain* across the genres, in terms of his oeuvre as a whole and the complex and highly significant interrelationships among its various components.

This initiative, prompted in part by the expanding range of interdisciplinary studies of late medieval European culture, responds also to the promptings of the oeuvre itself. It is a critical commonplace that Froissart may readily be situated, in terms of his precursors, in any one of the various genres he practiced. In the case of his lyric and allegorical poetry, that (unnamed) precursor, as the contributors in this volume frequently recall, is clearly Guillaume de Machaut;[3] for the *Meliador*, it is the long tradition of Arthurian romance; and the *Chroniques* originated as a *remaniement* and continuation of the *Chronique* of Jean le Bel. In most studies of Froissart's works, these conventional generic boundaries have generally been respected, resulting in discrete, sometimes rather artificial profiles of the writer in each of his authorial roles: as poet, or romancer, or historian. But these distinctions, in particular that between "history" and "romance," are themselves largely anachronistic, as a number of recent studies demonstrate;[4] and in Froissart's writings explored in this volume, we find that generic boundaries are often blurred within and among the individual texts, a tendency that becomes increasingly evident in his later works and that nearly always accrues to the depth and originality of the passages thus cross-fertilized. As Peter F. Ainsworth observes of the later books of the *Chroniques*, their texts "cut across our modern generic categories with a delightful *sans-gêne*, blending as they do memoir, autobiography, chronicle, interview, travelogue, legend, prophecy, supernatural tale, fabliau and diary." This "intergeneric" dimension, confirming Froissart's sophisticated and agile redeployment of multiple traditions, whether under the sign of lyric or narrative, of history or romance, comes to prominence in the essays in this collection as one of the defining characteristics of his oeuvre as a whole. It emerges, moreover, as a mark of the writer's long-disparaged originality.

While offering probing new readings of a number of single texts, each of the essays included here also presents a unique perspective on the intricate interrelationships within the Froissartian corpus. Part I, "Testimonial and Textuality in the *Chroniques*," opening with Peter F. Ainsworth's sensitive and generous tribute to Froissart and continuing with two complementary and nuanced explorations by Charles T. Wood and George T. Diller, examines not only the many affinities between the *Chroniques* and Froissart's poetry and *Meliador* but also the dialogic relations between the *Chroniques* and the kinds of oral and written texts from which they draw their substance and to which they in turn afford a new vehicle of expression. Froissart's early lyric and narrative-allegorical verse is well represented in Part II, "Framing Selfhood in Froissart's Poetry," in provocative new readings by William W. Kibler, Keith Busby, Douglas Kelly, and Rupert T. Pickens. Part III, "Verse Romance and Poetic Renewal," consists of a very stimulating essay by Michel Zink on how the extraordinarily long—and long-neglected—romance of *Meliador* constitutes a wholly new infusion of poetic sensibility into the genre of verse romance. In Part IV, "Froissart and His Contemporaries," are found two widely ranging papers that, from very different perspectives, reposition Froissart within the context of his time: in the portrayal of chivalry (Elspeth Kennedy), and in comparison with Chaucer, his contemporary (John M. Fyler). Finally, in Part V, "Image and Reception," Laurence Harf-Lancner studies the ideological biases of reception perceptible in the early manuscript tradition.

Among the critical generalizations subject to revision as a result of this collective enterprise is that of a Froissart constrained, both by the circumstances of patronage and by his own conviction, to a pervasively pro-aristocratic and conservative vision. Certainly his relation to patrons of the highest ranks cannot be ignored, and not only in the *Chroniques*, which brings to prominence his early service at the English court of Edward III and his queen, Philippa of Hainaut, as well as Froissart's later connection with nobles such as Gaston Fébus, count of Foix-Béarn. The lyric and allegorical poems, too, contain hints of the circumstances of patronage: The captive protagonist of *Le bleu chevalier*, it has been repeatedly suggested, may represent one of John the Good's hostages, and the *Prison amoureuse* the one-year captivity of Wenceslas of Luxembourg, duke of Brabant,[5] while *Meliador* incorporates some seventy-nine lyrics composed by that same Wenceslas. The essays in this book, however, collectively prompt us to reconsider the unduly restrictive judgment that Froissart's "ability to please his aristocratic patrons and protectors is his chief characteristic as man and writer."[6] The intense scrutiny to which Froissart's historico-ideological stance is subjected here, from a variety of critical perspectives, brings other distinguishing characteristics into sharp focus, while also suggesting an array of promising directions for future inquiry.

A number of these essays affirm, moreover, that the "subjectivity" often noted in Froissart's engagement with a fading world of chivalry and *courtoisie* is far from naive. While the terms "autobiography" and "pseudoautobiography" recur in the studies of the poetic texts, attention is repeatedly focused on self-examination, on the self-conscious nature of Froissart's enterprise, both literary and historical. Here Peter Ainsworth, who in his masterly recent study *Froissart and the Fabric of History* profoundly nuanced the standard characterization of the chronicler as conservative and nostalgic,[7] underlines on a broader scale the tensions, the "antiphonal, conflictual resonances" characteristic of Froissart's prose. From a complementary perspective, Douglas Kelly, in an authoritative scrutiny of elements of Froissart's rhetorical strategy, finds in his *modus tractandi* across a range of poems a practice much like that of Jean de Meun's *Roman de la rose*, whereby poetic images are "refracted through various voices that question, revise, or refute the literal lesson." William Kibler finds a critique of courtly culture in at least the two longest of the *dits amoureux*, the *Espinette amoureuse* and the *Joli buisson de Jonece*. In *Meliador* Michel Zink discerns not the ultimate program of medieval verse romance but the inception of a new poetic sensibility, one that owes far more to Froissart's lyric genius and social dexterity than to the heritage of a narrative genre. The awareness of disparities between the theory and practice of chivalry that Elspeth Kennedy finds in the immediately preceding period in both the Prose *Lancelot* and Geoffroy de Charny is not alien to Froissart, in whom, especially in the later work, we can perceive reservations concerning the relevance of the ideals he had long propounded to a world in evolution. In sum, these essays repeatedly correct in various ways for abusively general views of Froissart's attitudes toward the major sociopolitical and cultural issues that confronted his age.

For Peter Ainsworth, Seamus Heaney's defense of true poetry as "the imagination pressing back against the pressure of reality" inspires a focus on the poetic dimension of Froissart's oeuvre as a whole. Part of that reality is mortality, countered in a "dream of immortality" in which the writer aspires to afford both pleasure and profit to future generations. Explicitly rendered thematically in a number of his works in both verse and prose, in the handling of questions of inheritance and succession as well as in his emphasis on his own craft, this concern as it is developed throughout the corpus of works also affords many insights into how Froissart works "across the genres." Ainsworth argues convincingly that the moral and aesthetic tension in Froissart's work suggests neither an uncomprehending nor a complacent attitude but rather a search for some alternative in a world experiencing rapid change. At the same time, Froissart's purpose takes on the compelling nature of a mission, that of the transmission to posterity of "the heritage of Chivalry" as he understood it—much like

Walter Scott's Old Mortality, shoring up, against the passage of time, memorials to the great men of a troubled but heroic age.

A thoughtful and particularly focused inquiry into Froissart's practice as historian is offered here by Charles T. Wood. Froissart's avowed project in the *Chroniques*, he notes, is to record events "so that posterity might have the advantage of it." And the advantage, he finds, frequently lies in the manner of the recording, not only of events but also of informants: not only those encountered by chance but also those assiduously pursued as witnesses or as likely sources of authentication for the events he sets down for us. As an example of the preservation—not only of the facts of history but also of "readings" of history—Wood pays close attention to the account, most likely constructed from the vantage point of Joan of Kent or her circle, of the English Peasants' Revolt of 1381 and the contemporaneous "coming of age" of her son, Richard II. Wood's study demonstrates that "the lasting historical value of the *Chroniques* often lies in the way in which its participant-based narrative allows us better to understand contemporary assessments of crucial events"; Froissart's enterprise, even as it unfurls before us a vast panoply of the events of his troubled age, thus also affords many subtle insights into that age's own historical understanding.

George T. Diller, examining what he terms "autotextuality" in Froissart's works, begins with the often-discussed account of Froissart's voyage to Béarn in book 3 of the *Chroniques*. Here, frequently, much of the narration "is highly self-reflexive and concerns as much its own creation and status as it does the recording of a historical trip." Diller gives us a fascinating portrait of Froissart himself as questing, going out to his informants in order to record chivalric deeds, in a world that much resembles that of romance—as does the court of Gaston Fébus, where Froissart temporarily becomes the hero of his own work in recounting his reading, before the court, of his romance *Meliador*. Through close attention to the recalls of that reading in book 3 and in the *Dit dou florin*, Diller discloses apparent contradictions both in chronology and in detail. These, he concludes, "suggest that Froissart may have largely fabricated the passages in which he describes his reading his romance before Gaston and his court."

The play between texts is the focus of another suggestive new reading, in William W. Kibler's examination of the two longest of Froissart's dits amoureux. The *Espinette amoureuse* and the *Joli buisson de Jonece* both feature as protagonist the persona of "a poet-lover whose attempts at romance are thwarted"—apparently by the same courtly lady at a distance of some ten years' time. The older lover of the latter poem, through a dream of courtly interaction that re-creates the love service of his youth, awakens to a new awareness of the inappropriateness, the futility, of that service in a man of his mature age. Thus Kibler reads the *Joli buisson* not only as a farewell to a certain type of courtly poetry and *courtoisie* but also as the announcement of "a new and more mature lyricism, founded on sublimation and religious piety." The pseudoautobiographical pose of the narrator is read against the events of Froissart's life in the period immediately preceding the poem's composition, so as to affirm that that text marks a transition in self-consciousness that will "become the very stuff of his new poetry."

Keith Busby reads a broad poetic corpus that includes most of the dits and short narrative poems, restoring to prominence works that have long been subject, in Pickens's phrase, to "benign and not-so-benign neglect." Taking as point of departure the observation that few authors' poetic oeuvre "is quite so dominated on all levels by images of enclosure" as that of Froissart, Busby examines the principle of enclosure and confinement from a double perspective that includes close reading not only of individual poems but also, in keeping with much recent work on the manuscript contexts of medieval texts, of Froissart's ordering—enclosing—of the individual poems within the codex that contains them. The principle is evident not only in the most thematically focused example, the *Prison amoureuse*, which receives detailed analysis here, but also in most of the other dits and short narratives. Various forms of spatial and metaphorical confinement constrain the personages within the poems; in the narratives, poems and images are confined until they can be released—liberated—as creative energy. This thematic presence is doubled by textual confines. In the poems having lyric insertions, the tension between the narrative and lyric modes is itself suggestive of enclosure, in an arrangement doubled by the ordering of components within the codex. From this dual perspective, Busby proposes that "enclosure and confinement [are] a structuring principle of Froissart's aesthetic."

In "Imitation, Metamorphosis, and Froissart's Use of the Exemplary *Modus tractandi*," Douglas Kelly shows how Froissart, in his dits and some of his lyrics, makes use of mythological exempla as accessories of the production of meaning. While there are indeed instances of the straightforward and obvious kind of illustration, or "deductive exemplum"—whereby, for example, Achilles' love for Polixena, kindled suddenly by a single glimpse, illustrates the amorous *coup de foudre*—the passages Kelly cites, from several of Froissart's poems, are generally indicative of the writer's penchant for configurations of a subtler, more intricate nature.

Rather than specify precise equivalencies between an image and the concept to which it refers—a tactic that Rosemond Tuve qualified as "bad" allegory—Froissart tends to juxtapose multiple exempla that generate mutual, and sometimes discrepant, glosses, thus leading to an enriched perception of the subject matter from a plurality of perspectives. Froissart in fact cultivated numerous strategies designed to complicate, and thus deepen, the reader's intergeneric negotiation between an exemplum and the poem into which he rewrote it. For example, Kelly cites some particularly arresting examples of enthymeme, or "inductive exemplum," that is, "an incomplete syllogism in which the conclusion is left to whomever hears and evaluates the work, as in *jeux partis.*" We also see how Froissart sometimes contrived deliberate misprisions of his Ovidian sources in order to prompt reflective rereading and thus fresh construal of extremely familiar, and thus potentially banal, material. Yet, whether in order merely to illustrate meanings or else to exploit tensions between meanings and their contraries so as to induce a more profound reading born of ambiguity and indeterminacy, the integration of sets of analogous exempla into these poems, in Kelly's view, turns them into veritable "treatises," in the late medieval sense of that term, whereby subject matter is developed according to multiple "modes" of writing, including the exemplum, for the purpose of exploring both its explicit and its latent meanings.

Qualities of the "treatise" in this sense in fact emerge from Rupert T. Pickens's new and provocative reading of the *Bleu chevalier*. Like earlier readers, Pickens begins with the question: Why is the knight "blue"? Instead of the quest for historical referentiality that has characterized attempts to answer that question, he turns not only to heraldic treatises but to medieval lapidary tradition and medical theory, factors necessary in this case to divulge "the cultural literacy in terms of which the [Froissartian dits] must be read." Taken together, these suggest that the knight's condition—his mental derangement—has physical causes in his sanguine temperament, an example of the disordered condition classified by medieval theorists as "heroic love." Froissart's narrator, the clerk, offers in his *confort d'ami* a "therapy of a peculiarly learned and literary kind," drawing on the rich medieval tradition of consolation. The progressive engagement of knight and clerk sets up a "narcissistic mirror-play among Froissart, his narrator, the clerk, and the Blue Knight," relating this text in complex ways to other texts, notably Froissart's own *Espinette amoureuse.* Pickens's close attention to this brief poem of 504 lines is richly rewarding: he reveals the work to be "an ambiguous, plurivalent, culturally relevant text," one "that is deliberately structured to call attention to its own composition, to its own status as literary discourse, and to its place in the Froissartian canon."

The critical fortunes of *Meliador* have been relatively modest. It is a work of extraordinary length—more than thirty thousand verses in its unfinished state. One of its first readers after its discovery in a manuscript at the end of the last century commented, "Nous n'avons plus le temps pour les romans de cette taille."[8] Hence the particular interest of Michel Zink's contribution in this book. Despite the generic vitality suggested by such a lengthy work, *Meliador* was long perceived as the ultimate paroxysm of an effete genre, the Arthurian romance in verse. It is sometimes evoked, usually unfavorably, in contrast with the *Chroniques*, in book 3 of which we learn that Froissart read selections from it to his host in Orthez, the count of Foix. Only recently has *Meliador* begun to receive extended critical scrutiny on other grounds. Asking why Froissart, well into his career as a practitioner of prose, would have resurrected a form that had lain dormant for over a century, Zink brushes aside the traditional view of *Meliador* as a warehouse of crepuscular banalities, discovering instead the extent to which it serves as the vehicle of Froissart's gifts as poet. He shows how the attenuated Arthurian settings, the sparse sprinkling of Arthurian characters, and the banal devices of traditional romance all provide sporadic "window dressing" for a conventional plot, while in the foreground verse romance is constantly rejuvenated by the kind of sparkling originality and vigor that characterize Froissart's poetry. Zink finds extensive affinities of situation and style with the *Paradis d'amour*, the *Prison amoureuse*, the *Espinette amoureuse*, and the *Joli buisson de Jonece*. These features, along with the incorporation of poems and chansons at key junctures and the insertion of lyrics by Wenceslas of Luxembourg, make of *Meliador* a "romance in the spirit of verse narratives of the fourteenth century," as well as "a vast *dit* invested with lyrics." Moreover, for Zink they signal the emergence of a remarkably new poetic sensibility: "For the first time verse, as such—and not merely when it is associated with song in various lyric forms—is felt as the natural mode of effusiveness, of self-expression, and of a subjective outlook on the world. The notion of poetry as the modern world will know it begins to take shape." In sum, *Meliador* allows us to observe, extensively and in depth, Froissart's capacity to range creatively across the genres represented by his works in order to inject new vitality into the late medieval writing of history, fiction, and the self.

Froissart's remarkable receptivity to this kind of generic diversity is apparent from his affinities with other writers of his age, among them

Geoffroy de Charny and Geoffrey Chaucer. Of all the knights whose deeds are recorded by Froissart, Geoffroy de Charny, who died bearing the French king's standard at the battle of Poitiers, is extolled by the chronicler as "the most worthy and valiant of them all." And Charny not only epitomizes the chivalric career as recorded by Froissart; he explored its various dimensions in writings of his own. Elspeth Kennedy, who recently collaborated in the edition and translation of Charny's *Livre de chevalerie*, here examines both that work and Froissart's for their representation of the theory and practice of chivalry in the thirteenth and fourteenth centuries and its interplay with romance. In both writers she finds evidence of the reception of the great thirteenth-century prose romances, notably those of the *Lancelot-Grail* cycle. The historical knights in the Company of the Star, for which Charny's works may well have been composed, pledge to observe rules of conduct that echo the precepts set forth in the Prose *Lancelot*, while Charny himself, like the Prose *Lancelot*, includes the function of women in the formation of knights. The recording of chivalric exploits is a preoccupation both of the Arthurian court of the romances and of Froissart in the *Chroniques*; the *Lancelot-Grail* cycle too, Kennedy suggests, anticipates, in the "shadow areas" of its representation of knights and kings, some of the tensions in Froissart's later work that are identified by other contributors to this book.

John M. Fyler offers a comparison between Froissart and Chaucer, his almost exact contemporary. The relations between the literary production of the early period of each writer's career have received some critical attention, especially on the part of Chaucerians; in that regard, Fyler proposes that Chaucer's early appropriations from Froissart in the *Book of the Duchess* are suggestive, not of an "anxiety of influence," but of a "sibling rivalry" in which both poets are engaged in positioning themselves within established (French) lyric tradition. More suggestive still is Fyler's comparison of elements of their later works, of "their mature, nuanced, and darkening responses to their age." Fyler, who has elsewhere devoted intensive attention to Chaucer and Ovid,[9] focuses here in particular on the "Ovidian inclinations" of the two writers as found in the Béarn voyage episode in book 3 of the *Chroniques* and some of Froissart's earlier poems and in Chaucer's tales of the Squire and the Franklin. The chronicler's representation of the court at Orthez, he suggests, may be informed by Ovid's House of Fame as well as by vernacular romance models. Both Froissart and Chaucer, he demonstrates, are concerned with "the chivalric, the exotic, belatedness, the mysterious and the magical, the Golden Age, and the threats to it of contingency and death."

The question of the reception of the *Chroniques* is addressed by

Laurence Harf-Lancner in a detailed examination of the illustrations in the manuscripts of book 1. Taking as point of departure Alberto Varvaro's recent essays and making judicious use of a variety of studies of the manuscript tradition, she demonstrates that the manuscripts fall into two distinct groups, separated not only by their geographical provenance—Parisian and Flemish—and the varying temporal interval but also by their patronage. This classification affords an unusual opportunity to question the adaptation of iconographic elements to the circumstances of manuscript patronage. Froissart was chronicling a period of great political turmoil, and the reception of his *Chroniques* during his own lifetime is seen here to reflect the evolution of historical events. Although all the painters are found to be scrupulously faithful to the text of the *Chroniques*, the two different families of manuscripts nonetheless reveal in their illustrations differing perspectives on the narrated events; the differing iconographic traditions would appear to correspond to the two views of the continuation of French-English conflict: that of the French lords who commissioned the one group of manuscripts and that of the patrons within the Hainaut sphere of influence who commissioned the other.

In conclusion, we may reconsider a representative earlier critical judgment concerning Froissart. "Il a merveilleusement peint son époque," Gaston Paris tells us, "et il l'a peu comprise; il n'a pas réfléchi sur ces événements, dont le récit le plaisait tant. . . . Tout ce qui n'est point éclat, lumière, vie extérieure, lui échappe. Le bruit de l'histoire lui en a caché le sens."[10] The results of the collective inquiry recorded in this book suggest just the contrary. As George Diller has elsewhere observed of the *Chroniques*, Froissart's is "un idéal chevaleresque, et par conséquent romanesque et moral, qui se heurte constamment à sa quête de la vérité historique."[11] In these essays, Froissart's dedication to an ideal of chivalry and *courtoisie* emerges, not as a rosy lens that distorts his apprehension of the events of his tumultuous time, but as the source of a tension that accounts for much of the rich texture of the tapestry now more fully described and understood, and thus more suitable for further exploration.

From these essays emerges a whole gallery of portraits of Froissart as writer of history, of fiction, and of the self: Froissart as pseudoautobiographer in the *Bleu chevalier* and the *Espinette amoureuse* and then as artisan of a fictional resolution of his midlife crisis as man and author in the *Joli buisson de Jonece*; Froissart as quester seeking out informants both for the monumental events and for the obscure moments recorded in his *Chroniques*; Froissart as protagonist in the *Chroniques*, reading his *Meliador* before the court of Gaston Fébus. Taken together, read "across the genres," these images bring more precisely into focus an oeuvre that constantly engages the intricacies of representations, in an extraordinary and perhaps unique authorial performance: Froissart's works, read as an oeuvre, offer us insights not only into the fascinating complexities and paradoxes of the fourteenth century—hence their value as *témoignage*—but especially into the processes of construction, and revision, of selfhood, fiction, and history.

Notes

1. William Calin, *The French Tradition and the Literature of Medieval England* (Toronto: University of Toronto Press, 1994), p. 231. In particular, the *Chroniques*, translated by Lord Berners, "became a staple of English historiography. . . . A modern Plutarch in the fourteenth century, [Froissart] served to instill in the young and to remind the old of the myth of English chivalry, the joys of chivalric adventure, and the English vision of national history in the Middle Ages."

2. The editors would especially like to thank the collaborators in this volume for their enthusiastic support of the Amherst Colloquium "Froissart Across the Genres," held November 3–5, 1995. We are grateful as well to Margaret Switten of Mount Holyoke College, who was most helpful with arrangements for the colloquium and who generously provided valuable background for the work of the gathering, and to the performance ensemble, organized by Robert Eisenstein, that presented a much-appreciated selection of musical illustrations.

3. Machaut's work has attracted substantial critical attention in recent years. Among the many important studies, see William Calin, *A Poet at the Fountain: Essays on the Narrative Verse of Guillaume de Machaut* (Lexington: University Press of Kentucky, 1974); Kevin Brownlee, *Poetic Identity in Guillaume de Machaut* (Madison: University of Wisconsin Press, 1984); Jacqueline Cerquiglini, *"Un engin si soutil": Guillaume de Machaut et l'écriture au XIVe siècle* (Paris: Champion, 1985); Sylvia Huot, *From Song to Book: The Poetics of Writing in Old French Lyric and Lyrical Narrative Poetry* (Ithaca: Cornell University Press, 1987); Maureen Barry McCann Boulton, *The Song in the Story: Lyric Insertions in French Narrative Fiction, 1200–1400* (Philadelphia: University of Pennsylvania Press, 1993); and Jacqueline Cerquiglini-Toulet, *La Couleur de la mélancolie: La fréquentation des livres aux XIVe siècle* (Paris: Hatier, 1993).

4. As Laurence Harf-Lancner observes, "la distinction nette que l'on veut établir entre chronique et roman est étrangère à la conception de la littérature narrative au Moyen Age et l'opposition entre la prétendue vérité de l'historiographie et la fiction romanesque ne rend pas compte de la complexité entre histoire et roman"; see "Chronique et roman: Les contes fantastiques de Froissart," in *Autour du roman: Etudes presentées à Nicole Cazauran* (Paris: Presses de l'Ecole normale supérieure, 1990), pp. 51–65; here p. 51.

5. See, for example, William W. Kibler, "Poet and Patron: Froissart's *Prison amoureuse*," *L'Esprit Créateur* 18 (1978):32–46.

6. Peter Dembowski, "Froissart," in *Medieval France: An Encyclopedia*, ed. William W. Kibler and Grover A. Zinn (New York and London: Garland, 1995), p. 374.

7. *Jean Froissart and the Fabric of History: Truth, Myth and Fiction in the "Chroniques"* (Oxford: Clarendon Press, 1990).

8. Mary Darmester, cited in Peter Dembowski, *Jean Froissart and His "Meliador": Context, Craft, and Sense* (Lexington, Ky.: French Forum, 1983); on the critical fortune of the romance, see pp. 20–24.

9. John M. Fyler, *Chaucer and Ovid* (New Haven and London: Yale University Press, 1979).

10. Cited in George T. Diller, *Attitudes chevaleresques et réalités politiques chez Froissart: Microlectures du premier livre des Chroniques* (Geneva: Droz, 1984), p. 2.

11. Jean Froissart, *Chroniques. Dernière rédaction du premier livre. Edition du manuscrit de Rome Reg. lat. 869*, ed. George T. Diller (Geneva: Droz, 1972), p. 31.

I

Testimony and Textuality in the *Chroniques*

1

Configuring Transience

Patterns of Transmission and Transmissibility in the *Chroniques* (1395–1995)

Peter F. Ainsworth

An internationalist *avant la lettre*, Jean Froissart was familiar with most of the distinguished courts of his day, and he was always prepared to cross mountain range or saltwater on his perennial quest for new material. Amherst in the fall of 1995 thus proved a fitting time and venue for the first international colloquium on the poet-chronicler. His writing, moreover, ranges energetically across the generic boundaries that were the focus of the three-day *cour d'amour* held at the University of Massachusetts. Many of those attending the colloquium amidst the glories of a New England fall did so after a transatlantic journey, a fitting homage to Froissart's own preferred method of information gathering: traveling far afield in search of lively and informed conversation. The chronicler-poet of Valenciennes would have been pleased indeed to learn that *armes et amour* had found a new home amidst the forests of New England. The analogy is suggestive for yet another reason. In the *Chroniques*, descriptions of adventurous journeys overseas are often the cue for Froissart's thoughts on the theme that is the focus of this essay: the transmission to generations as yet unborn of the inheritance of Chivalry, as Froissart understood it—and all that threatens to prevent such a transmission.

The year of the colloquium was also auspicious, being a sexcentenary: 1395 was the year of the climacteric recorded by Froissart in book 4 of the *Chroniques*, when he took ship for a metaphorically autumnal visit to the fondly remembered England that in his youth had become the latest abode of knightly prowess. Midway through book 4 he shares his reasons for the journey:

Plusieurs raisons me esmouvoient à faire ce voyage. La première estoit pour ce que de ma jœunesse je avoie esté nourry en la court et hostel du noble roy Edouard, de bonne mémoire, et de la noble royne Phelippe sa femme, et entre leurs enfans et les barons d'Angleterre qui pour ce temps y vivoient et demouroient; car toute honneur, largesse et courtoisie je avoie veu et trouvé en euls. Si désiroie à veoir le pays, *et me sembloit en mon ymagination que, se veu l'avoie, j'en viveroie plus longuement.* (KL 15:140; my emphasis)[1]

[Several reasons inclined me to make this journey, the first that in my youth I had been brought up in the court and household of the noble King Edward of dear memory, and of Queen Philippa his wife, and amongst their children and the lords of England who dwelt there in those days; for I had found in them all honor, liberality, and courtesy. And so I longed to see the land, for I fancied that, if I were to see it again, I should live the longer for it.] (translations mine unless otherwise indicated)

The hope expressed—that a visit late in life to the English court might afford the poet a last, restorative draft from some *fontaine de jouvence*—echoes the equally well-known statement in the prologue to book 3, in which Froissart sets off the projected immortality of his written testimony against the ineluctable fate reserved for his flesh: "Car bien sçay que ou temps advenir, *quant je seray mort et pourry,* ceste haulte et noble hystoire sera en grant cours, et y prendront tous nobles et vaillans hommes plaisance et augmentation de bien" (SHF 12:2; my emphasis). [For well I know that, when I am dead and rotten in the grave, this noble and lofty history will be noised both far and wide, and all noble and valiant men derive pleasure and profit therefrom.] This antiphonal call and response, from threat of decay to dream of immortality, provides one of the deepest resonances in Froissart's writing. It forms part of a nexus of tensions in his work, all of which lend substance to the claim that he was not only a fine writer but also a poet—in prose as well as in verse.

All of these tensions have to do, this essay argues, with a longing for various kinds of *redress*. Fall 1995 proved once again to be a timely season for discussion of such ideas, in view of earlier events that year: the award to Seamus Heaney of the Nobel Prize in literature and the publication of his Oxford lectures under the title *The Redress of Poetry*. Heaney may seem an unlikely correlative for the fourteenth-century chronicler, but at least one illuminating parallel can be adduced, at a fundamental level: that which Heaney himself identifies as the very principle and foundation of the poetic act. Writing about Robert Frost's poem "Directive," Heaney remarks on the way in which Frost appears to suggest at one point that "the imaginative transformation of human life is the means by which we can most truly grasp and comprehend it."[2] Although such an imaginative transformation of observed reality was not one of Froissart's avowed purposes in the *Chroniques,* his prose does from time to time allow for the opening of such an imaginative window upon the world he depicts, in a manner that hints at the need to look beyond the limitations of the immediate world for some transcendent alternative—however elusive it may prove to be.[3]

The phenomenon is perhaps most palpable in the last two books of the *Chroniques,* in a number of intriguing episodes dealing with the problematic nature of the transmission (or *transmissibility*) from one generation to the next of power, nobility, and chivalry. This key theme is associated more and more frequently in the later *Chroniques* with that of the fate of the writer as self-conscious preserver of the past and as guarantor of tradition. From book 3 onward the two themes begin to coalesce in ways that are frequently arresting. As writer-protagonist, Froissart invades his own historiographical discourse, depicting himself in the execution of each evolution of his craft: his travels abroad for research purposes;[4] his interviews with eyewitnesses; his eavesdropping on the gossip of the bibulous; his late-night fireside conversations;[5] his making of quick notes at the close of each day;[6] and then, back at Valenciennes or Chimay, his preparation of initial, composite drafts, either by dictation or pen in hand.[7] Most important of all, we learn of his great purpose: the transmission to posterity—through the enduring record of the written word—of the deeds and values of the caste he served.[8] I explore these issues here.

This essay concludes that Froissart's great purpose found its first truly percipient modern commentator in Sir Walter Scott. His otherwise sensitive critical essay of 1805 is sympathetic in its understanding of the chronicler as writer and artist but not to the degree found in his novel of 1816, *Old Mortality.* Here is to be found the strongest expression of empathy on Scott's part for his fellow artist from an earlier age. It is surely fitting, early in this collection of essays, to celebrate the unique *translatio studii* wrought by Sir Walter Scott: He it was, more than anyone else, who revived the chronicler's reputation as writer and artist with the modern English-speaking republic of letters. As such, he deserves to be remembered at the threshold of a collection of essays that bears ample testimony to Froissart's continuing ability to find sensitive and discerning readers.

The passages from *Old Mortality* that I have selected for commentary fulfill at least one additional purpose: They provide a memorable summary of the arguments that follow.

Froissart's authorial voice as we hear its inflections across the genres is profoundly imbued with the ethic of service, from the traditional love service (sometimes articulated at secondhand) of the narrative *dits*, *ballades*, and virelays, to the prologue of the *Prison amoureuse*, which elevates service of the chivalrous aristocracy to a moral principle.[9] It is perhaps this sense of duty and commitment to a *ministerium* that best explains the sheer prolixity and richness of Froissart's legacy to us in verse and prose. However, service does not necessarily imply self-effacement. In the *Dit dou bleu chevalier*, for instance, the disconsolate, eponymous knight recognizes in the itinerant philosopher who seeks to console him a man undoubtedly sent by God to bring him both profit and wise counsel:

> Et dist: "Amis,
> Li bien venus soiiés, car je sui fis,
> Puis qu'aventure et Diex vous ont ci mis,
> Qu'il m'avenront et consauls et proufis
> De vo venue."[10]

[Saying, "My friend, you're welcome here; for I am sure, since God and adventure have brought you hither, nought but profit and counsel can come of this."]

This passage clearly suggests that Froissart the officiant or celebrant of Chivalry was not an entirely passive witness; his texts occasionally bear more than a hint of self-regard, and he is not averse to telling us how highly his credit stood with several of his noble contemporaries. On the other hand, there are instances in the later *Chroniques* of refreshingly self-deprecating irony. If we still read Froissart with profit and pleasure today, it is not so much on account of any wise counsel he may have to offer us as students of fourteenth-century history or verse; the reason is rather what I call the antiphonal, conflictual (ironic) resonances of his prose, the composite elements of which unite in providing that moral and aesthetic tension so peculiar to his best writing.

Mortality and immortality; Eros and Thanatos; past, present, and future and their interferences; verse and prose as vehicles for a partly fictional message that says more than can be said in or about real life without wholly betraying truth: These are some of the foci of tension that imbue Froissart's oeuvre with its most enduring poetic qualities. In the *Chroniques*, as suggested earlier, we have an intermittent glimpse of an alternative way of considering the world about which they are written. The same is true of the *Prison amoureuse,* which not only looks beyond the prison of the title but also guarantees a degree of transcendence for the servant-writer.[11] Fates are diverted for a while, compensations of various kinds adduced or suggested for a social vision espoused by a flawed society that insists on seeing itself as guided by an ideology of moral and military perfectibility.[12]

This, writes Seamus Heaney, is what true poetry has always been about: "The imagination pressing back against the pressure of reality" (*The Redress of Poetry*, p. 1). In the activity of poetry, he writes, "there is a tendency to place a counter-reality in the scales—a reality which may be only imagined but which nevertheless has weight because it is imagined within the gravitational pull of the actual and can therefore hold its own and balance out against the historical situation. This redressing effect of poetry comes from its being a glimpsed alternative, a revelation of potential that is denied or constantly threatened by circumstances" (pp. 3–4). The later books of the *Chroniques,* composed between 1389 and ca. 1405, provide—however intermittently—such a glimpsed alternative, the deeper resonances of which are rarely apprehended on a first reading. The texts of these later books cut across our modern generic categories with a delightful *sans-gêne,* blending as they do memoir, autobiography, chronicle, interview, travelogue, legend, prophecy, supernatural tale, fabliau, and diary. This fruitful blurring of boundaries and teleologies opens the door to a rich variety of readings, allowing for a pleasing deferral of the disclosure of meaning.[13] Indeed, the problematics of the transmission of meaning from author to successive generations of readers, via an ambiguous text complicated by all kinds of diegetic and intradiegetic games, becomes the arresting subtext of a work that I describe elsewhere as sitting provocatively between several muses (*Fabric*, p. 170).

In this respect, the most promising seam to quarry lies within the prose narratives composed after 1388, the date of the chronicler's celebrated journey to the court of Gaston Fébus, count of Foix-Béarn. The journey south to Orthez delineated in book 3 becomes a metaphor for the writer's own self-discovery and self-affirmation. It also opens up for exploration the human and ideological significance of his own work and its conscious purport: the remembrance of things past and the commemoration of the self-evidently glorious deeds of that past. The final transformation is wrought by stealth, as it were, as the chronicle text itself goes seriously—but poetically—astray (by dint of digression and increasingly complex diegetic convolutions), to the extent that it begins to convey more and more insistently the very opposite of its supposed message. This is the implication, here, of the phrase "glimpsed alternatives." *Contraire est vérité*.[14] At one end of the diegetic spectrum is the direct, tell-as-you-go syntax of "Or parlerons du roy Edowart, et de quel cose qu'il fist" [Now let us tell of King Edward and his deeds]; at the other, the complex textual constellations of books 3 and 4, incorporating sustained metaphor, subtle metonymic relationships between ostensibly unconnected episodes, nascent symbolism, and the progressive consolidation of identifiable fields of imagery and thematic association.

It is all the more surprising, in this connection, that some critics remain convinced that Froissart's *sole* working method was oral extemporization in the presence of a team of scribes at his *forge*, or workshop, at Valenciennes.[15] It is certainly true that, when not using a preexisting written source such as le Bel's *Chronique*, Froissart's raw materials were most

1.1. Wax tablets from Polling Abbey, Bavaria, measuring 170 mm x 88 mm x 6 mm. Late fourteenth century. Reproduced by permission of Sotheby's, New Bond Street, London.

likely the hastily scribbled notes taken down weeks earlier in foreign climes during interviews with eyewitness informants. However, much of this material would have been worked up immediately afterward in the bedchamber of some wayside inn, thus forming the preliminary draft for this or that episode. This conclusion is borne out by several passages in the *Chroniques* in which Froissart speaks directly of the writing process. The sheer scale of the enterprise, involving the collation of hundreds of such interviews and narrative episodes, is all the more breathtaking given the chronicler's lack of a laptop computer. What he almost certainly did have at hand were rolls of parchment scrap[16] and perhaps a collection of wax tablets, such as those found nearly ten years ago by archaeologists at York rummaging about in a medieval cesspit[17] or, more probably, like those that featured in a recent sale at Sotheby's of London (fig. 1.1).[18]

What Froissart certainly did have, as an Arthurian poet, was the compositional art of interlace. Close analysis of only a few passages makes it abundantly clear that he was aware of more than the limited patterns of the sentence, paragraph, or episode that he was currently dictating. As I have noted elsewhere, he was not averse on occasion to cannibalizing quite lengthy passages lifted from his own texts in true cut-and-paste mode and in what appears to be a calculated or at least conscious manner.[19] Study of the themes of inheritance, hereditary succession, and transmission, and of their handling in the *Chroniques*, confirms just how wrong it is to consider the later Froissart as little more than a dictating extemporizer or as the uncritical echo of his interviewees.

Since at least the Book of Job, human beings have worried lest their testimony vanish forever from the face of the earth, for want of a medium guaranteed to leave a truly permanent record of their passage. In Job 19:23–24, Job exclaims:

> Oh, that my words were written!
> Oh, that they were inscribed in a book!
> That they were engraved on a rock
> With an iron pen and lead, forever!

Transmission of the writer's creations to posterity is a major late medieval topos, finding expression, for instance, in the *Ubi sunt?* of Villon's poetry, as well as in the *Livre des fais du mareschal Bouciquaut*.[20] The difference in Froissart's work is the interest he evinces in the *supports d'écriture*, the very media that both permit and constrain the transmission. The theme occurs frequently in his verse compositions. The ballade or rondeau inscribed on a parchment leaf or collated with others within a manuscript codex—indeed, the manuscript book itself and all that it enshrines—clearly represented for Froissart (as for Christine de Pizan) a *bien précieux*. Froissart's poems occasionally depict an almost proprietorial concern for the fate of the parchment leaves or rolls bearing the poet-protagonist's virelays or ballades, and of course for the fate of the precious manuscript books that enshrined them. Jacqueline Cerquiglini-Toulet writes persuasively of their value in Froissart's poetry as amorous and artisanal currency. She has also highlighted the importance in Froissart's verse of images of fullness, emptiness, and containment—in contexts that have to do with the processes of writing and poetic creation.[21] A recurrent metaphoric pattern may thus be identified in his verse compositions, most visibly at work in the *Prison amoureuse* and *Joli buisson de Jonece* but found also in the *Meliador*. It can also be descried, from time to time, in the chronicler's prose.

In the verse works, an explicit or implicit connection is made between the fate of the material work and the financial and professional fortunes of its author. In the *Dit dou florin*, for example, the poet's last remaining coin comments explicitly on the fate of its departed fellows—many of whom have been thoroughly well spent, it must be allowed, on the production of history books:

> Tout premiers, vous avés fait livres
> Qui ont cousté bien .VII^c. livres.
> L'argent avés vous mis la bien;
> Je le prise sus toute rien,
> Car fait en avés mainte hystore
> Dont il sera encor memore
> De vous ens ou temps a venir,
> *Et ferés les gens souvenir*
> *De vo sens et de vos doctrines.* (my emphasis)[22]

[First of all, you have had books made costing a good seven hundred pounds. That was money well spent, and I cannot commend you too highly for it. It went into the making of many a history, for which you will still be remembered in years to come. You will cause people to recollect both your wisdom and your teachings.]

Part of the basis for such references is the writer's preoccupation with the uncertain fate awaiting the manuscript-book and the truth it enshrines (see Ainsworth, *Fabric*, pp. 2–3). Froissart had brought the count of Foix-Béarn a gift from his master and patron, Gui de Châtillon, count of Blois: a pair of greyhounds. His own "gift" to Gaston was a nocturnal cycle of readings from his romance *Meliador*, at a rate of some seven folios per sitting. Whether or not the poet intended to leave the volume itself with Gaston is not clear, but we sense Froissart's concern for this precious, handwritten repository for some thirty thousand lines of carefully crafted verse.[23] In fact the *Meliador* was lost to scholars between the end of the Middle Ages and the late nineteenth century, when it was rediscovered at the Bibliothèque Nationale.[24] What became of it between 1388 and 1895, the year in which Auguste Longnon published volume 1? Did Fébus keep it for any length of time? Did he hand it back again to the poet at the end of his stay with a polite affectation of gratitude, or did he use it as a political gift to cement some alliance or other?

In view of the writer's preoccupation with his professional status and financial position, several questions come to mind: Should the poet-secretary-chronicler be paid? How, exactly? Is high patronage to be prized more than financial reward? Will the creator's art go to people who may not appreciate it? Is it really desirable to part with beautifully crafted creations? We have already seen that the writer's creations could "go missing." As is well known, another of Froissart's manuscripts was intercepted on its way to England by Louis, duke of Orleans, for fear of its pro-English propaganda value.[25] Although we know of several working copies calligraphed on paper, most of the surviving manuscripts of the *Chroniques* are objets d'art, luxury items on vellum that was sumptuously illuminated and handsomely bound before being delivered to patron or prince. Such fates surely account in part for the hint of anxiety, in verse and chronicles alike, about the successful transmission of the written word to posterity and about its ultimate function. Cognate with this notion is another episode in book 4 of the *Chroniques* in which Froissart again depicts himself as protagonist. Visiting Richard II in 1395, the chronicler handed the king a splendidly bound volume containing his collected poems (possibly the manuscript BN fr. 831).[26] The king, we are told, took the volume, went into his private chamber, leafed through it for a moment, then handed it on to a chamberlain. It is the progressive material disappearance—or rather, the *recessional withdrawal*—of the volume (and of all that it encloses) that remains in the reader's mind at the end of the episode, together with a suggestion of the chronicler's anxiety that the collection may never be "properly" read by the king himself.

Texts of this kind, when compared with one another, encourage a metaphorical reading suggestive of the precarious, transient act of writerly creation and of the writer's need to see the preserved record of artistic endeavor consigned, bound, preserved, enshrined—yet not quite *entombed* or *embalmed*, for it must also be transmitted to posterity. We feel the unwritten desire of the writer to see immortality conferred upon a material work that will somehow stay vital and accessible to all future generations blessed with ears to hear and eyes to see. This links up in book 4 with the theme of the sea voyage and Froissart's return to his spiritual home, "out of time" as it were, in the wrong generation. Edward III has been succeeded by Richard II, and the chronicler evokes a sense of ghostly déjà vu as he describes meeting the heirs of those he had once known among the royal entourage. Hence the inspired title of Nicole Chareyron's evocative study "Froissart le revenant," prefaced with an *exergue* from Vladimir Jankélévitch: "L'homme qui retourne vieilli à ses sources—revient où il n'est jamais allé." [The man who returns in old age to his roots—revisits places where he has never set foot.][27] The last journey of 1395 is thus a late reworking of the theme of uncertain transmission. The burden is the writer's growing awareness of the passing of an ideology; namely, of the victorious, vigorous chivalry of Edward III and the Black Prince—which does not appear to have been transmitted to Richard himself.[28] When, in the passage quoted above, Froissart tells us that he is writing for a distant posterity, the ostensible self-confidence does not altogether mask the anguished thought that there may no longer be any readers in later generations able to appreciate it—or (more to the point) to grasp the ideology that subtends it.

The implication that this transmission can never be guaranteed is encoded in a number of ways in Froissart's verse and prose. It appears in the famous episode of metonymic transference (subsequently transmitted to Shakespeare via Holinshed) in which Richard II's hitherto faithful greyhound, Match, deserts him for Henry Bolingbroke (in Shakespeare's play the greyhound becomes the roan Barbary). Here again is the theme of vitiated, indirect transmission, this time in the context of royal lineage.[29] Usurpation is here transformed, by metonymic sleight of hand, into acceptable, publicly witnessed succession:

> Le roy Richart avoit ung lévrier, lequel lévrier on nommoit Blemach, très bel lévrier oultre mesure, et ne vouloit ce chien congnoistre nul homme fors le roy seulement, et lorsque le roy devoit chevauchier, celluy qui l'avoit en garde, le laissoit aler, et ce lévrier venoit tantost devers le roy et le festoioit et luy mettoit ses deux piés sus ses espaules. Et adont en advint que le roy et le conte d'Erby parlans ensemble emmy la place de la court du dit chastel et leurs chevauls tous ensellés (car tantost ils devoient monter), ce lévrier nommé Blemach qui coustumier estoit de faire au roy ce que dit vous ay, laissa le roy et s'en vint tout droit au duc de Lancastre, et luy fist toutes les contenances telles que en devant il faisoit au roy Richart,

et luy assist ses deux piés sus les espaules, et le commença moult grandement à conjouir. Adont le duc de Lancastre qui point ne congnissoit le lévrier, demanda au roy et dist: "Mais que veult ce lévrier faire?" —"Cousin, respondy lors le roy, ce vous est une moult grande signifiance et à moy une très-petite." —"Comment, dist le duc de Lancastre, l'entendés-vous?" —"Je l'entens ainsi, dist le roy. Cestuy lévrier vous recueille et festoie aujourd'huy comme roy d'Angleterre que vous serés, et j'en seray déposé et débouté, et le lévrier en a congnoissance naturelle; se le tenés delés vous, car il vous sieuvra et jà ne vous eslongera." Le duc de Lancastre entendy et notta bien ceste parole, et conjouy fort le lévrier, lequel oncques depuis ne le habandonna, car plus ne voulu sieuvir le roy Richart, mais très-bien le duc de Lancastre, et ce veirent et sceurent eulx plus de trente mille hommes. Tous montèrent incontinent à cheval et se départirent du chastel de Fluich et se retrairent sus les champs, et chevauchoit le duc de Lancastre (d'ores-en-avant nous ne le nommerons plus conte d'Erby, mais duc de Lancastre). (KL 16:187–88)

[King Richard had a greyhound whose name was Match, an exceptionally fine animal that recognized no man but the king himself. When the king was to ride out, the dog's handler would release him, and the greyhound would run to greet the king, placing both forepaws on his master's shoulders. And so it occurred that, as the king and the earl of Derby were in conversation together in the inner ward of the castle, their horses being saddled ready for departure, Match the greyhound, whose custom it had been to behave as I have described, deserted the king and made straight for the duke of Lancaster, showing him all the affection he was wont to show King Richard, and placing both forepaws on Duke Henry's shoulders; and he began to make a great fuss of him. Then the duke of Lancaster, who did not know the greyhound, asked the king, "What is this creature doing?" —"As I see it," replied the king, "my greyhound is greeting and honoring you this day as the future king of England that you shall surely be, whilst my fate will be to be deposed and cast down. The greyhound can sense all this instinctively. So keep him by your side, for he will follow you and never leave you." The duke of Lancaster heard and marked what was told him and made a great fuss of the greyhound, which never thereafter deserted him; for he no longer had any heart for serving King Richard, but would cleave, rather, to the duke of Lancaster. And this was witnessed by more than 30,000 men. All mounted forthwith, leaving

Flint Castle and setting out across the fields. And the duke of Lancaster rode forth (henceforward we shall call him no longer earl of Derby but duke of Lancaster).]

The high degree of poetic valency in such episodes is owing to their frequent connection with the theme of the vicissitudes of *literary* transmission—which, it is suggested, can be assured only with difficulty via the labors of the chronicler. He must endlessly resume and add to his great enterprise, refining and enhancing it through rewriting, through the acquisition of further testimony, and through the production, dissemination, and circulation (in the quasi-monetary sense discussed by Jacqueline Cerquiglini-Toulet and Michel Zink)[30] of *manuscrits de commande*, the basis for a whole livelihood and career: *compilatio, amplificatio, translatio.*

Another complicating factor is Froissart's growing need to talk about his craft. This is one of the features that render book 3's *Voyage en Béarn* so endlessly appealing. It is perhaps best approached via a short quotation from the *Joli buisson de Jonece*, another work that self-consciously foregrounds the artist as narrator.[31] Here, two traveling companions—the poet-narrator and "Venus"—are ambling along the road toward their destination, the Vigorous Bush of Youth of the poem's title, chattering away and exchanging virelays. The poet is a little troubled that they may be losing their way, despite the pleasure afforded by the journey. He observes that anyone who strays from his avowed purpose ("se fourvoie": to be taken here, I believe, in its moral as well as its literal sense) will never reach his goal.[32] Venus replies that to wander along in this fashion makes the journey all the shorter—paradoxically, by prolonging the enjoyment; there is in any case no danger of her losing the way:

> Et puis li di selonc mon sens:
> "Foi que je doi a Sainte Crois,
> Dame, je crieng et me mescrois
> Qu'a present ne vous fourvoiiés.
> Je vous en pri que vous voiiés
> Se noient nous nos fourvoions,
> A fin que nous nos ravoions,
> Car al homme qui se fourvoie
> Trop li est longe courte voie."
> Et elle respont en riant:
> "S'un petit alons detriant,
> Tant nous est li deduis plus lons;
> Mes je sçai bien que nous alons
> Droit au Buisson sans nul fourvoi." (*JBJ*, 1325–38)

[And then I said to her, as I saw the matter:
"By the faith I owe the Holy Cross,
I fear, my lady, and suspect, that
You are beginning to go astray.
I beg you consider
Whether we are indeed straying at all,
That we may find our way again;
For he who loses his way
Finds even a short road much too long."
Her reply came with a laugh:
"If we are dallying on the way,
It only makes the delight last longer;
For I know well that we are bound
Straight for the Bush—unerringly."]

This passage affords the perfect epigraph for the *Voyage* sequence, in which Froissart *goes astray* in quite spectacular fashion. He exchanges news and information with the Bascot de Mauléon, Espan de Lyon, and an "escuier ancien et moult notable homme" [an aged and most venerable squire]. Attempting to bring into the full light of day a series of somewhat obscure incidents involving his host, Gaston Fébus, and his family, the chronicler in fact opens a veritable Pandora's box, which he only partially manages to close once again as he turns to the narration of other matters later in book 3. Unable to resist the temptation to follow every potential twist and turn in the scandalous tales his interlocutors weave for him, the narrator contrives ultimately to aggravate the enigmas and compound the very mysteries he has sought to resolve. *Amplificatio* and *compilatio* thus result in *mystificatio* (see Ainsworth, *Fabric*, pp. 140–71).

The mystification is in large part determined by Froissart's recourse to intradiegetic narrators, some of them conveniently anonymous. The resulting construction of the narrative, like a set of Chinese boxes, opens up to the reader's scrutiny those very "facts" that Froissart purports to set forth so unambiguously. In sum, the writer plays out a brightly colored narrative skein of which the ultimate significance partly eludes him. The reader in turn proceeds to unravel this series of interwoven and embedded narratives, each of which seems to echo or query its neighbors in ironic fashion. The underlying tensions binding these threads together at a deeper level than that of the surface narrative only begin to emerge as the aesthetic patterns of the text progressively disclose themselves to the reader.

Perhaps because of Johan Huizinga's enduring influence, the darker notes in Froissart's work (stories of parricide, spirit possession, and political assassination, among other fare) have all too often been associated with the alleged waning of the Middle Ages. I would suggest that their presence betokens, rather, a dawning awareness on the chronicler's part that things are indeed changing, socially and politically, perhaps too fast for his liking—or in ways that are as yet only dimly understood. This textual mystification encapsulates much of the charm inherent in the later *Chroniques*, but the charm is surely only manifest when Froissart is read as he deserves to be: *in extenso*, rather than via selections of *morceaux choisis*. Froissart ought to be read in every possible direction—forward, backward, repeatedly, and of course across the metagenres of verse and prose. The reason is partly that some of the more significant resonances in the *Chroniques* are achieved progressively, as we have seen, and at a level probably far deeper than the writer himself would have owned. One of the most fascinating aspects of his prose has to do with the conflict between the different ways in which successive episodes actually link up with one another. Many literally succeed (follow) one another; others are interwoven and associated by interlace. But the most memorable connections—in aesthetic terms—arise when episodes are linked not so much by chronological or topical logic as by symbol, echo, or metonymy, or indeed when their most obvious textual or thematic correlative lies beyond the immediate episode concerned.

An illustration from book 4 is exemplary. Here the chronicler has recourse to deferred resolution and to a form of narrative convolution and frustration that is best approached from the perspectives afforded by Cerquiglini-Toulet's categories of fullness and emptiness and by Keith Busby's discussion in chapter 5 of Froissart's thematics of imprisonment. What is immediately at stake in this anecdote is the fate of the treasury of the late count of Foix and Béarn.

Upon Gaston Fébus's sudden death after a bear hunt (itself part of a narrative system abounding in metonymic, magical, and symbolic connotations, as Michel Zink and John Fyler argue in chapters 8 and 10), the late count's beloved but illegitimate son Yvain is encouraged by his father's knights to rush to Orthez in order to secure the Treasury and thereby guarantee the comital succession. What follows is a perversely inconsequential narrative that, however gratuitous it may seem at first, soon takes on metaphorical significance—as we realize that what is fundamentally at stake is the mortality of even the most consummate of chivalric heroes (Fébus), as well as the question of his succession by a bastard son, however beloved of his father and his father's household.

The story echoes an earlier narrative sequence that orchestrates, poetically and metonymically, the progressive contamination and extinction of Gaston Fébus's legitimate line and, by implication, of his alleged chivalry (see Ainsworth, "Knife," pp. 92–102). The later narrative thus has a poignant and indirectly didactic ring to it. In sum, both sequences are best read not only in succession but also as a palimpsest.

Yvain rides to the castle bearing tokens that he is sure will open all doors to him: his father's ring and knife (the use of ring and knife as totems of identification itself ought to be read within the wider symbolic and diegetic system operating in book 3; in particular, the "coutel" is *possessed* of both analeptic and proleptic resonances; see Ainsworth, "Knife," p. 111, n. 46):

Si s'en vint au chastel et appella le portier. Le portier respondy: "Que vous plaist, messire Yewain? Où est monseigneur?" —"Il est à l'ospital, respondy le chevallier et me envoie icy quérir certaines choses qui sont en sa chambre, et puis retourneray vers luy, et affin que tu m'en croyes de vérité, vecy les enseignes de son anel et de son coutel." Le portier ouvry une fenestre et vey les enseignes. Si les recongneut bien le portier, car autreffois les avoit veues. Si ouvry le guichet de la porte, et entrèrent luy et ung autre, et le vallet garda les chevaulx ou mena vers l'estable.

Quant messire Yewain fut dedens, il dist au portier: "Ferme la porte." Il la ferma, et quant il l'eut fermée, messire Yewain saisi les clefs et dist au portier: "Tu es mort, se tu sonnes mot." Le portier fut tout esbahy et dist: "Pourquoy, sire Yewain" —"Pour ce, dist-il, que monseigneur mon père est aujourd'hui dévyé, et je vueil estre audessus de son trésor avant que nuls y viègne." Le portier obéy, car faire luy convenoit, et si avoit aussi chier ung bien pour messire Yewain que pour ung autre.

Messire Yewain sçavoit bien où le trésor du conte son père estoit et reposoit. Si se traist celle part, et estoit en une tour grosse et forte où il y avoit trois paires de fors huis barrés et ferrés au devant, et tous les convenoit ouvrir de diverses clefs, avant que on [SHF: "ou"] y peuist venir, lesquelles clefs il ne trouva point appareilliement, car elles estoient en ung coffret long tout de fin achier et estoit fermé de une petite clef d'achier, et celle clef portoit le conte Gaston sur luy, quant il chevauchoit et partoit hors d'Orthais, et fut trouvée à ung juppon de soye pendant, lequel il avoit vestu dessus sa chemise, puis que messire Yewain fut departy, et quant elle fut trouvée des chevalliers qui estoient en la chambre à l'ospital de Rion, qui gardoient le corps du conte de Fois, moult s'esmerveilloient de quoy, ne à quoy celle petite clef povoit servir.

Adont dist le chappellain du conte qui là estoit, nommé messire Nicole de l'Escale, qui savoit les secrès du conte, car il estoit bien en sa grâce, et quant il estoit alé à son trésor, il y menoit son chappellain et non autruy: si dist ainsi, quant il vey la clef: "Messire Yewain perdera sa voye, car sans celle clef-cy il ne puet entrer ou tresor; car elle defferme ung petit coffret d'achier où toutes les clefs du trésor sont."

Or furent les chevalliers tous courrouchiés et dirent à messire Nicole: "Portés-la luy et vous ferés bien. Il vault mieulx que le chevallier soit au dessus du trésor que nul autre; il le vault, et son père, que Dieu pardoinst, l'amoit moult." Respondy le chappellain: "Puisque vous le me conseilliés, je le feray."

Tantost le chappellain monta à cheval. Si prist la clef et se mist au chemin pour venir vers Orthais, et messire Yewain qui estoit ou chastel d'Orthais, fut moult ensonnié de quérir les clefs, et si ne les povoit trouver, et si ne sçavoit viser voye, ne tour, comment il pourroit rompre les serrures des huys de la tour, car elles estoient trop fortes, et si n'avoit point les instrumens appareilliés pour ce faire. (KL 14:328–30)

[He came to the castle and called to the gatekeeper, who answered: "What do you want, my lord Yvain? Where is my master?" —"He is at the hunting lodge," replied the knight, "and has sent me to look for certain things that are in his room, after which done, I shall return to him. And so that you may believe that this is the truth, see, here are tokens: his ring and his knife." The gatekeeper opened a window and saw the tokens. He recognized them well, for he had seen them in earlier days. And so he opened the door in the gate and Yvain went in with one companion, while the servant stayed with the horses or took them to the stable.

When Sir Yvain was inside, he said to the gatekeeper: "Shut the door." He did so. When it was shut, Sir Yvain seized the keys and said to him: "If you utter so much as a word, you're a dead man." The gatekeeper was astounded, asking "Why, Sir Yvain?" —"Because," came the reply, "my father died today, and I want to take possession of his plate before anyone else comes along." The gatekeeper obeyed, having no choice, and because he would just as soon have Sir Yvain reap the advantage as anyone else.

Sir Yvain knew well where the count's treasure was kept, and so he set off in that direction. It was in a massive, strongly built tower that had three pairs of heavy doors secured on their outer sides with iron bars; each door had to be opened with different keys before one could gain access. These keys did not come to his hand easily, for they were in a long, rectangular casket made of tempered steel and locked with a tiny key of steel. The count used to carry this key on his person whenever he went riding forth from Orthez, and it was found, a little after Yvain's departure, hanging from a silk tunic that Gaston had put on over his shirt. When it was found by the knights who were in the count's chamber at the hunting lodge, guarding his body, they were greatly puzzled as to what purpose the little key might serve.

Then the count's chaplain, Nicholas de l'Escale, who was present, and who was privy to all his master's secrets because he enjoyed his full confidence and had been taken with him alone on visits that Gaston had made to his Treasury, said upon seeing the key: "Sir Yvain will lose his way, for without that key he cannot get into the Treasury; it unlocks a small steel box containing all the keys to the Treasury."

The knights were dismayed to hear this and said to Master Nicholas: "You would do well to take it to him. It would be much better for Sir Yvain to be in charge of the Treasury than anyone else. He is worthy of it, and his father, to whom God be merciful, loved him dearly." —"Since this is what you advise me to do," replied the chaplain, "I shall do it."

The chaplain mounted his horse, taking the key, and set out for the castle of Orthez, where Sir Yvain was earnestly searching for the keys but could not find them; nor did he know of any way or means whereby to break the locks of the doors in the tower, for they were very strong and he lacked the necessary tools to do it.]

The denouement is further delayed by Froissart's gleeful recital of the trouble experienced by Master Nicholas in getting through the throng that is by now surrounding the castle and clamoring for confirmation of the rumor that Yvain's father is indeed dead. The men of Orthez decide to let the chaplain in, then set about sealing the castle off to prevent anyone from getting in and making off with the contents of the Treasury. Yvain now finds himself imprisoned, locked inside the Treasury tower together with Master Nicholas (and the little key), and obliged to make a public speech to the crowd from a window—the second use, in this passage, of one of Froissart's most characteristic framing devices. Yvain beseeches his fellow subjects to allow him at least a share in the inheritance from his father (pp. 332–33). They assure him that they will do all in their power to guarantee that justice is done him, and that is all he is able to secure for now. For all that Master Nicholas has joined Yvain in the tower, bringing with him the precious key that was to unlock all doors, the narrative has by this stage repressed this detail. A few years later (a few folios later in the manuscript), Yvain is burned to death in the affair of the Wodehouses, or *Bal des Ardents*. The recital of the death of Gaston Fébus thus leads into a consummate example of the "biter-bit" algorithm, used elsewhere in the *Chroniques* to comic effect[33] but employed here with tragicomic overtones.

This examination of metonymic connections in the later *Chroniques* turns now to Sir Walter Scott. The author of the Waverley novels has long been recognized as a deft and perceptive critic of Froissart's prose style. However, if proof were wanted that Scott understood the fundamental aesthetic mainspring behind Froissart's most compelling writing, there is an even better guide to hand than his celebrated *Edinburgh Review* essay of 1805.[34] I refer to a handful of incidents from his 1816 novel *Old Mortality*,[35] which, I argue, will strike a chord in anyone possessed of a reasonable acquaintance with the *Chroniques*.

That Scott had Froissart in mind while composing *Old Mortality* is clear from chapter 35 of the novel, where Henry Morton has been captured and taken into custody by General Grahame of Claverhouse in the wake of an abortive Covenanters' rising. Claverhouse shows his prisoner both courtesy and respect, but Morton is coldly contemptuous of what he appears to view as affectation. Claverhouse retorts by chiding Morton, telling him that he had thought him to be "a different sort of person," sensitive, that is, to chivalrous behavior between equals on opposing sides, between victor and vanquished of equivalent social rank. Then comes Claverhouse's query and Morton's understandably laconic response: "'Did you ever read Froissart?' —'No,' was Morton's answer." Claverhouse parries with a jocular proposal—presented, ironically, as a penance: "'I have half a mind,' said Claverhouse, 'to contrive you should have six months' imprisonment in order to procure you that pleasure. His chapters inspire me with more enthusiasm than even poetry itself. And the noble canon, with what true chivalrous feeling he confines his beautiful expressions of sorrow to the death of the gallant and high-bred knight, of whom it was a pity to see the fall, such was his loyalty to his king, pure faith to his religion, hardihood towards his enemy, and fidelity to his lady-love!—Ah, benedicite! how he will mourn over the fall of such a pearl of knighthood, be it on the side he happens to favour, or on the other. But, truly, for sweeping from the face of the earth some few hundreds of villain churls, who are born but to plough it, the high-born and inquisitive historian has marvellous little sympathy,—as little, or less, perhaps, than John Grahame of Claverhouse'" (*Old Mortality*, p. 382).

Morton's response is to use this panegyric of Froissart's aristocratic values as a pretext for a dignified but scornful request to Claverhouse that he have mercy on his own lowly companion, the plowman Cuddie Headrigg, "'in despite of the contempt in which you hold a profession which some philosophers have considered as useful as that of a soldier'." As Angus Calder points out, Scott himself was not a liberal in the style of a Henry Morton. He had been willing to "endorse the use of severe force against working-class rebels in his own Scotland" (p. 37). At all events, the novelist was clearly aware of the deficiencies of Froissart's history and social vision, even as he extolled the ineffable poetry of the *Chroniques* through the panegyric uttered by a man who, in Scottish history (depending on which side one favored), was both "Bonnie Dundee" and "Bloody Claver's."[36]

Of more direct relevance to the subject of this essay, however, are the passages from the novel that introduce the "Old Mortality" of its title. That is in fact the nickname of an aged Covenanter who rides from cemetery to cemetery in a resolute attempt to keep alive memorials to the glorious, martyred dead and to preserve from oblivion the last, chiseled trace of their passage here on earth. Not unlike the chronicler of Valenciennes, "He considered himself as fulfilling a sacred duty, while renewing to the eyes of posterity the decaying emblems of the zeal and sufferings of their forefathers, and thereby trimming, as it were, the beacon-light, which was to warn future generations to defend their religion even unto blood" (*Old Mortality*, pp. 64–65).

Here is Scott the romantic historical novelist reaching out *across the genres*, down through some five or six centuries of literary and political history, so as to provide us with a wonderfully discreet, encoded but surely quite unmistakable homage to Jean Froissart—chronicler, writer, and poet:

> To talk of the exploits of the Covenanters was the delight, as to repair their monuments was the business, of his life. He was profuse in the communication of all the minute information which he had collected concerning them, their wars, and their wanderings. One would almost have supposed he must have been their contempo-

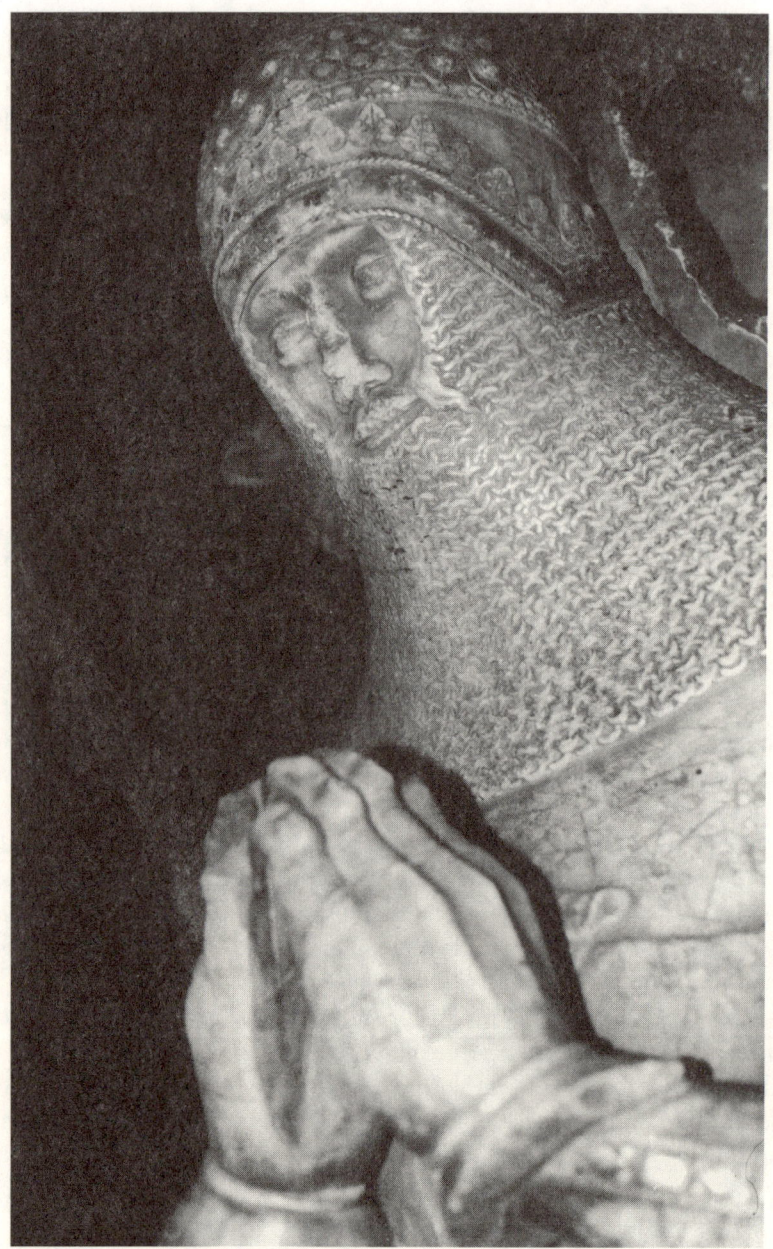

1.2. Detail of funeral effigy from the tomb of Hugh de Calveley (d.1390s), Parish Church of St. Boniface, Bunbury, Cheshire. Photograph, J. Rudderforth. Reproduced by permission of the vicar and churchwardens.

rary, and have actually beheld the passages which he related, so much had he identified his feelings and opinions with theirs, and so much had his narratives the circumstantiality of an eye-witness. (p. 66)

One might even venture to suggest that the inspiration for the figure of Old Mortality himself was none other than Jean Froissart, in his guise as protagonist of his own memorializing narratives. Like those responsible for commissioning the alabaster *gisants* still to be found in many an English village church (fig. 1.2), Froissart was intent upon leaving a lasting memorial to the *souverains preux* and their feats of arms.[37] Just how successful either Froissart or Old Mortality may ultimately prove to have been at *redressing* their respective memorials to the heroes of the past is perhaps suggested by another quotation from Scott's novel:

The common people still regard his memory with great respect; and many are of opinion, that the stones which he repaired will not again require the assistance of the chisel. They even assert, that on the tombs where the manner of the martyrs' murder is recorded, their names have remained indelibly legible since the death of Old Mortality, while those of the persecutors, sculptured on the same monuments, have been entirely defaced. It is hardly necessary to say that this is a fond imagination, and that, since the time of the pious pilgrim, the monuments which were the objects of his care are hastening, like all earthly memorials, into ruin or decay. (p. 68)

Notes

I am grateful to the organizers of the Amherst Froissart Colloquium, Donald Maddox and Sara Sturm-Maddox of the University of Massachusetts, and to Margaret Switten of Mount Holyoke College, for generous assistance with costs associated with my participation. I also thank the Research Support Fund and the Graduate School of the Arts Faculty, University of Manchester, for the subventions that allowed me to travel to the United States to deliver this paper and carry out research at libraries in Chicago and New York. Thanks are also due to friends and colleagues in the Department of French, University of Edinburgh, before whom an initial version of this essay was read in March 1995 as part of that department's centenary celebrations; it was published as "Froissart the Writer and Walter Scott: Chivalry and Its Inheritance in the *Chroniques* and *Old Mortality*," in R. Wakely and P. E. Bennett, eds., *France and Germany in Scotland: Studies in Language and Culture* (Edinburgh, 1996), pp. 65–80. I thank the editors for kind permission to reproduce some of the material.

1. References to the *Chroniques* are either to the Société de l'Histoire de France edition (abbreviated SHF, followed by volume and page numbers) or to the Belgian Royal Academy edition (abbreviated KL, followed by volume and page numbers): Jean Froissart, *Chroniques,* ed. Siméon Luce, Gaston Raynaud, Léon and Albert Mirot, 15 vols., in progress (Paris: Société de l'Histoire de France, 1869–); Jean Froissart, *Oeuvres,* ed. Kervyn de Lettenhove, 28 vols. (Brussels: Académie Royale de Belgique, 1867–77).

2. Seamus Heaney, *The Redress of Poetry* (London and Boston: Faber and Faber, 1995), p. xv.

3. Douglas Kelly reminds us in chap. 6 of this book how, in verse compositions such as the *Prison amoureuse,* Froissart intimates that a true representation of things is to be secured, above all, via the imagination. Philip E. Bennett argues that Froissart was at least to some extent aware of the limitations of his world of *armes et amours* and felt the need for an alternative vision; Bennett, "Female Readers in Froissart: Implied, Fictive and Other," in *Women, the Book and the Worldly,* ed. Lesley Smith and Jane H. M. Taylor (Cambridge: D. S. Brewer, 1995), 13–23.

4. As Elspeth Kennedy points out in chap. 9, Froissart's journeys far and wide in search of supplementary information and eyewitness informants constitute an interesting, centrifugal reversal of the "return to court" motif of Arthurian romance.

5. Peter F. Ainsworth, *Jean Froissart and the Fabric of History: Truth, Myth, and Fiction in the Chroniques* (Oxford: Clarendon Press, 1990), pp. 143–45.

6. "Des paroles que messire Espaeng de Lyon me comptoit estoie tout rafreschi, car elles me venoient grandement a plaisance et toutes très bien les retenoie, et si tost que aux hostelz, sur le chemin que nous fesismes ensamble, descendu estoie, je les escripsoie, fust de soir ou de matin, pour avoir en tou[t] temps advenir mieulx la memoire, car il n'est si juste retenue que cest d'escripture" (SHF 12:65). See also Ainsworth, *Fabric,* pp. 146–48.

7. Cf. SHF 12:238–39: "Or retournay depuis à Bruges et en mon pays, si ouvray sus les paroles et relations faites du gentil chevalier messire Jehan Ferrant Percok, et cronisay tout ce que de Portingal et de Castille est avenu jusques à l'an de grace MYCCC III^{xx} et X."

8. See Ainsworth, *Fabric,* p. 72, n.6, and book 1, prologue, SHF 1:2–3; B MSS: "Or doient donc tout jone gentil homme, qui se voellent avancier, avoir ardant desir d'acquerre le fait et le renommée de proèce, par quoi il soient mis et compté ou nombre des preus, et regarder et considerer comment leur predicesseur, dont il tiennent [leurs] hyretages et portent espoir les armes, sont honnouré et recommandé par leurs biens fais. Je sui seurs que, se ilz regardent et lisent en ce livre, que il trouveront otant de grans fais et de belles apertises d'armes, de durs rencontres, de fors assaus, de fières batailles et de tous autres maniemens d'armes qui se descendent des membres de proèce, que en nulle hystore dont on puist parler, tant soit anchiienne ne nouvelle. Et ce sera à yaus matère et exemples de yaus encoragier en bien faisant, car la memore des bons et li recors des preus atisent et enflament par raison les coers des jones bacelers, qui tirent et tendent à toute per-

fection d'onneur, de quoi proèce est li principaus chiés et li certains ressors."

9. "On est tenu par droite honneur/ D'amer et servir son signeur,/ Ne on ne se puet escuser/ Qu'on li doie riens refuser,/ Corps et biens, avoir et chavance." *La prison amoureuse*, ed. A. Fourrier (Paris: Klincksieck, 1974), ll. 111–15; cf. ll. 1–44 and 138–51. We are reminded of the fierce devotion of Marie de France's Bisclavret to his feudal overlord or indeed of Yvain's lion in Chrétien's *Chevalier au lion*.

10. "Le dit dou bleu chevalier," in Jean Froissart, *"Dits" et "Débats,"* ed. A. Fourrier (Geneva: Droz, 1979), ll. 216–20. As Rupert Pickens suggests in chap. 7, *Clergie* here serves *Chevalerie*. However, *Chevalerie*, it is implied, cannot live without *Clergie*. Compare George Diller's remarks in chap. 3 concerning Froissart's power over his listeners—the military aristocracy—as evinced by his narrative's consecration of his own nocturnal readings of *Meliador*.

11. Cf. Douglas Kelly's and Philip Bennett's observations in note 3 above.

12. It is interesting to compare Froissart's ironic or critical mode with that of the Knight in Guillaume de Machaut's *Dit dou lyon*; see *Oeuvres de Guillaume de Machaut*, ed. E. Hoepffner, vol. 2 (Paris: Firmin-Didot, 1911), ll. 853–1800.

13. Compare Douglas Kelly's observations in chap. 6 concerning Froissart's recourse, in works such as the *Dit dou bleu chevalier*, to enthymeme (meaning "a syllogism in which one premise is not explicitly stated," *New Shorter Oxford English Dictionary* [1993]). Kelly also identifies the use of parallel or analogous images in Froissart's verse compositions as a hallmark of his particular variety of poetic montage.

14. See chap. 6 for Douglas Kelly's percipient remarks on this theme and chaps. 3 and 10, by George Diller and John Fyler, respectively, for further thoughts on the metaphorical properties of the *Voyage*.

15. See KL 14:1–3.

16. Such as those held by the young huntsmen receiving instruction from their master in a miniature from the Paris MS of the *Livre de chasse* (BN fr. 616, folio 51v, "Gaston Fébus enseignant la chasse aux jeunes garçons").

17. For references to wax tablets and styli, see J. Alexander and P. Binski, *Age of Chivalry: Art in Plantagenet England 1200–1400* (London: Royal Academy of Arts, 1987), p. 383; E. Lalou, in J. Glénisson, ed., *Le livre au moyen age* (Paris: Presses du CNRS, 1988), pp. 30–31; Lalou, *Les comptes sur tablettes de cire de la chambre aux deniers de Philippe III le Hardi et de Philippe IV le Bel (1282–1309)* (Paris: Boccard, 1994); Lalou, "Les tablettes de cire médiévales," *Bibliothèque de l'Ecole des Chartes* 147 (1989):123–40; Lalou, "Un compte de l'hôtel du roi sur tablettes de cire, 10 octobre–14 novembre [1350]," *Bibliothèque de l'Ecole des Chartes* 152 (1994):91–127; J. Trenchs Odena and M. J. Carbonell, "Tablettes de cire aragonaises (XIIe-XVe siècles)," *Bibliothèque de l'Ecole des Chartes* 151 (1993):155–60; R. H. Rouse and M. A. Rouse, "Wax Tablets," *Language and Communication* 9 (1989):175–91; B. Bischoff, *Latin Palaeography* (Cambridge: Cambridge University Press, 1990), pp. 13–14. Also S. O'Connor and D. Tweddle, "A Set of Waxed Tablets from Swinegate, York," *Bibliologia* 12 (1987):307–22. The eight boxwood tablets found at Swinegate are small; each measures only 50mm x 30mm x 0.20mm. Their Middle English and

Latin inscriptions, in Cursiva Anglicana, are written in "landscape mode"; a single side of only seven lines holds little more than five or six words per line. See also *Interim* (a quarterly published by the York Archaeological Trust), vol. 14, no. 4 (1989); vol. 15, nos. 3 and 4 (1990); and vol. 17, no. 2 (1992). I am indebted to R. A. Hall of the York Trust for this information and to Godfried Croenen for the references to works by E. Lalou and Trenchs Odena/Carbonell.

18. I am grateful to Sotheby's of London, in particular to Christopher De Hamel, keeper of Ancient Manuscripts, for permission to reproduce the photograph of this item from their sale catalogue.

19. Peter F. Ainsworth, "Collationnement, montage et *jeu parti:* le début de la campagne espagnole du Prince Noir (1366–1367) dans les *Chroniques* de Jean Froissart," *Le Moyen Age* 100 (1994):369–411.

20. *Le livre des fais du bon messire Jehan le Maingre, dit Bouciquaut, mareschal de France et gouverneur de Jennes*, ed. D. Lalande (Geneva: Droz, 1985), pp. 8–10. This passaage is discussed in Ainsworth, *Fabric*, pp. 72–73.

21. Jacqueline Cerquiglini-Toulet, "Fullness and Emptiness: Shortages and Storehouses of Lyric Treasure in the Fourteenth and Fifteenth Centuries," in Daniel Poirion and Nancy Freeman Regalado, eds., *Contexts: Style and Values in Medieval Art and Literature,* special issue of *Yale French Studies* (1991):224–39, esp. p. 236. See also Keith Busby's remarks (chap. 5) on images of imprisonment and Froissart's claustrophilia: enclosed places as propitious for the making of poetry. Philip Bennett, in contrast, points to Froissart's awareness of "the prison that love had become for writers" ("Female Readers," p. 22), a prison that he, in some measure at least, sought to transcend via the ironic viewpoint of male behavior furnished by his implied or virtual female readers.

22. "Le dit dou florin," in Jean Froissart, *"Dits" et "Débats"* (Geneva: Droz, 1979), ll. 199–207.

23. Here p. 95; Peter F. Ainsworth, "Knife, Key, Bear and Book: Poisoned Metonymies and the Problem of *Translatio* in Froissart's Later *Chroniques,*" *Medium Aevum* 59 (1990):91–113.

24. See Peter F. Dembowski, *Jean Froissart and his "Meliador": Context, Craft, and Sense* (Lexington, Ky.: French Forum, 1983), pp. 18–19.

25. Henri Moranvillé, *Manuscrit de ses chroniques destiné par Froissart à Richard II, roi d'Angleterre*, Besançon, Bibliothèque Municipale, S.l.n.d. In-fo, 6 pp. non numérotées. pl. h.t., cote BrB.1 (1). Moranvillé's identification of the manuscript in question as Besançon 864 is no longer accepted by Froissart scholars.

26. KL 15:141–42, 167. See also Jean Froissart, *Le paradis d'amour / L'orloge amoureus*, ed. Peter F. Dembowski (Geneva: Droz, 1986), pp. 3–4.

27. Nicole Chareyron, "Froissart le revenant," *Perspectives Médiévales* 15 (1989): 66–73. See also Marie-Thérèse de Medeiros, "Voyage et lieux de mémoire: Le retour de Froissart en Angleterre," *Le Moyen Age* 98 (1992):419–28.

28. The topic is explored in chap. 8 of Ainsworth, *Fabric*, "Creating an Image: Edward III in the Rome Manuscript."

29. Ainsworth, "Knife," pp. 104; 112, n.50.

30. See n. 21 and Michel Zink, "Le temps, c'est de l'argent: Remarques sur le *Dit du florin* de Jean Froissart," in *Et c'est la fin pour quoy sommes ensemble,* Mélanges J. Dufournet, vol. 3 (Paris: Champion, 1993), pp. 1455–64.

31. Jean Froissart, *Le joli buisson de Jonece,* ed. A. Fourrier (Geneva: Droz, 1975); hereafter *JBJ.*

32. Again, one is reminded of Machaut's *Dit dou lyon* and its paradisal island domain, accessible only to those completely innocent of dissembling in matters of the heart.

33. Ainsworth, *Fabric,* pp. 114–18.

34. Sir Walter Scott, "Johnes' Translation of Froissart," *Edinburgh Review* 5, no. 10 (1805):347–62. For astute comments on auditory and dramatic features of Froissart's style, see esp. p. 347.

35. Sir Walter Scott, *Old Mortality* (1816; reprint, ed. Angus Calder, Harmondsworth: Penguin Books, 1975).

36. I am indebted for this reference to Janis Spurlock, sometime associate editor of *French Studies.*

37. I thank the vicar and churchwardens of St. Boniface's Church, Bunbury, Cheshire, for permission to reproduce the photograph of Sir Hugh Calveley's funeral effigy (fig. 1.2). I am grateful to Charles Wood of Dartmouth College for allowing me to see the unpublished presidential address "Froissart's Chronicles, Memorial Field, and the Concept of Chivalry," which he delivered at Dartmouth College in 1994. Wood adduces a parallel between the understandable decline in the popularity of the *Chroniques* as suitable reading material for young men in post–Great War Europe, on the one hand, and the building in the United States of numerous memorial sports stadiums (such as Soldier Field, Chicago), on the other—a case of heroism migrating from battlefield to playing field, yet another metonymic shift. In this regard, Wood argues that Froissart's *Chroniques* has been unjustly stigmatized for its allegedly unthinking militarism. In his view, it "memorialize[s] not everyone, but only those whose *beaux gestes* in the face of impossible odds define a chivalry that allows men possessing it not just to rise above the sheer awfulness of their age, but also to speak to a vision of humanity perhaps nobler in its values. Only such men and *their* chivalry are worthy of being remembered forever." While this interpretation does not, in my view, account for every shade of meaning to be found in the *Chroniques* under the heading of chivalry, it is an interesting hypothesis concerning the nature of their memorializing function and their glimpse of a possible transcendence in regard to the *souverains preux.*

2

Froissart, Personal Testimony, and the Peasants' Revolt of 1381

CHARLES T. WOOD

Of all the Roman gods, Mercury is surely the one who would have most appealed to Jean Froissart, courtly poet and chronicler of chivalry. Mercury was, after all, the inventor of the lyre and that deity who had bestowed on Pandora, the first woman, her arts of persuasion. Even more strikingly, perhaps, it was he who had guided Priam to Achilles' tent and who had reminded Aeneas in Carthage of the war-filled high destiny for which he was to abandon the delights of Dido's embraces. In short, as the god of persuasion, dexterity, and eloquence, Mercury had attributes useful to lovers and warriors alike, and if he was also the "patron of . . . rogues, vagabonds, and thieves," these, too, were types of men whom Froissart would meet, and write about, in the course of his own wanderings.[1]

Above all else, however, Mercury was Jupiter's messenger, the god whose contacts with mortals were not infrequently their source of the information needed to set history in motion. Thus, even though Froissart was a maker of history only in the sense that he created it in his *Chroniques*, the fact remains that his achievement as a historian, not to mention the value we can derive from him as a primary source, ultimately depends less on written documents than on the typically oral stories he relentlessly sought from those who had been participants in, and shapers of, the events in which he was interested. In effect, he often becomes their messenger.

Such a statement could not be made about the earliest version of the *Chroniques*, for it was little more than a deft reworking of the writings of Jean le Bel.[2] Yet later versions departed more and more from Jean le Bel, not just because they began to cover events that had happened only after

Jean had written, but more because Froissart began to seek out people whose own recollections could provide him with new information. As a result, the shape of his *Chronicles* began to change, becoming less reflective of the dictates of time and space as we moderns would understand them than of the complex layering of encounters he had had with various people whom he had met, some by chance, others by design. In the words of Peter Ainsworth, Froissart's approach is one in which "all his interlocutors tend to find their way into the *Chroniques* as its protagonists."[3]

The nature of the process involved is most apparent in Froissart's account of the journey he took in 1388 to meet the count of Foix in his Béarnaise capital of Orthez, a trip he quite specifically made in order to learn from foreign participants about "the truth of distant transactions."[4] Several days from Orthez, however, he finds himself joined in the journey by Sir Espan de Lyon, one of the count's knights who, as it turns out, participated in various relevant campaigns. When the knight remarks: "'See, yonder is Malvoisin: have you not inserted in your history (of which you have been speaking to me) how the duke of Anjou, when he was in this country, advanced to Lourdes [and] besieged and conquered it . . . ?'" Froissart replies: "'I believe I have not mentioned it, nor have I ever been informed of such an event. I therefore pray you to relate the business, to which I shall attentively listen . . . that posterity might have the advantage of it, for there is nothing like writing for the preservation of events'" (Johnes 2:80, 91).

In much the same way, when Froissart reaches his hotel in Orthez, he finds that the bascot de Mauléon is also a guest there, staying with a cousin. Since Sir Espan de Lyon had commented favorably on the bascot's military exploits only days before, Froissart is naturally anxious to meet him, and the following incident soon takes place:

> One night, as we were sitting around the fire chatting. . . , [the bascot's] cousin began a conversation relative to his former life, and asked him to tell of his adventures and success in arms, without concealing loss or profit, as he knew he could well remember them. Upon this [the bascot] said, "Sir John, have you in your chronicle what I am going to speak of?" "I do not know," replied I; "but begin your story, which I shall be happy to hear; for I cannot recollect every particular of my history, nor can I have been perfectly informed of every event." (Johnes 2:102)

That Froissart often failed to be "perfectly informed" is a reality on which most scholars would readily agree. James Sherborne has argued, for example, that his treatment of Richard II's early reign "is permeated with ignorance or error," that it "would be difficult to imagine ... greater ignorance of English political life at this time" than that displayed in his comment "that after the death of Edward III John of Gaunt 'had the government of the kingdom'."[5] Correct as such judgments may be, they nevertheless overlook a crucial point, that insofar as Froissart increasingly based his narrative on the personal testimony of participants, the viewpoints of those participants—their assessment of crucial events, why they were significant, and why those involved had acted as they did—also find themselves embedded in that narrative, factually inaccurate though the result may often be. As is perhaps nowhere better demonstrated than in Froissart's account of the English Peasants' Revolt of 1381, his *Chronicles* takes on its greatest value when studied less for narrative precision than for what the narratives reveal about the outlook of those on whose evidence they depend.

Although Froissart had long lived in England, from 1361 to 1369 frequently serving in the retinue of Edward III's wife, Philippa of Hainault (Brereton, 10), he himself was not an eyewitness to the tumultuous events of 1381. Rather, he specifies that his version is based on "information I had at the time" from unnamed sources (Johnes 1:652). His specifics make it likely, however, that this information came from the circle of Joan of Kent, Richard II's mother, if not from Joan herself. She appears in Froissart's story with greater frequency than anyone else, and it is also the case that some incidents involving her, notably the peasant attacks she experienced as she returned to London from a pilgrimage to Canterbury, appear in no other chronicle (Sherborne, 53). Moreover, since Joan had spent her formative years in the household of Philippa of Hainault, there being treated almost as a daughter,[6] she had more reasons than most for putting her trust in Philippa's former retainer and fellow countryman Jean Froissart. If so, what can the shadings in his story tell us about the king's mother and how she viewed both the revolt and its outcome?

Froissart assures his readers that he is writing of "all that was done" by the "evil-disposed" among "the lower ranks of the people" so that the uprising "may serve as an example to mankind" (Johnes 1:652). As is so often the case in his *Chroniques*, then, he intends a universal lesson to be drawn from uniquely particular data. In his view, too, England was normally a part of what would later be termed "the great chain of being," a well-ordered realm in which a divinely ordained king rules while "[t]he prelates and gentlemen are ... served ... [by] the commonalty, whom they keep in bondage." But this tranquillity was suddenly shattered when "[a] crazy priest in the county of Kent, called John Ball," began to preach on disquieting themes that Froissart is far from alone in reporting: "'My good friends, things cannot go well in England ... until everything shall be held in common, when there shall be neither vassal nor lord..., when the lords shall no more be masters than ourselves. ... Are we not all descended from the same parents, Adam and Eve?'" That much is familiar, surely, but what follows is unique to Froissart, namely Ball's explanation for all England's social ills: "'We are called slaves,'" his Ball is made to say, "'and, if we do not perform our services, we are beaten, for we have no sovereign to whom we can complain, or who wishes to hear us and do us justice'" (Johnes 1:652–53).

In objective terms, Ball's claim that England lacked a sovereign had considerable merit since Richard II had been only ten at the time of his accession in 1377. Moreover, even though at least two bishops had likened him to Christ in the course of that year—Adam Houghton, for example, dilating on the biblical text "This is my beloved son" to arrive at the conclusion that all should "'do him honor in the same manner as the pagans, that is the three kings of Cologne, did to the Son of God'"[7]—soon after the coronation the Commons had made it clear in a petition that he was to have no role in the composition and policies of his governing council until he had become "'of full age to know both good and evil'" (Wood, 36). Understandably, then, it had been the council, not Richard, that had ruled right down to 1381, a reality that must have increasingly grated on the royalist sensibilities of a woman like Joan of Kent.

Given that fact, what becomes striking about Froissart's ensuing account is the extent to which his revolting peasants take action primarily against those who had governed in the absence of a viable king—and specifically in retaliation for all the evil deeds they had committed, and were continuing to commit, during Richard's minority. For example, when "the common people of London" heard of Ball's preaching, they "began to say among themselves that the kingdom was too badly governed and the nobility had seized on all the gold and silver coin" (Johnes 1:654). Little wonder, then, that these men and their allies should ultimately have sacked and burned John of Gaunt's Savoy Palace, thereby proving with their deeds that they differed from the modern view that Gaunt had had nothing to do with governmental policies.[8] Similarly, when Froissart's Kentish peasants reached Canterbury and the palace of Archbishop Simon Sudbury, also the chancellor of England, "they pillaged the apartments of the archbishop, saying as they were carrying off different articles, 'This chancellor of England has had this piece of furniture very cheap: he must now give us an account of the revenues of England, and of the large sums he has levied since the coronation of the king'" (Johnes 1:654, 655).

Not content with these actions, when the rebels reached Blackheath they decided to send an emissary to Richard at the Tower "to tell him that what they were doing was for his service, for the kingdom had been for several years wretchedly governed, to the great dishonour of the realm and to the oppression of the lower ranks of the people, by his uncles, by the clergy, and in particular by the archbishop of Canterbury, his chancellor, from whom they would have an account of his ministry" (Johnes 1:655–56). Lastly, when the rebels took the Tower, they immediately "entered the apartment of the princess [Richard II's mother], and cut her bed, which so much terrified her that she fainted, and in this condition was by her servants and ladies carried to the river side, when she was put into a covered boat, and conveyed to the house called The Wardrobe, where she continued that day and night like a woman half dead, until she was comforted by the king her son, as you presently shall hear" (Johnes 1:659). In the interim, the rebels in the Tower had also executed four men discovered there, notably the hated archbishop and chancellor, Simon Sudbury (Johnes 1:659). Moreover, "execution" seems the proper term, not "murder," since the way in which the victims were decapitated suggests that their judges had the specific rituals and penalties of a treason trial very much in mind, an impression that is strengthened by the additional specifics recorded in Froissart's report of how "these scoundrels" then "fixed those four heads on long pikes, and had them carried before them through the streets of London; when they had sufficiently played with them, they placed them on London Bridge, as if they had been traitors to their king and country" (Johnes 1:659).

In short, everything about Froissart's account thus far demonstrates that while he and his sources had no sympathy with the peasants and their urban allies, they appear to have thought that the principal cause of the Peasants' Revolt lay in the oppression and fiscal mismanagement of Richard II's minority government. It looks, too, as though Froissart's sources agree with this negative judgment even while disagreeing with the peasants' solution. That being the case, one last aspect of Froissart's John Ball needs emphasis, for if his preaching stressed that all the evils in England had arisen because "'we have no sovereign to whom we can complain'," its solution was for all those aggrieved to "'go to the king, who is young, and remonstrate with him on our servitude, telling him we must have it otherwise, or that we shall find a remedy for it ourselves. If we wait on him in a body, all those who come under the appellation of slaves, or who are held in bondage, will follow us in the hopes of being free. When the king shall see us, we shall obtain a favorable answer'" (Johnes 1:653).

There is, of course, a seeming anomaly in Ball's reported position here, but only if one assumes that Froissart based his version on testimony received from followers of the renegade priest. On the one hand, Ball stresses that England is without a sovereign, but, on the other, like Father Gapon on Bloody Sunday he seems also to believe that all will be well if only the oppressed can meet personally with their king and tell him of their miseries. That view makes no sense if Richard remained too young to be a sovereign, but an explanation emerges when one recalls the likelihood that Froissart's information came from Joan of Kent or her circle. For even though Ball's followers would neither have known nor appreciated the point, on January 6, 1381, Richard II had turned fourteen, in canon law the age of discretion and, in France, the age at which King Charles V had proclaimed, only seven years before, that his eldest son should attain his full majority (Wood, 35). Thus, if England had long suffered from the consequences of a minor king, from a maternal point of view it need do so no longer. Richard was now an adult, a man finally graced with the authority needed to restore justice to his realm.

Here, however, a practical problem arises, one to which the remaining portions of Froissart's account of the Peasants' Revolt are quite consciously designed to speak. As a matter of law, England had never formally recognized an age of majority for its kings, and the record in both England and France makes clear that, no matter what the law might provide, most child kings came of age and had their authority effectively recognized only at such times as they themselves seized the initiative—and then made their decisions stick, often by forcing others to accept them (Wood, 29–44).

In other words, royal majority demanded practical proof of its existence, and that Froissart recognized this reality is nowhere better demonstrated than in his story of how Edward, the Black Prince and Richard II's father, had attained adulthood. Born in 1330, Edward had received nominal titles at a tender age and had further been made Prince of Wales a month before his thirteenth birthday. Nevertheless, he proved his capacity to lead, and with it his full manhood, only at the battle of Crécy in 1346, when he had reached the age of sixteen (although, be it noted, our chronicler thought him to be just fourteen). In Froissart's version, Edward III makes his son commander of the English first division, but when it is hard pressed by the French, a knight is dispatched to the king to plead for assistance. Having heard him out, the king replies: "'Is my son dead, unhorsed, or so badly wounded that he cannot support himself? . . . [R]eturn back to those that sent you, and tell them from me not to send again for me this day . . . as long as my son has life; and say that I command them to let the boy win his spurs; for I am determined, if it please God, that all the glory and honor of this day shall be given to him'" (Johnes 1:167). Even more strikingly, after the battle is won, Froissart's Edward III searches out his heir and, after finding him, embraces and kisses him, all the while exclaiming, "'Sweet son, God give you good perseverance: you are my son, for most loyally have you acquitted yourself this day; you are worthy to be a sovereign'" (Johnes 1:168).

Given that story and Froissart's treatment of the Peasants' Revolt and its denouement, it is not too much to say that the sources for this part of his *Chroniques* saw that revolt as Richard II's Crécy. In this reading, Froissart's informants believed that misgovernment during the minority had largely caused the uprising, though this is not to say that they sympathized in any way with its participants. Insight has its limits, after all, and whatever grievances Froissart's contacts may themselves have felt against Sudbury, the royal uncles, and all others responsible for the formulation of policy, they remained true to their aristocratic values in seeing Wat Tyler, Jack Straw, John Ball, and their followers as little more than a godless rabble, to be struck down as such. At the same time, however, they saw Richard II's performance in putting down the rebellion as persuasive proof that he had finally come of age and could therefore begin to rule in his own person. This is, moreover, a conclusion with which Froissart himself heartily agrees.

Richard's first personal test comes on Corpus Christi, June 13, but its results prove inconclusive. After hearing mass in the Tower, he is rowed down the Thames in a barge, accompanied by the earls of Salisbury, Warwick, and Suffolk, but they soon encounter "upwards of ten thousand men" on the banks. Although the king is advised not to land, still he insists on having the barge rowed up and down the river as he shouts out, "'What do ye wish for? I am come hither to hear what you have to say.'" Nevertheless, when the rebels insist that he land first, "The earl of Salisbury then replied for the king, and said, 'Gentlemen, you are not properly dressed, nor in a fit condition for the king to talk with you,'" after which Richard returns to the Tower, leaving the mob to move on to Blackheath, "inflamed with passion" (Johnes 1:657–58).

In this first encounter, then, Richard shows signs of a promising initiative, but at the crucial moment he fails to prevent one of his advisers, Salisbury, from taking command and speaking in his name to end all possibility of fruitful negotiations. Literarily, the indecisiveness of this outcome serves to increase the level of suspense, a quality much prized by Froissart, and he allows it to be resolved only two days later, on June 15, when there is a quite different outcome. By that point, Wat Tyler has retired to Smithfield with "upwards of twenty thousand" of the most obdurate of his followers (Johnes 1:661), and while the story is familiar, it bears repeating in Froissart's terms in order to reemphasize the extent to which the lasting historical value of his *Chroniques* often lies in the way in which its participant-based narrative allows us better to understand contemporary assessments of crucial events. If Froissart had not so relentlessly pursued his sources, insisting on personal testimony from them that was both oral and written, these views would otherwise have been lost to us.

At Smithfield, Wat Tyler and his reprobate supporters have just agreed to pillage the city of London when Richard suddenly "appear[s] in sight, attended by sixty horse." The famous shouting and scuffling match ensues, during the course of which the lord mayor of London strikes Tyler dead. The "crowds of evil men begin to mutter, 'They've killed our captain. Come on, we'll slay the lot'."

> Then the king did an extraordinarily rash thing, but it ended well. As soon as Tyler was dispatched, he left his men, saying, "Stay here, no one is to follow me," and went alone towards those half-crazed people, to whom he said: "Sirs, what more do you want? You have no other captain but me. I am your king, behave peaceably." On hearing this, the majority of them were ashamed and began to break up. (Brereton, 227)

Help then arrives; the last of the mob is dispersed; and Richard returns to London, where he hastens to comfort his mother:

> When she saw her son, she was overjoyed and said: "Ah, my son, how anxious I have been today on your account!" "Yes, my lady," the King answered, "I know you have. But now take comfort and praise God, for it is a time to praise Him. Today I have recovered my inheritance, the realm of England which I had lost."
>
> The King remained with his mother for the whole day and the lords and nobles went back peaceably to their houses. A royal proclamation was drawn up . . . ordering all persons who were not natives of London . . . to leave at once. . . . All the people from the distant counties who had flocked there at the summons of those wicked men set off hurriedly for their own places, and never dared to come back again. (Brereton, 228–29)

Appropriately, then, there is a happy ending. Through what Froissart would doubtless have called the king's "honorable example," not to mention his "great prowess," Richard II has come of age (Johnes 1:3). After years of turmoil caused by the ill-considered policies and greed of a minority government, the vacuum is filled, the great chain of being restored. England has a true sovereign once more, and, after his practical demonstration of leadership, "the nobles" go "back peaceably to their houses" while the "wicked men set off hurriedly for their own places." At least that's how it appears to have looked to those who gave Froissart "information . . . at the time."

And that, in the end, is a statement that may best convey the true historical value of Froissart's *Chroniques* at its best. With patient research and the wisdom of hindsight, modern historians may know, as Joan of Kent in 1381 did not, just how many challenges yet remained, just how many more years Richard II would have to wait before becoming fully king. They know, too, of the disaster with which he would be visited when he began to insist, perhaps too zealously, on all those prerogatives he had come to believe were no more than his due. In the present context, however, such knowledge is irrelevant. What matters, rather, is that the nature of Froissart's interactions with others, the very basis for his *Chroniques*, allows the reader to gain unexpected insight into the thoughts of at least some of those who actually made the history that this wandering canon and treasurer of Chimay worked so hard to record, so "that posterity might have the advantage of it." Froissart may have lighted no candles for Mercury, but his principal value to history, like that god's, may lie in the fact that he, too, served many times as a messenger.

Notes

1. Thomas Bulfinch, *Bulfinch's Mythology* (New York: Avenel Books, 1979), pp. 7–8, 13, 226, 263, 926.

2. Jean Froissart, *Chronicles*, ed. and tr. Geoffrey Brereton (Harmondsworth: Penguin Classics, 1968), p. 13. Hereafter cited as Brereton.

3. Peter F. Ainsworth, *Jean Froissart and the Fabric of History* (Oxford: Clarendon Press, 1990), p. 157.

4. Sir John Froissart, *Chronicles of England, France, Spain, and the Adjoining Countries*, tr. Thomas Johnes (London: W. Smith, 1839), 2:68; hereafter cited as Johnes. Since the *Chroniques* is not a literary text, technically speaking, for economy's sake I do not cite its original French in the text, but in all instances I have checked the translations used against the original for their accuracy. In general, I have used the Johnes translation because of its familiarity, but in two later instances I have used the more recent Brereton since in those cases it better captures the nuances of the original.

5. J. W. Sherborne, "Charles VI and Richard II," in *Froissart: Historian*, ed. J. J. N. Palmer (Woodbridge, England: Boydell Press, 1981), pp. 51, 52. On p. 53, however, Sherborne stresses that Froissart's treatment of the Peasants' Revolt is "one of the more informed sections of the *Chronicles*."

6. Michael Packe, *King Edward III*, ed. L. C. B. Seaman (London: Routledge & Kegan Paul, 1983), pp. 113–14.

7. As cited in Charles T. Wood, *Joan of Arc and Richard III* (New York: Oxford University Press, 1980), p. 80.

8. For a discussion of similar perceptions about Gaunt that are based on quite different evidence, see Wood, pp. 29–31.

3

Froissart's 1389 Travel to Béarn
A Voyage Narration to the Center of the *Chroniques*

GEORGE T. DILLER

Froissart opens book 3 of his *Chroniques* by recounting how, some 607 years ago, he set out from Pamiers for Gaston de Foix's castle in Orthez, the chief city of Béarn on the French side of the Pyrenees.[1] His narration converges on this city and its lord in a number of ways that show that his ambitions for his literary work are no less important than his historiographical goals. Outwardly, Froissart composes the travel log of his six-day voyage (SHF 12:21)[2] in such a manner as to heighten with each successive day the reader's anticipation of the account of his arrival and encounter with the elegant, proud, and independent lord of Foix, Gaston Fébus, at Orthez. The suspended narration of the death of Gaston's only son and successor thus adds a powerful dramatic goal to the journey and to the text. We remember how Espan de Lyon, Froissart's guide and usually garrulous travel companion, puts an end to Sir John's persistent questioning by declaring the events too awful for him to recount and by advising the chronicler to find another informant at Orthez: "La matiere en est trop piteuse, si ne vous en vueil pas parler; quant vous venrez à Ortais, vous trouverez bien, se vous le demandez, qui le vous dira" (SHF 12:75). [The subject is too pitiful, so I do not want to talk to you about it; when you come to Orthez, you will well find, if you ask, someone who will tell you.](translations mine unless otherwise indicated)

But along the written voyage from Pamiers to Orthez Froissart examines and illustrates other literary goals. First, the glorious reputation of Fébus and of his court, we are told, was attracting men of arms and adventurers from every corner of Europe, and that repute had strongly motivated the chronicler's trip: "Nouvelles de quel royaume ne de quel païs que ce feust la dedens on aprenoit, car de tous païs, pour la vaillance du seigneur, elles y aplouvoient et venoient. La fu je enformez de la greigneur partie des faiz d'armes qui estoient avenuz."[3] [News from every kingdom, from every county was learned of there, for from all countries, because of the lord's (Gaston's) valiance, news came raining in. There was I informed of the greater part of the deeds of arms that had occurred.]

Indeed, the information that the chronicler garners from his interviews at Orthez supplies the greater part of the third book's subsequent narrative, historical material. In an immediate sense, then, the journey account serves as an entry point into itself (book 3), much as his trips to England and to Scotland are gateways to book 1[4] and as Isabeau de Bavière's entry into Paris will serve book 4.[5] This text, which takes us to the *Chroniques*'s distant informants, becomes then a voyage to its own sources.

Second, the dialogues the writer composes between himself and his first informant, Espan de Lyon, assert and test the work's own narrative reliability just as much as they extend into the Pyrenees region the reader's knowledge about the great, tentacular Anglo-French struggle. It is with this intent that Froissart repeatedly affirms that his text is the integral, faithful reproduction of Espan's words, as for example in this well-known passage: "Si tost que aux hostelz, sur le chemin que nous fesismes ensamble, descendu estoie, je les escripsoie, fust de soir ou de matin" (SHF 12:65) [As soon as I had gotten off at the hotels along the way we traveled together, I would write (my accounts), whether evening or morning.]

In another instructive passage, Espan starts out recounting an episode from the siege of Derval dating from some fifteen years earlier, but then he hesitates: "'[J]e croy bien que tout ce vous avez en vostre hystoire'." [I do believe that you have all this in your history.] Let that be no cause for omission, responds the chronicler: "'Je ne sçay . . . , il ne me souvient pas du tout; mais dictes-moy de l'escarmuche et du siège comment il en ala, espoir le savez-vous par autre maniere que je ne sçay'" (SHF 12:36).[6] [I don't know . . . , I don't remember everything; but tell me about the skirmish and siege, how it went: perhaps you know it in a different way than I do.] Here Espan assumes authorship to the second degree, as both informant and reflective reader of the *Chroniques*.

Froissart also uses his dialogue format to proclaim before Espan his oft-expressed belief in the power of the written word to conserve events in perpetual memory: "'Saincte Marie, sire, di-ge au chevalier, que vos paroles me sont aggreables et que elles me font grant bien, tandis que vous les me comptés, et vous ne les perdez pas, car toutes seront mises en memoire et en ramembrance et croniquiés en l'istoire que je poursieu'"

(SHF 12:70; cf. 75).[7] [Saint Mary, sire, I said to the knight, how agreeable your words are to me and how they do me good, as you recount them to me, and you don't lose them, for all will be set in memory and membrance and chronicled in the history I am pursuing.] In short, much of this narration is highly self-reflective and concerns as much its own creation and status as it does the recording of a historical trip.

Yet for the author of book 3 the crowning moment of this opening voyage narration will be to recount how he read his immense Arthurian romance, *Meliador*, before the assembled heroes and informants of his *Chroniques*. For a short moment in the composition of his *Chroniques*, during these late winter night readings of his romance, Froissart portrays himself as hero in his own work, who by his words commands the silence and complete attention of Gaston Fébus and his court, thus successfully bridging the time between the prose of his *Chroniques* and the ideal, verse universe of his *Meliador*.

Certainly, reaching Orthez at last permits Froissart to meet the enlightened but impulsively cruel prince whom he has already admired and celebrated in his text. His arrival has brought him to the heralds and men of arms upon whose accounts he depends to complete his narrative of the assassination of Gaston's son and to write his third book. However, in terms of the hierarchy of narrative values, Orthez is above all the crowning point of the voyage because it is here that Froissart inserts, into the matrix of his *Chroniques*, the account of his performance of his own recently completed Arthurian romance; it is here that he inserts into book 3, dedicated to Gui II of Châtillon, count of Blois (d. 1397), this huge *verse* work dedicated to Wenceslas of Bohemia (1337–88), the principal former patron of his poetic works. Here then we read about the author's reading of his own verse work, commanded by the hero, Gaston Fébus (Phoebus), of the very work into which it is a part (book 3). In turn, we learn that in his immense verse romance—30,771 extant octosyllabic couplets—Froissart implanted 79 poems by Wenceslas.[8]

In an oft-quoted passage, Froissart records how his words commanded total silence over Gaston's court during his nightly torch-lit readings: "En lisant nul n'osoit parler ne mot dire" (SHF 12:76). [As I read, no one dared speak or say a word.] At night, *Meliador* the romance gives to the chronicler's words authority over those men of arms whose words in turn, during the day, Froissart will solicit, and that by the clerk's pen will transform the deeds and destinies of their companions into written eternity, words upon which the existence of book 3 depends. The empowerment gained by reciting the Arthurian courtly adventures of Hermondine and Meliador is not limited to the knightly *auditeurs* gathered in Gaston's castle. In his texts, the writer weakens the boundaries between *Meliador* and book 3, between romance and chronicle. We also find inserted into *Le dit dou florin* another description of the reading of *Meliador*. The verse *Meliador*, its reading described by Froissart—both its author and the author of the englobing prose work, creates a virtual *prosimètre*. Indeed, the anticipated introduction of the Arthurian romance colors the way the writer composes the preceding trip narrative, as well as his description of Gaston and his court, to whom he read the questing adventures of the Chevalier au Soleil d'Or and his knightly companions. We are in the presence of a very self-conscious literary construct here, influenced by the complex layering in Guillaume de Machaut's *dits*.

Consider, thus, the affective landscape that Froissart introduces into the preceding voyage narrative. Though he set out from Blois (*Le dit dou florin*, 270), he omits entirely from his narration the longest part of his trip across France, from Blois to Carcasonne. He begins his sustained travel text only when, after having left all the cities of the Kingdom of France, he arrives in Pamiers, that is, in territory governed by the count of Foix. Then once he sets out from Pamiers, he crosses from this world into a land of *adventure et merveilles*, much as the questing knight who crosses the *Borne de Galway*[9] or the *Pont de l'Épée*.[10] And so it is that when Froissart describes his, the writer's, travel to Orthez, his landscape will connote space suggestive of the danger and the unknown through which knights quest in the *Lancelot en prose*. Thus, "et chevauchames unes landes qui durent en alant devers Thoulouse bien XV. lieues, et apppele-on ces landes *Landes Bourc*, et y a moult de *perilleux passaiges*" (SHF 12:35, my emphasis; cf. 27). [And we rode on a heath that extends going toward Toulouse a good fifteen leagues, and they call this heath *Landes bourc*, and there are many perilous crossings there.] To this he adds, almost as a personal aside, "Pour gens qui seroient avisez." That is, it's a perilous land if you know how—as I do—to read the signs properly. In similar manner, Froissart notes his arrival at the Pas au Larre: "Adont avisai-ge et regarday le pays; si me sembla moult estrange et me comptoie pour perdu et en très grand aventure, se ne fust la compaignie du chevalier" (SHF 12:48). [Then I took in and looked over the country; and it seemed most foreboding to me and I considered myself done for and in great peril, had it not been for the knight's company.] Successful passage through otherworld landscape, as Dante had shown, depends on a precious companion and experienced guide (Virgil). And so our chronicler must introduce Espan de Lyon to serve as narrator-guide and *compagnon* through the prose of the *Chroniques* and the lands of Gaston Fébus.

Though Froissart records with reasonable accuracy the sequence of towns and places through which he passed, individual, real details of those towns and the country merit recognition in his text only in the most limited terms, as for instance Tarbes, which is merely a good horse town: "c'est une ville trop bien aisie pour séjourner chevaulx de bon foins, bonne avoines et de belle rivière" (Diverres, 50). Even the descriptions of fortifications are so general that they exclude most identifiable reality. But Froissart is not interested here in familiar space; to reach Orthez and the romance universe of *Meliador*, his voyage must lead through the undefinable dangers of quest adventure.

As Froissart begins composing book 3, he sets in motion a stratified, retrospective process. First there had been the act of writing *Meliador*, an act itself founded on the composed memories of Arthurian texts, of Jean le Bel's texts, and of Froissart's own early travels in Scotland; then comes the memory—imagined?—of reading his verse work coincidentally with his recent stay at Orthez. All these memories blur with memories of the courtly universes read in other texts. Thus, while Froissart's description of Gaston's reign over Béarn and Foix invariably gives emphasis to the count's political and fiscal astuteness and to his cruelty, when the chronicler's text reaches the nocturnal courtly site where he relives or enshrines his glorious triumphs as a performing, reading writer, Gaston and his court partake in that illumination of the *Chroniques* and share the perfections of Hermondine and the Chevalier au Soleil d'Or:

> Avant que je venisse en sa court, je avoie esté en moult de cours de roys, de ducs, de princes, de contes et de haultes dames, mais je n'en fu onques en nulle qui mieulx me pleust, ne qui feust sur le fait d'armes plus resjouys comme cil conte de Fois estoit. On veoit en la sale et es chambres et en la court chevaliers et escuiers d'onneur aler et marcher, et d'armes et d'amours les oioit on parler; toute honneur estoit la dedens trouvee. (Diverres, 68)

> [Before I had come to his court, I had been in the courts of many kings, dukes, princes, counts, and high ladies, but I was never in one that more greatly pleased me, nor that was as joyful by deeds of arms as was the court of the count of Foix. In the hall and the chambers and in the court, knights and squires of honor were seen going about and walking, and you could hear them speaking of arms and of love; every honor was there found.]

Froissart also uses *Meliador* as originating text in his *Dit dou florin*, a short, alert, and entertaining narrative poem. This dit also takes its inspiration from the chronicler's stay with Gaston and from an incident on his return route, in Avignon, where he was following Joan of Boulogne's nuptial travel party. In Avignon, most of the eighty florins that the writer had received from Gaston, supposedly for his reading of *Meliador*, disappear, stolen. After debating his misfortune with a lone residual coin discovered at the bottom of his nearly emptied purse, the author-narrator returns again to Orthez and commemorates a second time his romance reading in self-encomiastic verse (ll. 343–83). As in the prose description of the same scene in the *Chroniques*, Froissart dwells here upon the brilliant light that illuminated the nocturnal recital scene in which he, the writer, read his romance to Gaston:

> Et aussi d'entree premiere
> En la sale avoit tel lumiere
> ou en sa chambre a son souper,
> Que on y veoit ossi cler
> Que nulle clarté poet estre:
> Certes a paradys terrestre
> Le comparoie souvent. (359–365)[11]

[And also from the first, as one entered into the hall or into his chambers at his evening dinner, there was such light that you could see as clearly as any light could have made it: indeed, I often compared it to a paradise on earth.]

Reading *Meliador*, Froissart tells us, resuscitated the writer's fictive heroes and their courtly universe; the accompanying bright light evokes the worldly paradise that the reader's words recreate in his and in his public's imagination. There can be no doubt also that, for a moment, this near-blinding light partakes of the light of the Grail Castle, which manifests the ultimate power and fate of the Arthurian universe. But here it is a bookish illumination, gained by writing the memories of one's own literary glories.

Froissart also resurrects *Meliador* in one of his earliest poems, *Le paradis d'amour*,[12] an allegorical dream poem, in which the lover-poet-dreamer approaches the residence of the God of Love, near the fountain of Narcissus. On a wide plain appear a great number of beautiful ladies and handsome noblemen, dressed in green and about to dance. Among the male figures that the lover first distinguishes are Troilus, Paris, Lancelot, Tristan, Perceval, Mordred, Agravain, Yvain, and Gauvain. Then, in four lines (985–88) that only Froissart could have inserted later, are named Meliador, Tanghis, and Camel de Camois.[13] Among the ladies that the text enumerates next are the chatelaine de Vergi, Guenièvre, Iseut, Echo, and

Medea (but not Hermondine). By setting the heroes of his romance squarely in the center of this renowned assembly, Froissart can again be seen to seek for his ill-known heroes and romance the identity and prestige reserved for the great heroes of antiquity and Arthurian romance.

It can even be argued that the *Meliador* episode in the *Chroniques* exists principally as a literary, fictional construct. To begin with, the texts related to his *Voyage en Béarn* contain a number of odd chronological and "factual" disjunctions and inconsistencies. In the "prologue," which he composed undoubtedly after completing the main body of book 3, Froissart reviews his reasons for traveling to Béarn, explains how Guy de Blois had provided him with letters of introduction for Gaston Fébus, and how Gaston had then welcomed and honored him when he arrived at Orthez on November 25, 1388, as the renowned historian of his age. He insists on the well of information that Gaston and the men of arms at his court supplied, information that is going to permit him to extend his great prose monument, or as he more expressively states: "pour rengrossier nostre matiere" (SHF 12:3). It is, therefore, quite unexpected to find no mention of *Meliador* here in this presentation of book 3 and Froissart's trip to Orthez. It was, after all, he proudly states some fifty pages later (SHF 12:75–76), a crowning personal literary triumph to be asked to read his romance, every evening during his twelve-week stay, before the great lord and his court. Could it be that over the months that separated the early writing of the *Voyage en Béarn* episode and the completion of book 3, Froissart's enthusiasm subsided for some reason? When we next try to piece together, from the chronicler's different texts, the calendar of his reading and his stay at Orthez, we observe that these passages, in the third book and in the *Dit dou florin*, offer quite divergent accounts.

If we start by adding the twelve weeks given as the duration of his stay at Orthez (SHF 12:75) to the November 25, 1388, arrival date, found here in the prologue (SHF 12:2), we can place the chronicler's departure from Orthez at about the third week of February 1389. In the *Dit dou florin* (349–50), it is stated that the reading of *Meliador* lasted ten weeks, starting six weeks before Christmas and ending four weeks after. Does this mean that, completing his reading at the end of January, Froissart prolonged his stay at Orthez for a month, to the end of February, or did he, as he reports in the *Dit dou florin*, leave directly following the completion of the reading (378–81)? At the end of book 3, in a passage that achieves the greater closure of the whole book, Froissart describes his departure in circumstantial detail. The dates and details are at major variance from those of the opening section of the book. Here, some thousand pages distant from the glowing memories of the *Meliador* performance, we read, to our great surprise, that shortly after Christmas of 1388 (Fourrier 1979, 64) it was Froissart who requested to leave Orthez in the company of King Charles VI's maréchal, Louis de Sancerre (SHF 15:224), and it was Gaston Fébus who refused to give him leave. Surely, if Gaston had kept the chronicler so that he could complete his reading of *Meliador* before leaving, Froissart would not have failed to record such a flattering detail. The chronicler offers no explanation for Gaston's decision to retain him, and it is only in May 1389 that he at last leaves Orthez for Avignon, in the nuptial travel party of Joan of Boulogne (SHF 15:234; Fourrier 1979, 63, n.140)—a good three or four months *after* reading *Meliador*. Gaston does reward the departing writer "generously" ("me fist grant prouffit," SHF 15:234) with the eighty florins to whose disappearance in Avignon we owe the composition of *Le dit dou florin*. It is in this narrative poem that we learn of the quite unexpected sequel to the destiny of *Meliador:* The chronicler had to bring the book back to Avignon because Gaston had not wanted to keep the codex containing glories that the writer had described in such glowing terms: "mon livre ... m'ot laissié, / ne sçai se ce fu de coer lié" (387–88). This admission of the "rejection" of his work—by the lord whom the writer, only ten lines earlier in the dit (and at the beginning of book 3), describes as his most glorious admirer and patron—is indeed startling.[14] In their aggregate, the dissonant elements that compose the *Meliador* episode suggest that Froissart may have largely fabricated the passages in which he describes reading his romance before Gaston and his court. In addition, there is evidence to suggest that Espan de Lyon, the principal "voice" of the *Voyage* and a recurrent hero of books 3 and 4, may be a fictional creation.[15] Such a deep fictional construct would attest again to the *Chroniques* as history subordinated to oeuvre.

The text passages we have discussed illustrate certain organizing features of Froissart's works, with particular application to his prose *Chroniques*. For Froissart, the initial act of committing contemporary events to written memory is almost always followed by a self-conscious, mirroring observation or commemoration of that same writing gesture. The advantage of these *mise en abyme* techniques for a work that thus becomes a record of itself, a chronicle of the *Chroniques,* lies in the illusion they afford the reader of participating in the genesis of the text.

Thus, as I and others have noted elsewhere, Froissart introduces events and persons into his work because they contribute to it: "Facts" are subordinate to the work. The wars of Brittany, for instance, "illuminate" the work: "Les guerres de Bretaigne de saint Charles de Blois et de messire Jehan de Montfort ont grandement renforcié et renluminé ceste haulte et noble hystoire" (SHF 13:121–22) [The wars between Saint Charles of Blois and Sir John of Montfort have greatly strengthened and illuminated this high and noble history.] Froissart recalls them for the glory and honor they have brought to the work.

Frequently the use of one event recalling another told previously in the *Chroniques* becomes an organizing principle of the narration. Thus the battle of Poitiers becomes intelligible, legible, in terms of knowledge of earlier text of the *Chroniques:* "Vous avés ci dessus en ceste hystore bien oy parler de le bataille de Creci, et comment fortune fu moult mervilleuse por les François: ossi à le bataille de Poitiers, elle fu moult diverse et très felenesse pour yaus, et auques parelle à ceste de Creci" (SHF 5:42). [You have well heard, here above in this history, spoken of the battle of Crécy, and how strange fortune was for the French; in like manner, at the battle of Poitiers, fortune was very mean and cruel for the French, and quite similar to that of Crécy.]

As we have seen, in the cases of Espan de Lyon and of Gaston Fébus, Froissart also enjoys composing dialogues and scenes with his protagonists and informants in which he has himself recognized as the author-historian of his renowned work. Such is the manner in which the writer relates in book 4 his encounter with Henry Cristede, a squire of King Richard II: "si s'accointa de moy pour la cause de ce que il . . . avoit veu le livre lequel j'avoye présenté au roy, et ymagina, si comme je vey les apparans par ses paroles, que j'estoye ung historien" (KL 15:168). [And he made my acquaintance because he . . . had seen the book that I had presented to the king, and he imagined, as I could deduce from his words, that I was a historian.]

Again, Froissart freely introduces into the body of his *Chroniques* accounts of the voyages he makes to gather information for the work. Sometimes, these are trips made to revisit events or sites already inscribed in the work. Thus he reports how, a year after his return from Béarn, he set out to the Low Countries to get from John Ferrant Percock the Portuguese view of matters related to the battle of Aljubarrota (August 15, 1385), about which he had previously written, using French-Castilian informants, while at Orthez. Into his account, which Froissart composes in book 3, Percock inserts dialogues between the chancellor of King John I of Portugal, Fogaça, and the duke of Lancaster, dialogues into which Percock, in turn, inserts himself (SHF 12:237–38). Such successive mirroring, or *mise en abyme*, is similar to the technique at work in the text relating Froissart's reading of *Meliador*. Again, when he visits Scotland in 1365, he is in fact revisiting Jean le Bel's texts; but unlike Percock's account, which he adds to the *Chroniques*, Froissart expands and alters le Bel's narration as he implants it in his successive rewritings of book 1.

Finally, as we have seen, Froissart encloses a named version of his own work *Meliador* in his *Chroniques* as a narrated offering to his patron, Guy de Blois—an offering that he had composed for a previous patron, Wenceslas of Brabant, and very possibly a fictional, villonesque gift for Gaston Fébus. Froissart enhances the prestige and authority of the *Chroniques* at two other sites similar to the book 3 account, first in one version of the prologue of book 1, where he recounts how in 1361 he brought his rhymed historical work to England, where he presented it to Philippa of Hainaut: "Et le presentay adonc à très haulte et très noble dame, dame Phelippe de Haynault, royne d'Angleterre, qui doulcement et lieement le receut de moy et me fist grant proffit" (SHF 1:210: prologue, MS A). [And I presented it then to most high and most noble lady, Lady Philippa of Hainaut, queen of England, who sweetly and joyfully received it from me and greatly rewarded me for it.] The third and last gift account, this time of his lyric works, occurs near the end of book 4, when Sir John describes the gift he made to Philippa's grandson, Richard II, who

> ... l'ouvry et regarda ens, et luy pleut très-grandement et bien plaire luy devoit, car il estoit enluminé, escript et historié et couvert de vermeil velours à dix clous attachiés d'argent dorés et roses d'or ou milieu, a deux grans frumaus dorés et richement ouvrés ou milieu de roses d'or. Adont me demanda le roy de quoy il traittoit. Je luy dis: "D'amours." De ceste response fut-il tous resjouys.[16]

> [... opened it, and looked in it, and it greatly pleased him as well it should have, for it was illuminated, written and composed, and covered with red velvet, with ten gilded silver studs and golden roses in the middle, with two great and richly worked clasps in the middle of the gilded roses. Then the king asked me what the book treated of. I said to him: "Of love." This answer filled him with joy.]

Notes

This essay is particularly indebted to chap. 6, "Froissart," of William C. Calin's *The French Tradition and the Literature of Medieval England* (Toronto: University of Toronto Press, 1994), 229–49.

1. Pamiers, Ariège, is a town some forty miles south of Toulouse. Froissart and Espan averaged about twenty-five miles a day on horseback to accomplish their 150-mile trip east to Orthez (Basses-Pyrenees).

2. Jean Froissart, *Chroniques*, books 1–3, ed. Siméon Luce, Gaston Raynaud, Léon Mirot, and Albert Mirot (Paris: Société de l'Histoire de France, 1869–1975); hereafter, SHF.

3. Jean Froissart, *Voyage en Béarn*, ed. A. H. Diverres (Manchester: Manchester University Press, 1953), 68–69.

4. *Chroniques*. Début du premier livre. Edition du MS de Rome. Reg. lat. 869 par George T. Diller (Geneva: Droz, 1972), 127; SHF 1:268; Rome, 779; SHF 4:235.

5. See G. T. Diller, "Froissart, Historiography, the University Curriculum and Isabeau of Bavière," *Romance Quarterly* 41 (1994):148–55.

6. He does in fact add a dramatic scene to the hostage killing of 1373: cf. SHF 8:158–60.

7. Michel Zink observes well that "Ce qui frappe dans le *Voyage en Béarn*, qui est supposé raconter des faits réels, c'est l'enchâssement et en même temps les rencontres des voix du récit: voix 'fondamentale' de Froissart le narrateur et, à l'intérieur de sa narration, voix de Froissart le voyageur, interrogeant ses informateurs, commentant leurs récits insérés dans celui du narrateur, voix de ces interlocuteurs . . . et voix des personnages de leurs récits"; see "Froissart et la nuit du chasseur," *Poétique* 41 (1980):76.

8. See Peter F. Dembowski, *Jean Froissart and His "Meliador": Context, Craft, and Sense* (Lexington, Ky.: French Forum, 1983), pp. 92–96.

9. Chrétien de Troyes, *Perceval* (Paris: Fayard, 1994), 6520–28: "La Borne de Galvoie."

10. *Lancelot*, same edition, 3005ss.

11. Froissart, *Le dit dou florin*, in *"Dits" et "Débats,"* ed. Anthime Fourrier (Geneva: Droz, 1979), 186.

12. *Le paradis d'amour*, ed. Peter F. Dembowski (Geneva: Droz, 1986).

13. See Dembowski, *Froissart and His "Meliador,"* 57–59; 117, note.

14. For Jacqueline Cerquiglini-Toulet, these lines from the *Dit dou florin* confirm the historical evidence concerning Gaston: "Le livre n'a pas été reconnu par Gaston Phoébus comme un objet digne d'être possédé. Gaston Phoébus n'est pas sur ce point un prince moderne. Il est surtout, les documents d'archives en témoignent, un prince avare." See *La couleur de la mélancolie: La fréquentation des livres au XIVe siècle, 1300–1415* (Paris: Hatier, 1993), 48. However, the care with which this prince produced his own *Livre de chasse* must occasion some reserve about these assertions.

15. The observation was made by Peter Ainsworth during the Amherst Froissart Colloquium, November 3–5, 1995.

16. Jean Froissart, *Oeuvres*, ed. Kervyn de Lettenhove (Reprint, Osnabrück: Biblio Verlag, 1967), 15:167.

II

Framing Selfhood
in Froissart's Poetry

4

Le joli buisson de Jonece
Froissart's Midlife Crisis

WILLIAM W. KIBLER

We have finally reached a time when we can discuss the poetry of Jean Froissart without first apologizing for doing so. Indeed, the very name of the Amherst 1995 colloquium—"Froissart Across the Genres"—is indicative of an awakened interest in works other than the justly celebrated *Chroniques;* and two-thirds of the papers presented were primarily concerned with his poetic production, either the *dits amoureux* or *Meliador*. In the wake of Robert Guiette's seminal *De la poésie formelle en France* and Daniel Poirion's monumental thesis, *Le poète et le prince: L'évolution du lyrisme courtois de Guillaume de Machaut à Charles d'Orléans*,[1] a new appreciation of conventional poetry in the *formes fixes* has led to a number of important studies of fourteenth-century poets and poetry, but until the Amherst colloquium comparatively little of it has been devoted to Froissart. Most critics who have discussed Froissart's poetry have either mined it for its presumed autobiographical details or fulminated against its conventionality and prolixity. Compared with Machaut, the principal beneficiary to date of the renewed interest in late medieval poetics, Froissart inevitably comes out second best. His *pastourelles* are admired for their unique politico-social import rather than for their poetry; his *Meliador* is praised by its most sympathetic critic, Peter Dembowski,[2] for its stolid conservatism and dogged attempt to revitalize a bygone era of chivalric glory; his lyric poems are viewed as "shallow ... platitudinous, repetitious, and conventional" by their most recent editor, Rob Roy McGregor Jr.[3]—who, incidentally, although writing ten years *after* the publication of Poirion's study, seems to have been blissfully unaware of it. The dits amoureux have not fared much better.

While I am not proposing to argue here against the fundamentally conservative nature of *Meliador* and the *Chroniques,* nor even against the deferential and proaristocratic stance of Froissart's numerous courtly lyrics in *formes fixes,* I would like to suggest that in at least the two longest of his dits amoureux, the *Espinette amoureuse* and the *Joli buisson de Jonece,*[4] Froissart is offering a perhaps uncharacteristic critique of courtly culture through his conscious manipulation of the persona of his narrator-poet-lover.

In the *Espinette amoureuse,* as I have argued elsewhere,[5] Froissart creates a poet-lover persona who plays court unsuccessfully to a fictional lady. The lover adheres obstinately to the courtly tradition, sighing and pining for his lady, sending her gifts of letters and poems, communing with mythological and allegorical figures, and generally making a fool of himself. But this fool is *not* Froissart the poet, who clearly sees beyond the love rhetoric that he himself has created in the name of the poet-lover and who works into his poem any number of indications that the protagonist is intent upon deluding himself in spite of manifest opportunities to see through the constraints of the conventions and thereby escape from them. His lady, too, plays the game for all it is worth, but she—like Froissart the poet—is conscious all the while that it is only a game, and a game that, in this "calamitous fourteenth century,"[6] has lost its former pertinence.

In the *Joli buisson,* as in the *Espinette amoureuse,* Froissart creates a poet-lover persona whose attempts at romance are thwarted, ironically, it would seem, by the self-same lady who had made a mockery of his advances in the *Espinette.* The *Joli buisson,* composed at least three years after the *Espinette*[7] but, in diegetic action, set some ten years after that of the earlier work, takes the same pseudoautobiographical pose as its predecessor and, like the earlier poem, reveals an author masterfully in control of his poetic means and fully conscious of the ironies of his characters' actions. It differs, however, from the former work by having the poet-lover come to a realization within the fiction of the futility and vaingloriousness of love service to a courtly lady. At the end, service to the imperious and unsympathetic courtly lady is transmuted into service of Our Lady, the generous and patient mother of Christ.

In the only study devoted exclusively to the *Joli buisson de Jonece,* Michelle Freeman has characterized the work as Froissart's "Farewell to Poetry."[8] And Peter Dembowski, in his valuable study of *Meliador,* has most perceptively labeled our poem "Froissart's mid-life crisis."[9] Fourrier likewise has recognized that the *Joli buisson* "exprime un cheminement intérieur, à la fois intellectuel, sentimental, et spirituel" (28). I unblushingly acknowledge my debt to these prior critics, and I would like here to explore in more detail some of the implications of their insights for our understanding of Froissart the poet.

The *Joli buisson de Jonece*, which has 5,442 lines in Anthime Fourrier's remarkable 1975 edition, is the longest of Froissart's dits, the only other of comparable length being the *Espinette amoureuse*, with which it has often been paired. But whereas the *Espinette* tells of the passion of its youthful narrator-lover for a young woman who is not inclined to return his affection, the *Joli buisson* recounts a failed attempt by the narrator to rekindle that same passion some ten years later. Our poem falls naturally into three parts of unequal length, which Fourrier has compared to a triptych with a large central panel framed by two smaller panels.[10] In the initial section, lines 1–837 of Fourrier's edition, the narrator discourses with his thoughts, at first called simply Pensee but later magically transformed into Dame Philozophie. The second and by far the longest part, lines 838–5081, narrates a dream vision in which the poet-lover is transported by Venus into "Youth's Pretty Bush." In the third and final division, lines 5082–442, the narrator is abruptly awakened and composes a prayer to the Virgin Mary in the form of a *lai*.

In the period immediately preceding the composition of the *Joli buisson de Jonece*, Froissart had apparently come to a watershed in his career. He was about thirty-five years of age, as he himself tells us in the opening section of the poem ("Si ai je en ce monde aresté / .XXXV. ans, peu plus, peu mains" [793–94]); he had just completed the first redaction of the first book of his *Chroniques* for Robert de Namur; he had apparently just failed in a business venture; and he had recently taken holy orders and been granted the benefice of Les Estinnes in Hainaut, no doubt through the good graces of one of his numerous benefactors, Guy de Blois.[11] In the opening section of the *Joli buisson*, the poet-narrator hints that the frivolities of youth are past, the time for poetry is over, and that he has turned over a new leaf in life: "Or voi je cangié mon afaire / En aultre ordenance nouvelle" (458–59). [Now I see my situation changed into a new and different state.] (translations mine unless otherwise indicated)

Although he certainly did not abandon poetry altogether—the more than thirty thousand lines of his unfinished *Meliador*, a number of occasional poems, and at least two dits, the *Plaidoirie de la rose et de la violette* and the *Dit dou florin*, were yet to come—nonetheless, the *Joli buisson* does seem to mark a turning point in his career. According to the chronology widely accepted for his poetry,[12] the *Joli buisson* was the last of Froissart's major dits amoureux. Where his younger years had been spent composing love poetry in the tradition of his unacknowledged master, Guillaume de Machaut, in which Froissart celebrated chivalry and *courtoisie* in dits amoureux and numerous shorter lyrics, the later years of his life would be devoted in large measure to his prose chronicles of the Hundred Years' War.

The *Joli buisson* seems to me to reflect the inner struggles of a hitherto successful poet who, like his mentor Machaut, associated youth with love and love with poetry. As a poet in the tradition of the *Roman de la rose* and Machaut, Froissart had always associated lyricism and a certain type of lyric poetry—both the narrative poetry of the dits amoureux and the fixed-form verses of the post-Machaudian poetic tradition—with the flames of youthful passion. This association is especially clear in the *Espinette amoureuse* and the later *Meliador,* and the central movement of the *Joli buisson* is an artificial and ultimately unsuccessful attempt to rekindle this flame. For Froissart, love was the only true source for poetic inspiration; but as he approached middle age and took on new social and religious responsibilities, the season for love and the types of poetry inspired by love seemed to belong to the past. It is certainly not by coincidence that the *Joli buisson* is set on the thirtieth night of November in the year 1373—"Le trentisme nuit de novembre / L'an mil .CCC.XIII. et sissante" (859–60)—when Froissart was about thirty-five years of age.[13]

In the *Joli buisson,* Froissart associates the different ages of a person's life with traditional astrological signs. The first four years are watched over by the Moon; from five to fourteen, the period of childhood is overseen by Mercury. Then Venus ushers in the time for love, the fifteenth to the twenty-fourth year. From twenty-five to thirty-four, a man is under the sign of the Sun, which "le fet a toute honneur tendre/ Et a plainne cavanche entendre" [makes him desire every honor and seek all manner of wealth] (1648–49). Next, the age of Mars helps a person recognize true worth and true power: "Car par lui [Mars] prent le congnissance/ Que c'est d'avoir et de poissance" (1654–55). [For Mars helps him understand the true meaning of wealth and power.] The later years are under the aegis of Jupiter and Saturn.

In the *Joli buisson,* thus, the poet-narrator is just entering the age of Mars, an age of reflection and taking stock. He rejects, on the one hand, the vain pursuit of wealth through commerce, symbolized by the age of the Sun, while on the other he senses that the carefree time of youth dedicated to cultivating love and the poetry of love is over for a man in his mid-thirties.

As early as the opening section of his poem, Froissart suggests that the direction his life is to take will turn him away from earthly pleasures, whether those of wealth or of love, and toward a more mature contemplation of eternal verities. In lines 59–97, he alludes pointedly to a period in which he abandoned his natural gift for poetry to pursue mercantile profit: "Or me cuidai trop bien parfaire / Pour prendre ailleurs me calandise; / Si me mis en le marcandise" (92–94). [I thought I could succeed better by seeking my clientele elsewhere, so I went into business.] And he acknowledges that his vain pursuit of wealth and profit has brought him only shame: "Dont grandement m'abestioie / Car mieuls vault science qu'argens" (84–85). [Which degraded me greatly, for wisdom is more valuable than riches.]

Lady Philozophie urges him not to abandon Nature—that is, not to abandon his gift for poetry—but to use his God-given talents to best advantage: "Et il t'a donné le science, / De quoi tu poes par conscience / Loer Dieu et servir le monde" (185–88). [And He has given you the wisdom by which you can in good conscience praise God and serve your fellow man.] Even in this early part of the work the poet's mind is inclined toward praising God, but first he must overcome the temptation to revert to the vaingloriousness of his youthful attempts at self-satisfaction through amorous dalliances and courtly passions.

If we pause now to look very briefly at the principal events of Froissart's life, we can understand better, I believe, what the poet is trying to communicate in this most personal and most complex of all his poetic works. Although the lover-narrator of the *Joli buisson*, like that in the *Espinette amoureuse*, is a poetic persona created and controlled by the poet Froissart, who is himself acutely aware of the lover's foolish naiveté in even attempting to recreate the mood and season traditionally associated with love, I believe that the Froissart who authenticates himself by listing within the first section of this poem his principal poetic works[14] and some thirty of his past patrons, is acutely conscious of the intensely autobiographical nature of what he is poeticizing. Indeed, that self-consciousness will become the very stuff of his new poetry.

Many of Froissart's formative years had been spent in the service of Philippa of Hainaut, daughter of Count William of Hainaut and wife of England's King Edward III. While he was still in his early twenties, Froissart's precocious poetic skills had apparently brought him to the attention of someone in Count William's household,[15] who recommended him to the queen, who received him warmly as her personal secretary. He served Philippa in England from 1361 until her death from a resurgence of the Black Plague in 1369, and it was during this decade of the 1360s, while Froissart served as a court poet in England, that he appears to have composed the majority of his dits amoureux and much of his occasional love poetry. The graceful elegance of his *virelais* and rondeaux, as well as the courtly and chivalric tone of many of his longer poems,[16] all seem to reflect the refined and noble English court. Moreover, in the prologue to the fourth book of his *Chroniques*, Froissart himself speaks of his poetic activities at the English court: "Et si m'a Dieu donné tant de grâce que j'ay esté bien de toutes parties et des hostels des roys et par espécial du roy Edouard et de la noble royne d'Angleterre sa femme madame Phelippe de Haynnau, royne d'Angleterre, dame d'Irlande et d'Aquitaine, à laquelle en ma jeunesse je fus clerc et la servoie de beaulx dittiers et traitiés amoureux."[17] [And God has so favored me that I have been well received in all quarters and in the households of kings, particularly by King Edward and the noble Queen of England, his spouse Lady Philippa of Hainaut, Queen of England, Lady of Ireland and Aquitaine, whose secretary I was in my youth and whom I provided with beautiful poems and amorous treatises.]

After Philippa's death, which Froissart lamented in a famous lai, the poet returned to his native Hainaut and entered the service of Wenceslas de Brabant, a great lover of poetry and himself an amateur poet. It was perhaps for Wenceslas that Froissart composed his *Espinette amoureuse* (ca. 1370), and it was certainly Wenceslas's imprisonment after the battle of Bastweiler in 1371 that inspired the *Prison amoureuse*, an allegorical poem visibly modeled on Machaut's *Voir dit*.[18] Finally, it was almost certainly for Wenceslas that Froissart composed his enormous Arthurian romance, *Meliador*, into which he inserted all of Wenceslas's lyric poems.[19]

Wenceslas was the son of John, the Blind King of Bohemia, one of the most celebrated chivalric heroes of the fourteenth century, who was killed in the battle of Crécy in 1346. Like his father, Wenceslas was a paragon of chivalric virtues, with a special predilection for pomp, pageantry, tournaments, and feats of valor. It should not surprise us that Froissart, as a member first of the elegant English court and then of the chivalric entourage of Wenceslas,[20] was himself imbued with a special love for chivalry and *courtoisie*, whose thematics dominated his early poetic production. It was also during these years that Froissart began work on what has remained his principal claim to fame, his *Chroniques*, which covers the opening period of the Hundred Years' War. The *Chroniques* is noted for its conservative celebration of the past and present glories of an already outmoded chivalry.[21]

Sometime shortly after Philippa's death—the date is unknown—Froissart took holy orders and became a priest. Thanks probably to the good graces of Guy de Blois, he was named in 1373 to the parish of Estinnes-au-Mont, about thirteen kilometers from present-day Mons, Belgium. Later, Froissart was made Guy de Blois's personal chaplain and named to the canonicate of Chimay. His ecclesiastical income gave him the means and necessary leisure for literary work. Thus, in 1373, at the very time of the *Joli buisson*, Froissart was not only enjoying the patronage of the courtly Wenceslas and the chivalric Guy de Blois, but he could also count for the first time on a steady income from his priestly benefice at Les Estinnes.[22]

It seems to me that it is precisely out of this amalgam of courtly and religious service that the *Joli buisson* arises, for it skillfully combines the two functions of the clerk-cleric quoted earlier: "Loer Dieu et servir le monde" (187). [Praise God and serve your fellow man.] While Froissart seems to have sensed that the courtly poetry of his youth was no longer appropriate to a man of his maturity, he was not yet sufficiently sure of the success of his prose *Chroniques* and was searching, I believe, for a new source of poetic inspiration. In the *Joli buisson*, he comes to grips with his present situation, recognizes that he cannot recreate the carefree days of youth, and seeks and finds a new type of love service, a new form of *courtoisie*. He does not abandon poetry altogether, as Freeman seems to imply, but seeks a new source of poetic inspiration now that he senses that the courtly mode is closed to him.

With this understanding of the personal situation of Froissart the poet, we can approach the poem with a new appreciation both of where Froissart is coming from and of what he is seeking to achieve through the composition. It seems to me that through this poem Froissart comes to terms with his own past and sets a moderate course for the future, placing his trust in God rather than in the empty formulas of courtly poetry.

In the first part of the *Joli buisson*, the poet-narrator enters into dialogue with his alter ego in the person of Dame Philozophie. He states cogently his present situation, lamenting his age and his lack of poetic inspiration. He senses that his life is changing, that it is time to try something different. Were he to attempt now to return to the England of Philippa's court,

... je serai lors tous chenus,
Foibles, impotens, mas et sombres.
Mes temps s'en fuit ensi q'uns ombres:
Vis m'est de quanq que j'ai esté
Que j'aie noient aresté. (374–78)

[Then I will be all white-haired, weak, sad, helpless, and blue. But time flies by like a shadow: it seems that whatever I've been, I've not been for long.]

These lines also contain important biblical echoes, as Fourrier has pointed out. In Wisdom 2:5 we read, "Yes, our days are the passing of a shadow," and in Psalm 144:4, David reminds us that "Man's life [is] a mere puff of wind, / his days, as fugitive as shadows." The early lines of the poem seem to anticipate and prepare us for the religious resolution.

The man who has just described himself as white-haired, weak, sad, and impotent then goes on to recall the lost creative energy of his youth:

> Mais j'estoie lors pour le tamps
> Toutes nouveletés sentans
> Et avoie prest a le main
> A toute heure, au soir et au main,
> Matere pour ce dire et faire. (453–57)

[But then because of the season (of youth) I felt fresh inspiration (in love) and had ready to hand, at any hour, whether night or day, subject matter for composing.]

Yet he is fully cognizant that his situation is now quite altered: "Or voi je cangié mon afaire / En aultre ordenance nouvelle" (458–59). [Now I see my situation changed into a new and different state.] And he seems prepared at this point to abandon altogether the "vainne glore" (387) he has now come to associate with the service of Eros, and to dedicate himself henceforth to the salvation of his eternal soul: "S'est bien heure de che tamps clore / Et de criier a Dieu merchi / Qui m'a amené jusqu'a chi" (388–90). [It is well time to put an end to this season and to beg mercy of God, who has brought me this far.]

Although the narrator-poet senses that the season for love and love lyrics is past, he cannot abandon it without a struggle. Thus, his alter ego, Dame Philozophie, admonishes him not to go against Nature and reject his God-given talent for writing:

> "Et te di en nom de castoi:
> Ce que Nature a mis en toi,
> Remonstre le de toutes pars
> Et si largement le depars
> Que gré t'en puissent chil savoir
> Qui le desirent a avoir." (425–30)

[And I admonish you: make plain to one and all what Nature has given you, and manifest it so generously that those who wish to benefit from it will thank you for it.]

Dame Philozophie further reminds the poet-lover of the favor he has experienced at the courts of his many patrons, whom she requests that he acknowledge. In a justly celebrated litany, Froissart names some thirty former patrons. Yet in spite of the obvious pride and pleasure the poet feels in recalling their generosity and their many gold florins, he remains personally discouraged on two counts. First, he feels that poetry is no longer appreciated and rewarded as once it was (196–221); and second, he recognizes that the time of experienced adventures is past: He is too old to love, and since love has traditionally been the sole source of lyric inspiration, he feels that he can no longer write.

The question now turns to the search for new material to inspire the mature poet. Dame Philozophie suggests that he look to his past works and seek inspiration there: "Il te couvient penser / Au temps passé et a tes oevres / Et voel que sus cesti tu oevres" (462–64). [You must think of the past and your (poetic) works; I want you to take inspiration from them.] This, as we shall see, will prove to be a false trail, but it is one that the poet must first explore in order to come to terms with his past. Encouraged by Dame Philozophie, the narrator takes from a little chest an image of his lady which he had placed there some ten years earlier. Symbolically, this image reflects his present attempt to regenerate his former love experience as a source of poetic imagination. But, unlike Pygmalion, he is unable ultimately to give life to an artistic image, and his attempt to find new poetic inspiration through a courtly love affair will be doomed to failure.

The recovery of the ten-year-old and long-forgotten image of his lady is accompanied by a mythological tale, largely of Froissart's own concoction, that ironically anticipates the ultimate failure of his enterprise: Achilles, after slaying Hector in the Trojan War, caught a glimpse of Hector's sister Polyxena in the Temple of Apollo, where she had come to mourn her brother, and fell madly in love with her. Because of his lovesickness, Achilles lost his prowess and failed to pursue knightly exploits. He had an image made of Polyxena that he kept with him at all times, since it was the only way he could see her. But Fortune turned against him, and Achilles was killed, ironically and pointedly, in the very temple in which he had seen Polyxena for the only time.[23]

Having rehearsed this mythological tale, the poet-narrator is led to recognize the folly of his ways, although he is still cognizant of his human weakness: "Et toutes fois je l'en [Fortune] mescroi, / Car je m'areste en grant folie; / Et se sçai bien que je folie; / Si n'en puis je mon coer retraire" (717–20). [But I do not believe in Fortune, for I wallow in great folly and know that I behave as a fool; yet I cannot control my heart.] The first section of Froissart's triptych ends, significantly, in a lengthy and extremely orthodox meditation on the Last Judgment (795–826), a meditation that will find its echo in the poem's epilogue.

The artificiality of the portrait, the failure of the attempt to recreate youth through its contemplation, and absence of inspiration are the subjects of the central section of the *Joli buisson*. Here love will be transformed by art and artifice into a literary experience, rather than being an actually lived affair. The mature poet, with pen, paper, and ink at hand, too old for *aventures* and *nouveleté*, is seeking a new accommodation with love, a new source of poetic expression.[24]

It is at this point that the poet falls asleep and has a dream vision in the manner of Machaut or the *Roman de la rose*. It occurs on a wintry night, the thirtieth of November in the year 1373, we are told—the kind of night that seems hardly propitious to love, which traditionally flourishes best in the warm days of spring and summer. In his vision he is visited by the goddess Venus, who chastises him for having abandoned the ways of love and insists that it is his fault, not hers, if his love has remained unsatisfied. Going one better than Dame Philozophie, who had merely modified her mythological tale of Achilles and Polyxena to suit her purposes, Venus invents from whole cloth the tale of Téléphus, Juno, and Diana in order to persuade the narrator-lover that winter is really spring. Not only does he succumb to the power of these words ("Rentrés estoit en se caverne / Yviers" [1226–27]), but the tale momentarily seduces him away from the Christian God to whom he had just dedicated himself and into the false love service represented by the pagan Venus and the allegorical figure of Youth. He claims that he is no longer able to say his Christian daily prayers: "Hui l'ai commenchiet pluiseurs [sic] fois, / Mes, ensi m'aÿt sainte Fois, / Je ne l'ai peüt a chief traire" (1110–12). [Today I began my prayer several times, but so help me St. Foy, I was unable to finish it.] Venus actually congratulates him, reassuring him that God will have His chance later: "Une aultre heure rara [Dieus] son lieu! / Toutdis s'aquite on bien a Dieu" (1116–17). [God will have his time later! One can always make it up to God.] The blasphemous character of this exchange could hardly have passed unnoticed.

With the narrator now rejoicing in the false springtime, Venus leads him easily into the "Joli buisson de Jonece," where she introduces him to Jonece himself, who gives him a learned explanation of the mysteries of the *buisson*, including an allegorical explanation of its seven branches, which figure the seven planets and the seven ages of man. The lover, however, is impatient with such intellectual discourse and eager to pursue his pleasure; he tells Jonece:

"Dont, chiers compains, c'est mieulz mes hes
A moi deduire et resjoïr
Que ce ne soit a vous oïr
Parler de grant astronomie." (1721–24)

[Wherefore, dear friend, my enjoyment in pleasure and rejoicing is better than listening to you speak of grand astronomy.]

Like the fool he is, he rejects wisdom and learning in favor of dalliance and ignorance, and allows Jonece to lead him to a "lieu delitable et biel" (1898) [fair and delightful spot] within the *buisson,* where the naive narrator-lover is granted a vision of his lady, just as she was ten years earlier. He cannot believe his eyes and compares this vision of her to the image on his parchment to convince himself that she has not aged a day.[25] The poet's astonishment is the occasion for Jonece to narrate two pseudo-Ovidian tales, the first of Ydrophus and Neptiphoras and the second of Architelés and Orphane, which ostensibly explain how it is possible for a lover not to age. The vanity of the poet's hope that he will ever be able to recreate the past is confirmed by the obvious falseness of these mythological tales. Froissart the author, I believe, treats these tales ironically and expects his sophisticated readers to recognize that they are fraudulent, whereas the naive narrator-lover is apparently taken in by them and allows himself to be convinced at least temporarily of the truthfulness of his counterfeit dream.[26]

His lady, however, is constantly guarded by Refus, Dangier, and Escondit, who discourage the lover from approaching or speaking with her. Desirs, however, finally persuades him to join hands with her in a *carole,* together with her more favorable qualities of Maniere, Atemprance, Franchise, Pitié, Plaisance, Cognoissance, and Humilités. The dance is performed to the a capella singing of rondeaux and virelais by the lover and the various allegorical personages, but the lady's only reaction is a brief smile after his song:

Tous li plus grans biens que je pris
De ma droite dame de pris,
Fu que je vi apriés ma note
Sa belle bouchette mignote
En riant un petit mouvoir. (2919–23)

[The very best reward I received from my right noble lady was that after my song I saw her pretty little mouth smile ever so slightly.]

Following the dance, the lady and her court join in a game of *pince meurine*. This otherwise unknown game allows the lover to absent himself from her immediate presence and hide in a *buisson* within the "Joli buisson," while Desirs, Pitiés, Jonece, and Franchise plead his cause. The curious result is that the lady agrees to suffer his presence since he is compelled to love her, but she will never dismiss Refus, Dangier, and Escondit. She tells Desirs and Douls Samblant:

> "Et puis qu'amer il li couvient
> Et qu'il dist et vous met en voie
> Que ches pensers je li envoie,
> Je le voel un peu resjoïr . . .
> Liement, sans li dechevoir,
> Le vorrai je huimais rechevoir.
> Mes que j'acorde ne ordonne
> Qu'a mes .III. varlés congiet donne
> Qui m'ont servi tres loyaument,
> Je ne le ferai nullement." (4313–25)

[And since he must love, and since he tells and convinces you that I am responsible for this feeling, I want to cheer him up a bit. . . . Joyfully, without deceit, I wish to receive him this very day. But to agree to, or command, the dismissal of my three young men who have served me so faithfully, this I will never do!]

After the game of *pince meurine*, the lover is able to approach and address his lady. He repeats the platitudes and empty promises proffered by every suitor, stresses the sufferings occasioned by his faithful service to the God of Love, and promises eternal fidelity to his lady. Her enigmatic reply both promises a reward and suggests the folly of love service; it is an almost coquettish mixture of come-on and rejection:

> "Fols est qui sert qui son tamps pert,
> Mes services fais loyaument
> A personne d'entendement
> Ne fu onques mors ne peris
> Qu'en le fin ne soit remeris." (4556–60)

[He's a fool who serves and wastes his time; but a service loyally rendered to a person of discernment was never lost or wasted or left unrewarded in the end.]

As if to punctuate her words, Refus, Dangier and Escondit immediately interpose themselves between the lady and the poet-lover. The lady of the *Joli buisson* behaves exactly like the lady in Froissart's earlier *Espinette amoureuse:* She refuses to be deceived by the flattering but empty words of an outmoded *courtoisie*. The lover, however, has matured considerably. Although he is besotted while in the *buisson* itself and led temporarily astray by Desirs and Jonece, we see in the final section that he has learned the lesson of the *Espinette*. Where in the earlier poem the narrator-lover remained faithful to the end to the empty tenets of courtly love, lamenting his frustrations in a final lai that repeated the major themes of the poem, in the *Joli buisson* he abruptly snaps out of his dream and returns to reality. In the very observant words of Douglas Kelly in his fine analysis of the Ovidian inventions in the *Joli buisson*, "La vision fait place à une autre vérité."[27] The narrator awakens from his dream to discover himself as he really is: "La réflexion amène Froissart à chercher non une autre Péronne d'Armentières, la fontaine de jouvence de Machaut (*Joli buisson* 786, 792), mais une dame plus assortie à son âge" (Kelly, 91). That lady, of course, is none other than the Virgin Mary.

The sudden finality of this awakening can best be appreciated in the original. While the lover and his lady and a company of allegorical figures are on their way to seek out the God of Love to serve as judge for a traditional poetic competition,

> En cheminant sus ce voiage,
> En pais, en joie et en reviel . . .
> Parés d'uns noes solers a las,
> Ensi qu'amant vont a la velle.
> On me boute, et lors je m'esvelle. (5073–81)

[As I was traveling along, peacefully, joyfully, and gaily . . . dressed in new lace-up shoes, like lovers headed for a late night, someone shoves me and then I awake.]

The springtime of the *songe* turns suddenly back into the winter of reality; again it is late November, the air is crisp and the season "yvreneuse et froide" (5088) [wintry and cold]. The poet comments on the illusionary aspects of the dream experience: The flames he felt in his dream have left no scars in reality (5150–55). More significantly, the emptiness of the dream experience leads the now mature poet to reflect more deeply on his present situation:

> En ceste ymagination
> Fis un peu de collation
> Contre ma vie et mon affaire
> Et di je n'euïsse que faire
> De penser a teles wiseuses,
> Car ce sont painnes et nuiseuses
> Pour l'ame, qui noient n'i pense
> Et qui il faut, en fin de cense,
> Rendre compte de tous fourfais
> Que li corps ara dis et fais,
> Qui n'est que cendre et poureture.
> Et la bonne ame est noureture
> De joie et de perfection. (5156–68).

> [In this imagination I made a little comparison between my life and my dream, and I said (to myself) that I had no business thinking of such idle things, for they are painful and harmful to the soul, which is not responsible for such things, yet which in the final accounting must make amends for all wrongs that the body—which is only dust and debris—will have said or done, while the good soul is the path of joy and perfection.]

Comparing life ("vie") with the dream ("affaire"), he reaches full awareness of the position with which he was experimenting and uncertain at the beginning of the poem: namely, that his eternal soul is more important than his mortal heart and that love service and *courtoisie* ought not to be directed to an illusionary earthly image on parchment but to the perfect Image of Mary, who can intercede with her Son on the lover's behalf. Recognizing, then, the vanity of all earthly attachments, the poet turns in humility to Our Lady in the very moving "Lay de Nostre Dame."

There can be no doubt that the *Joli buisson* marks a turning point in Froissart's career and that it is one of his richest and most complex works. It may well be seen as his farewell to a certain type of courtly lyricism rooted in sexual experience, whether real or imagined; but it announces, I believe, a new and more mature lyricism, founded on sublimation and religious piety. The *Joli buisson* can be read as an artificial and ultimately unsuccessful attempt to rekindle and relive the old *courtoisie*, the *courtoisie* of youth, of *noveleté*. The attempt to revive *courtoisie* in the old, courtly sense—artificially through a dream poem and through a painted image within that poem—was doomed to failure. Only after this experiment fails can the poet turn in his final section to a new lyricism and a new *courtoisie* that is not sexually based but that in effect banishes Desirs from the courtly world. As Douglas Kelly has shown in another context, the type of love fueled by Desirs that animated Arthurian fictions and the *Roman de la rose* was replaced by Machaut, in his *Remede de fortune*,[28] and Froissart, in his *Joli buisson de Jonece*, by a new *courtoisie*, a new aristocratic world view. The old *courtoisie* was sexually oriented; the new is a sublimated passion for an unattainable lady.

In the *Joli buisson* Froissart has created, like Machaut and Chaucer before him, a narrator who is fully cognizant of the game of love. In spite of the abundance of autobiographical details early in the dit—details that tempt us to associate the narrator-lover with Froissart the poet—the protagonist of the *Joli buisson* must not be equated with the poet. The poet, Froissart, controls his lover-narrator and is conscious of the foolishness he propagates. Froissart the poet, through his manipulation of his protagonist and his mastery of conventional poetry, seems to be suggesting here that there is more to life than love service. The poetry goes much deeper than the conventions. In discussing the earlier *Espinette amoureuse*, I argued that the protagonist in that dit deluded himself by trying to live out the conventions of the poetry, whereas Froissart the poet-creator was able to observe the action with ironic distance. In the *Joli buisson*, the protagonist once more seeks relief in delusion, but Froissart is telling us here in a more definitive manner that there is no "salvation" in courtly love service. Froissart uses the *Espinette amoureuse* and the *Joli buisson* as vehicles for self-examination as well as for an examination and critique of the courtly code. Through these poems he works through his own midlife crisis and successfully liberates himself from a convention that in his day had indeed become sterile and outworn.[29]

Notes

1. Guiette's study was first published in the *Revue des Sciences Humaines* 14 (1949):61–69; reprinted in *Questions de littérature* (Ghent: Romanica Gandensia 7 [1960]); published as a monograph, with additions, under the title *D'une poésie formelle en France au moyen âge* (Paris: Nizet, 1972); then reprinted in *Forme et senefiance: Études médiévales* (Geneva: Droz, 1978), 1–24. Poirion, *Le poète et le prince* (Paris: PUF, 1965).

2. *Jean Froissart and His "Méliador": Context, Craft, and Sense* (Lexington, Ky.: French Forum, 1983).

3. McGregor, *The Lyric Poems of Jehan Froissart: A Critical Edition*, Studies in Romance Languages and Literatures (Chapel Hill: University of North Carolina, 1975), pp. 59, 60.

4. The editions used are those by Anthime Fourrier, *L'Espinette amoureuse* (Paris: Klincksieck, 1963) and *Le joli buisson de Jonece* (Geneva: Droz, 1975).

5. Kibler, "Self-Delusion in Froissart's *Espinette amoureuse*," *Romania* 97 (1976): 77–98.

6. My descriptive phrase is taken from the subtitle of Barbara Tuchman's insightful study of the period, *A Distant Mirror: The Calamitous Fourteenth Century* (New York: Knopf, 1978).

7. The *Joli buisson* recounts a dream that the narrator-poet ostensibly experienced on the night of November 30, 1373—whence the traditional dating of the work. However, it is difficult to imagine Froissart composing a poem of more than five thousand lines in a single month. The *Espinette amoureuse* is usually dated to about 1370, following the conclusion of Froissart's service at Philippa of Hainaut's court in England. If the manuscript order reflects the order of composition of the dits, and the *Joli buisson* immediately precedes the *Dit dou florin* of 1389, the *Joli buisson* could have been composed at any time between late 1373 and 1389. Within the poem, Froissart tells us that there has been a ten-year gap between the action of the *Espinette* and that of the *Joli buisson*, so one can easily conceive of a date in the late 1370s or early 1380s for the latter.

8. Freeman, "Froissart's *Le Joli Buisson de Jonece*: A Farewell to Poetry?" in *Machaut's World: Science and Art in the Fourteenth Century*, ed. Madeleine Pelner Cosman and Bruce Chandler (New York: New York Academy of Sciences, 1978), 235–47.

9. I gratefully recognize here the source of my subtitle: Dembowski's section on the *Joli buisson* in *Jean Froissart and His "Méliador,"* 36–41.

10. "On a donc très nettement une composition en triptyque, avec un large volet médian encadré par deux volets de dimensions plus restreintes" (21).

11. See Dembowski, *Jean Froissart and His "Méliador,"* 46–47.

12. By Ernest Hoepffner, "La chronologie des 'pastourelles' de Froissart," in *Mélanges offerts à Monsieur Emile Picot par ses amis et ses élèves*, 2 vols. (Paris: Damascène Morgand, 1913), 2:27–42, and subsequently confirmed by Anthime Fourrier (29) and Daniel Poirion (206) in their works previously cited.

13. "Si ai je en ce monde aresté/ .XXXV. ans, peu plus, peu mains" (*Joli buisson*, 793–94) [I have been in this world / thirty-five years, more or less].

14. Voirs est qu'un livret fis jadis
   Qu'on dist l'*Amoureus Paradis*
   Et ossi celi del *Orloge*,
   Ou grant part del art d'Amours loge;
   Apriés, l'*Espinete amoureuse*,
   Qui n'est pas al oÿr ireuse;
   Et puis l'*Amoureuse Prison*,
   Qu'en pluiseurs [sic] places bien prise on,

Rondiaus, balades, virelais,
Grant fuison de dis et de lais. (443–52)

[It is true that once I composed a little work called "Love's Paradise" and also one called "The Clock," which contains much of the art of Love; afterward, "Love's Briar," which is not unpleasant to hear; then "The Prison of Love," which is much praised in many parts; rondeaux, ballades, virelays, and a great number of dits and lays.]

15. The commonly accepted opinion is that this someone was the younger brother of Count William, John of Beaumont, who was the patron of Jean le Bel and one of the chief heroes of his *Chroniques*. Dembowski, however, points out that John of Beaumont had died in 1356, fully five years before Froissart entered Philippa's entourage in 1361 (41).

16. *Paradis d'amour, Temple d'onnour, Le joli mois de mai, L'orloge amoureux, Le dit de la margherite, Le dit dou bleu chevalier,* and the *Debat du cheval et dou levrier*. See Poirion, *Poète et prince*, 207–8, and Dembowski, *Jean Froissart and His "Méliador,"* 42–43.

17. Cited by Dembowski, 163, n. 43.

18. Consult Froissart, *La prison amoureuse (The Prison of Love)*, ed. and trans. Laurence de Looze (New York: Garland, 1994).

19. "que fist jadis . . . Wenceslas li bons dus de Brabant" (301–3) [which Wenceslas the good king of Brabant formerly composed].

20. Froissart continued in the service of Wenceslas until the latter's death in 1383, which was every bit as severe a blow to the poet as had been Philippa's death in 1369.

21. See, among many others, Peter F. Dembowski, "Chivalry, Ideal and Real, in the Narrative Poetry of Jean Froissart," *Medievalia et Humanistica*, n.s., 14 (1986): 1–15.

22. As Poirion has pointed out, it was not particularly difficult in the fourteenth century to combine a secular and a clerical career: "Les deux tâches se complètent à cette époque sans trop s'opposer: le curé de Lestines continuera d'émarger aux comptes de Wenceslas, et c'est Guy de Blois qui donnera à son chapelain le canonicat de Chimay" (*Poète et prince*, 206).

23. The story of Achilles and Polyxena is the first of several ostensibly Ovidian tales modified or even created out of whole cloth by Froissart to give authority to the arguments of Dame Philozophie and, later, to those of Venus and Jonece, in their efforts to tempt the poet to turn from the ways of reason and religion in order to rekindle his lost love. Venus, for example, invents the story of Téléphus, who was tempted away from his service of Juno by Diana, with the promise that he would have dominion over all the birds of the air.

24. The opening lines of the *Joli buisson* refer directly to his clerkly role as scribe of love:

Des aventures me souvient
Dou temps passé. Or me couvient

> Entroes que j'ai sens et memore,
> Encre et papier et escriptore,
> Kanivet et penne taillie,
> Et volenté apparellie
> Qui m'amonneste et me remort,
> Que je remonstre avant me mort
> Comment ou Buisson de Jonece
> Fui jadis, et par quel adrece. (1–10)

[I recall adventures of days gone by. Now while I still have sense and memory, I need ink, paper, and a writing desk, a knife and sharp quill, and a ready will that admonishes and warns me to reveal before my death how and in what manner I once entered into the Bush of Youth.]

25. Mais trop grande m'est la mervelle
> De che que je le voi tousete,
> Jone, friche, lie et douchete
> Et del ëage dont ja fu
> Quant, pour s'amour, del ardant fu
> D'Amours je fui pris et atains. (1985–90)

[But I was quite astounded to see her as a young woman, youthful, playful, happy, and sweet, and the same age she was when, for love of her, I was enkindled and engulfed by the burning fire of Love.]

26. When the narrator himself relates a mythological tale, that of Acteon transformed into a stag after catching sight of Diana and her nymphs bathing nude, it is appropriately genuine.

27. Douglas Kelly, "Les inventions ovidiennes de Froissart: Réflexions intertextuelles comme imagination," *Littérature* 41 (1981):82–92.

28. See Douglas Kelly, *Medieval Imagination: Rhetoric and the Poetry of Courtly Love* (Madison: University of Wisconsin Press, 1978), esp. chap. 6, "Guillaume de Machaut and the Sublimation of Courtly Love in Imagination" (121–54).

29. Peter Ainsworth ("The Art of Hesitation: Chrétien, Froissart and the Inheritance of Chivalry," in *The Legacy of Chrétien de Troyes*, ed. Norris J. Lacy, Douglas Kelly, and Keith Busby [Amsterdam: Rodopi, 1988], 187–206) has argued cogently that Froissart, who is traditionally and rightly lauded as the chief defender of an outmoded chivalry in his *Chroniques*, did in fact harbor hesitations with regard to "the relative ethical viability of the ideals of the knightly caste" (187). Ainsworth senses a growing tension, particularly in the later recensions of the *Chroniques*, between the dominant tone of chivalrous celebration and more problematic strands of narrative suggesting that all is not well in the kingdom. In like manner, I have tried to suggest here that Froissart, who in his poetry has been nearly universally seen as derivative and conventional, expresses through his *Joli buisson* some serious doubts with regard to the ethical viability of courtly love service. Within the skillfully constructed tapestry of conventional poetry run counterstrands of narrative suggesting the inconsistencies and absurdities of a convention that was in its dying days.

5

Froissart's Poetic Prison
Enclosure as Image and Structure in the Narrative Poetry

Keith Busby

Images of imprisonment and enclosure are among the most commonplace in medieval literature: Knights are imprisoned during their adventures, and the *hortus conclusus* is central to a multitude of works written both before and after the *Roman de la rose*. It could even be argued that Arthur's court in the romances of Chrétien de Troyes is a kind of prison that not only absorbs defeated opponents sent back by victorious heroes but that also attempts to constrain and sequester those same heroes by appropriating them and their reputation as its own. Some of Chrétien's most memorable episodes are also variations on the theme of imprisonment: the masterly Joie de la Cort from *Erec et Enide*, Jean's tower and the idyllic orchard in *Cligés*, the abduction of Guenièvre in the *Charrette*, the Pesme Aventure from *Yvain*, and the Castle of Marvels in *Perceval*. Yet there can be few authors whose poetic oeuvre is quite so dominated on all levels by images of enclosure as those of Jean Froissart. This essay examines the narrative poetry of Froissart in its manuscript context in an attempt to show how it is articulated and subtended by such imagery and patterns textually, structurally, and codicologically.

This chapter considers most of Froissart's *dits* and longer narratives, in the order in which they occur in B.N. fr. 830, the most complete of the two manuscripts of Froissart's poetry; the other, B.N. fr. 831, is similar, albeit not identical, in structure.[1]

B.N. fr. 830 opens with *Le paradis d'amour*.[2] The very substance of this piece is enclosed within a dream: At the beginning, Morpheus sends his son, Enclinpostair, to put the poet-narrator to sleep (13–32); at the end, the poet-narrator thanks Morpheus for having brought about his dream (1696–723). Moreover, the poet-narrator is the whole time in his chamber

(29). Froissart often seems to repair at crucial moments to the safety of his chamber in a kind of "claustrophilia."[3] In his dream, the desperate poet-narrator finds himself in the comforting surroundings of a wood (39), later said to be a "clos" (enclosure) and a "vregié" (orchard) constructed by the God of Love (251). He leaves it only to visit the God of Love, who resides in another "clostre" (enclosure; 318) or "clos" (818), in which is another "praiiel / ... / Tous enclos de vermauls rosiers, / D'anqueliiers et de lissiers" (1455, 1457–58) [a meadow, enclosed by red rose-trees, by columbines and lilies]. It is perhaps not insignificant that the collection of happy lovers (from classical antiquity and Arthurian romance, including Froissart's own *Meliador*) are disporting themselves in an open "lande" [plain] (957) and not in a restricted space (although the plain is inside the God of Love's domain). Admission to the *Paradis d'amour* has removed the shackles of earthly social conventions and liberated the likes of Tristan and Iseut, Lancelot and Guenièvre, who are now—albeit somewhat ambiguously—free to love in a paradisal enclosure. There is thus an implicit contrast between the unhappy poet-narrator in his multiple enclosures and the happy lovers in an apparently open space.

Within the octosyllabic couplets of the narrative of *Le paradis d'amour* are enclosed a *complainte* (75–202), two rondeaux (851–59, 888–96), a lengthy *lai* (1079–354), a *virelai* (1423–44) and a ballade (1627–53). The phenomenon of lyric insertion into romance narrative has received a good deal of attention recently, and a simple glance at most of Froissart's narrative poems, long and short, will reveal its presence.[4] The mere disposition of lines on the parchment of the manuscripts or on the pages of a printed edition endows the poems with an iconicity that suggests that the metrical variation is significant beyond ornament alone. To say that lyric insertions occur at moments of emotional intensity is stating the obvious, but what strikes me as more structurally significant in much of Froissart's lyrico-narrative (or narrato-lyric?) poetry is the appearance of one form attempting to escape from or dominate another. In other words, lyric may be seen as trying to escape from the prison of narrative, or occasionally, in such poems as *Le joli mois de mai*, *Le dit de la marguerite*, or *Le dit dou bleu chevalier*, narrative may be struggling to impose discipline on an underlying lyric form.

Le temple d'honneur, which immediately follows *Le paradis d'amour* in both B.N. fr. 830 and fr. 831, is in essence a long moral sermon on love and marriage.[5] Although it contains no lyric insertions, it is doubly predicated on images of enclosure and imprisonment. First and most obviously, the principal section of the poem takes place in the temple after all entrance barriers have been removed:

> Ens ou temple qui ouvers fu
> Entrames, bien seuins par u,
> Car ostee estoit la barriere
> Et ouverte la porte arriere.
> Sans deffense et sans contredi
> Fumes ou temple, je vous di. (177–82)

[We entered the temple, which was open, we could see the way for the barrier had been removed and the back door opened. Without resistance and without argument, we were in the temple, I assure you.]

The removal of the barrier and opening of the rear door only lead, of course, to the enclosed space of the temple. Second, Froissart uses a telling image at the beginning of the poem that makes the writing of poetry dependent on the liberation of his subject matter from incarceration. Every day, says the poet-narrator, one hears of or (better still) witnesses "aucune nouvelle" (6), a new noteworthy event:

> Encor m'en avint awan une
> Qui n'a pas esté trop commune
> Ne remonstree jusqu'a chi,
> Dont grandement j'en remerchi
> Mon sentement qui l'a gardé
> Et si bellement retardé
> Que tenu close et en prison
> Jusques atant que j'ai raison
> Dou dire et dou remettre avant. (11–19)

[The other day one happened to me that is not very common and that has not been seen much; I am most grateful to my "sentement" for retaining it and delaying it so well, keeping it enclosed in prison until such time as I have the ability to compose and disseminate.]

The use of the verb "avint" in line 11 would probably authorize us to consider "nouvelle" the equivalent of "aventure." Douglas Kelly has underlined the importance of *sentement* in the genesis and composition of Machaut's *Le voir-dit* and in Froissart's *Meliador*,[6] and it here acts as a prison warden until such time as the "nouvelle" can profitably be released under the safe conduct of "raison," which I here take to mean the ability to transform subject matter into poetry. The poetic process is complete only when the poem has been disseminated ("remettre avant"), but the retention of the "nouvelle" in prison until the right time is crucial to the whole enterprise.

Anthime Fourrier has written of *Le joli mois de mai*: "Nous sommes ici à la limite entre poésie narrative et poésie lyrique. En effet, l'élément narratif se réduit à la plus simple expression et l'on peut dire qu'il n'y a pratiquement pas de récit au sens littéraire du mot."[7] Fourrier concludes that the originality of this piece lies both in its transforming the *reverdie*, normally a simple *entrée en matière*, into the subject of the whole poem, and in its formal novelty, namely in its use of widely different strophes (44–46). One might add that the use of what are essentially lyric forms permits Froissart to avoid the universal narrative octosyllabic couplet. The locus of the extended reverdie is, of course, the standard garden ("vregiet" [25]), but note the terms in which it is introduced:

> Entrai l'autre jour en un clos
> Ou la dedens avoit enclos
> (Bien l'avisai)
> Rosiers, osiers et joli glai. (16–19)

> [I came the other day into an enclosure, in which had been placed (I saw it clearly) rose-trees, willows, and pretty rushes.]

Once again, an enclosed space proves conducive to the production of poetry.

L'orloge amoureus is an extended allegory that compares the poet-narrator's love for his lady with the workings of a clock.[8] The lover's heart serves the clock as housing (the "maison," "loge," or "chambre" [house, lodge, or chamber]), in which the mechanism, representing the workings of love, resides (51–70, 1152–53). Continually in motion like the clock, night and day, the lover's movements and desires are nevertheless restricted to the boundaries of the housing. Froissart's allegory does, however, look outside the "orloge" itself and call upon the services of an "orlogier" (clockmaker) (931) to regulate the workings of the clock:

> Selonc l'estat dont j'ai parlé premiers,
> Souvenirs doit estre li orlogiers.
> Car Souvenirs qui ens ou coer s'enfrume
> Toutes les fois qu'il li plaist, il desfrume
> Le Doux Penser qui les broquetes porte,
> En quoi le vrai amant moult se deporte. (949–54)

> [In accordance with the state of which I first spoke, Remembrance

should be the clockmaker. For Remembrance, which encloses itself
in the heart whenever it wishes, unlocks the Sweet Thought that
bears the pins and in which the true lover delights.]

We might compare the function of "Souvenir" in *L'orloge amoureus* to that
of "sentement" in *Le temple d'honneur:* As "sentement" controls "nouvelle" until "raison" can generate poetry, so "Souvenir" regulates and
releases "Doux Penser," the bearer of the pins that strike the chimes and
produce melody:

> Car quant Desirs premiers mon coer feri,
> Par la vertu de vostre grant beauté,
> De puis n'a heure, en yver n'en esté,
> Que Doulx Penser, qui porte les broquetes,
> N'ait fait sonner en mon coer les clochetes
> De divers chans et de diverses notes. (914–19)

[For since Desire first struck my heart through the virtue of your
great beauty, there has not been an hour, in winter or in summer,
when Sweet Thought, which bears the pins, has not made the bells
in my heart ring with diverse songs and notes.]

In *L'orloge amoureus,* too, the entire process is subject to "raison": "Tout
ensi sui gouvrenés par raison" (1151). [Thus am I completely governed by
reason.]

Although *Le dit de la marguerite* (*"Dits" et "Débats,"* pp. 147–53) might
be considered a slight piece, it embodies many aspects of Froissart's poetic oeuvre. Written in strophic form, it has a narrative potential that remains largely unexploited and that hovers between lyric and narrative, in
a manner similar to that of *Le joli mois de mai.* Like much of Froissart's
work, it is largely indebted to Machaut (who had written two marguerite
poems), and seems to hold a personal significance for the poet beyond the
literary tradition of the marguerite.[9] The core of the poem is a pseudo-Ovidian transformation myth, invented by Froissart, according to which
the marguerite was born from the tears shed by Hero on the tomb of her
lover Cepheus. Touched by their love, Jupiter makes the flowers bloom
with the aid of Fébus's rays; Mercury makes a crown from the blossoms,
which he sends to Ceres, convincing her to reciprocate his affection. On a
smaller scale, this is precisely the kind of *inventio* wrought elsewhere by
Froissart's imagination, for example, in the story of Pinoteus and
Neptisphelé from *La prison amoureuse.*[10] Once more, images of imprisonment dominate: Hero's tears are released from the prison of the earth, but

only into the "encloseüre" (93) that surrounds Cepheus's tomb; and at the end, Froissart's poet-narrator wishes to sequester himself in some secluded spot—an enclosure with a tower—with his marguerite:

> Et di ensi: "Pleuïst au dieu d'Amour
> Que je veïsse enclos en une tour
> O le closier la gratieuse flour.
> Et si n'euïst homme ne femme au tour
>   Qui sourvenir
> Peuïst illuec, et fust en un destour
> A mon cuesir, n'ai cure en quel contour!" (148–54)

[And I spoke thus: "Would that it pleased the God of Love for me to see enclosed in a tower with a watchman the gracious flower. And would that no man or woman could come there, and would that it were in a secluded place, I care not where!"]

Whether or not the interlocutor in *Le dit dou bleu chevalier* can be identified as the young duke of Berry imprisoned in England,[11] the figure's incarcerated state is crucial to the nature of the poem. While the writing of poetry and the identification of *matière* is usually a matter of skill and effort, Froissart claims to have been merely lucky in this case:

> Car il m'avint, n'a pas grant temps, ensi
> Que sans cerchier je trouvai devant mi
> Une aventure. (5–7)

[For it so happened to me not long ago that, without seeking, I found before me an adventure.]

The adventure, of course, is the encounter with the Bleu Chevalier, a manic depressive if ever there was one.[12] If the poem as a whole, again in strophic form, can be seen as the knight's *complainte*,[13] lines 130–34 shed light not only on the poem itself but also on others in Froissart's oeuvre that incorporate lyrics:

> Et dist ensi: "Aprés plours et regrés
> Doit on chanter chançons et virelais
> Pour oublier
> Ce qu'as amans voelt Fortune envoiier:
> Trop est diverse, on ne s'en doit changier."

[And he said: "After tears and regrets, one should sing songs and virelays to forget whatever Fortune sends lovers: it is too fickle and one should not waver."]

In *Le dit dou bleu chevalier,* lyric insertion and its purpose are virtual and are wholly restrained by the narrative, not even actualized within its confines, as is normally the case. The Bleu Chevalier is said to sing (32–40, 135–40), but his songs are not reproduced.

Often in Froissart, imprisonment leads directly to the composition of poetry and its dissemination. Here, however, the route is indirect, as the Bleu Chevalier's prison seems to be more than usually oppressive and disabling during the downswings of his cyclothymia:

> Car, tout ensi qu'un oizelet on tient,
> Me tient on ci.
> . . . .
> Et d'autre part aussi, je pense tant
> A mes amours, dont je n'ai maintenant
> Solas ne joie, esbatement ne chant. (274–75, 289–91)

[For just as one keeps a bird, I am kept here. . . . And on the other hand, I think so much about my love that I now have neither solace nor joy, diversion nor song.]

And again:

> Ci sui enclos com dedens une tour.
> . . . .
> Il n'i aroit encores se bien non,
>   Se je sentoie
> Que de venir a chief de ceste voie,
> Ou pour paiier raençon, me pooie
> De ci partir: je me deliveroie
>   De ci pour voir.
> Mes je n'i voi nulle fin ne espoir
> De delivrance. Ensi me desespoir. (346, 359–66)

[I am enclosed here as in a tower. . . . It could do only good if I thought that by reaching the end of this path or by paying a ransom, I could leave this place: I would truly free myself from here. But I can see no end or hope of deliverance. Thus I despair.]

If indeed the imprisonment of the subject here is real rather than merely part of the metaphor of amorous and poetic rhetoric, its debilitating effects may be equally genuine. It is precisely the permanent nature of his confinement that prevents the Bleu Chevalier from being like the Arthurian lovers (Tristan, Yvain, Lancelot, Guiron le Courtois, Perceval) quoted by the poet-narrator as models of patience (295–326). The mechanism that leads from prison to poem here requires the intermediary of Froissart's poet-narrator, whose encounter with the captive Bleu Chevalier becomes not only the cause but also the "matere" of the final "dittié":

> Je vous requier
> Que vous voeilliés ordonner .I. dittier
> Com d'aventure avés, et sans cerchier,
> Dedens ce bois trouvé un chevalier
>   De bleu vesti . . . (424–28)

[I ask you to compose a poem about how, without seeking, you perchance met in this wood a knight dressed in blue . . .]

The poet-narrator will put the "matere" [subject matter] (463) of the "dittié" (462) into rhyme applying "sentement" (463) and "pourpos" [intention] (464) before having it performed ("recordés et dis" [443, 482]) in several locations in the hope that its intended recipient will be present.

Le debat dou cheval et dou levrier ("Dits" et "Débats," 171–74) is to all intents and purposes Froissart's Aesopic fable: A horse and a hound argue as to which of them has the worst of it, but the dispute is cut short as they realize they will both be fed in the next town, animal instinct being more powerful than debate. It would be easy to claim that since both are domestic animals, both have had their natural liberty taken from them by man and are thus imprisoned. This is true, if self-evident. What might be regarded as the hound's good fortune in having access to the house is in fact confinement ("derriere un huis" [behind a door] [65]), and it turns out to be a curse, as he is often blamed and beaten for stealing food (68–78). When the horse claims that the hound would not appreciate being pricked as he is with spurs, the horse swears by St. Anastasia ("sainte Honestasse" [49]). Anastasia was a Roman brought up as a Christian but married to a pagan who, when he discovered she was visiting Christian prisoners, shut her away. After surviving two more forced marriages to Roman prefects, she is cast into prison to die of hunger but is fed by St. Theodora. Finally, Anastasia is burned alive at the stake.

At 4198 lines, *L'espinette amoureuse* is Froissart's second longest narrative poem, and one that contains a good deal of material relevant to his *art poétique*.[14] In the grip of winter, the young Froissart spent his time reading "rommans" (romances) (314) and "traitiers / D'amours" (treatises about love) (315–16); the theory of love provided him with a head start when it came to practical application. Here, then, is a view of the function of reading that justifies it directly as a preparation for life. The basis of *L'espinette amoureuse* is an "aventure" (347) that happens to the poet-narrator one "joli mois de may" (351) and that takes place, of course, within the confines of a "gardinet" [little garden] (353), a *hortus conclusus*. Following on Venus's promise that he will fall in love with a woman more beautiful than Helen of Troy, the poet-narrator encounters a damsel engrossed in the romance of *Cleomadés* (696–709), which the pair then take turns in reading, until, in a moment redolent of Dante's story of Paolo and Francesca, they read no more: "Adont laissames nous le lire" (746) [thereupon we stopped reading]. Within the confines of the text are held not only the usual inserted lyrics (five ballades, 926–44, 1256–76, 1469–93, 3538–61, 3834–60; three virelais, 1021–45, 2436–52, 3087–127; a long complainte, 1556–2355; a set of rondeaux, 2485–97, 2498–530, 2531–40; the *Reconfort de la dame*, 2757–996; and a concluding lai, 3915–4146), but also references to fragments of the wider intertext: the young Froissart's winter reading, Adenet le Roi's *Cleomadés*, and Mahieu le Poirier's *Cour d'amour* (called the *Baillieu d'amours* [871]), a copy of which the poet-narrator sends to the damsel. Moreover, the complainte and the *Reconfort de la dame* rewrite tales from Ovid (or the *Ovide moralisé*) within the intercalated pieces. The complainte is central, both thematically and structurally, as Nancy Bradley-Cromey has shown, and is mathematically close to the midpoint of the poem.[15] As a "reduced model of the whole *dit*," it seems to expand both backward and forward, thereby creating its own confinement. Kibler, indeed, calls it "an imposing enclosure of rhetoric" ("Self-Delusion," 89).

The "real" love of the poet-narrator is clearly prefigured both by Ovidian mythography and by the matter of contemporary literature (Bradley-Cromey, 208). Figures from Arthurian romance and from *Les voeux du paon* (for example in the complainte [2308–23]) are also cited as models for the lover's amorous martyrdom, and Male Bouche from *Le roman de la rose* even appears as a participant in the poem (3724 ff.). If literature relates in this manner to life, then the containment of personal experience within fiction is symbolized by the poet-narrator's literally enclosing the first ballade between the covers of the copy of the *Cour d'amour* he lends his beloved. His decision to compose a poem rather than the letter he had initially considered (883–87) itself envelops reality in the cloak of literary artifice. The ballade is thus an inserted lyric on two levels: within the book of the *Cour d'amour* within the text of *L'espinette amoureuse*. This expedient is something of an easy option: "N'est nuls ne nulle qui mal disce / D'une cançon, se on le troeve / En un rommanch qu'on clot et oevre" (900–902).

[No man or woman will say ill of a song if it is found in a romance that one closes and opens.] Unfortunately, when the book is returned, the ballade is still there, between the covers, not having been released by the beloved to perform its function. At the same time, this paradoxically constitutes her rejection of his surrender as proposed in the last two lines of the ballade: "Vis me rench pour le prison / La belle que tant pris'on" (943–44). [I surrender alive as the prisoner of the fair one who is so praised.] Somewhat later, when the beloved's friend informs the poet-narrator of her possible marriage, his first reaction is to lock himself up in his room:

> Et tous seulés sans plus atendre
> En une cambre m'encloÿ.
> Je ne sçai se nulz homs m'oÿ,
> Mais je fis la des biaus regrés,
> Ensi com loyaus amans vrés,
> Plain de jalousie et de painne
> Et qui Amours a son gré mainne. (1422–28)

> [And without delay I shut myself up all alone in a room. I do not know if anyone heard me, but I there uttered sweet regrets, like a true loyal lover, full of jealousy and pain, and whom Love leads at will.]

It is probable that the phrase "biaus regrés" is here to be taken as meaning "poetic laments." They are the ballade that follows (1469–93) and the central complainte, both written during a period of delirious self-confinement in the chamber.

La prison amoureuse, which follows *L'espinette amoureuse* in fr. 830, is not surprisingly, given its title, the most acute and focused expression of the imagery of enclosure in Froissart's oeuvre.[16] The significance of the title—it relates both to his love and to that of the character Rose—is explained by Flos in letter 12 toward the end of the work:

> [Je] di ensi que vous sejournés et demorés en prison, car coers jolis et amoureus, qui aimme en le fourme et maniere comme vous fetes, ne poet vivre ne resgner sans estre emprisonnés. Or vous est ceste prison jolie et amoureuse, car, Dieu merci, entre vostre souverainne et vous n'a nul discort ne soussi, ains sont vo doi coer assés en unité parfete, ensi qu'il appert par le teneur de vos lettres fiablement tramises a mi; de quoi tel vie doit estre appellee amoureuse et prisons ossi. Et se je l'i adjouste, elle y est moult bien seans, car voirement estes vous pris et emprisonnés ou service de vostre dame, non

obstant toutes grasces; se ne vous poés vous escuser que vous ne soiiés son prisonnier et ossi je n'i ai point veü le contraire . . . Ja soit ce cose que en ceste prison je languis attendans la grasce de ma dame, se m'en est la vie et li esperance si joieuse que je le doi bien appeler amoureuse et prison, car je me rench a ma dame et me tien son prisonnier. (20:25–38, 43–47)

[I thus say that you stay and remain in prison, for a fair and amorous heart, which loves in the way and manner you do, cannot live and prevail without being imprisoned. This prison is so fair and amorous to you for, thank God, there is between your sovereign lady and yourself no discord or care so that your two hearts are in quite perfect unity, as it appears from the tenor of the letters sent in confidence to me; for this reason such a life should be called amorous and prison. And I may add that it is quite appropriate, for you are truly captured and imprisoned in the service of your lady, all favors notwithstanding; and you cannot argue that you are not her prisoner, and I have seen nothing to contradict it. . . . And even though I languish in prison waiting for the grace of my lady, my life and hope are so joyful that I might well call it amorous and prison, for I surrender to my lady and consider myself her prisoner.]

As elsewhere in Froissart's poetic oeuvre, literature and reality interact, here not so much because actual love affairs are the subject of poetry, but rather because the figure of Rose can be identified with Wenceslas of Luxembourg, duke of Brabant, held captive between August 1371 and July 1372 by Guillaume, duke of Juliers, in his castle at Nideggen on the Ruhr.[17] Wenceslas's amorous prison is therefore also political, the one perhaps providing consolation for the other.

From the opening sequence, it would appear that Froissart intends to use the usual devices and images of enclosure. For example, there are inserted lyrics (two virelays, 295–326, 429–60) and the as yet unnamed poet-narrator's (later Flos) responding to his lady's poem by repairing first to a "requoi" [refuge] (482) and then to his chamber ("En une cambre m'enfermai" (490). [I shut myself up in a chamber.]). But the "aventure" (627) of *La prison amoureuse* embeds a second story, that of Rose, in the first. The epistolary exchange that forms the basis for the rest of *La prison amoureuse* (the idea for which Froissart seems to have taken from Machaut's *Le voir-dit*) is full of images of containment. The prose letters often contain lyrics, and both are, of course, contained in parchment.[18] Their dispatch often has a liberating effect on the writer:

> La lettre, et la balade ossi,
> Tout en un volume escripsi,
> Puis le ploiai et saielai
> Et au messagier le baillai,
> Qui se parti, Diex le convoie!
> Je ne sçai ou il prist sa voie,
> Mes je sçai bien ou je remés:
> Dedens mon hostel enfremés,
> *Non que g'i soie trop enclos,*
> Mes pour l'amour du joli clos
> . . . .
> Volentiers je m'i esbatoie. (786–95, 800)

[The letter along with the ballad I wrote in a volume, then folded and sealed it and gave it to the messenger who then left, may God be with him! I do not know which direction he took, but I do know where I remained—shut up in my lodgings, not that I was too closed in, but because I liked the fair enclosure, I amused myself willingly.]

Flos can feel free only when locked up! Rose's first letter to Flos is then placed in a purse suspended from Flos's belt (802–7). Reading the letters is tantamount to liberating them, but has to be done in secret:

> Et puis si me tournai a part.
> Des lettres le signet rompi
> Et tout bellement les ouvri. (915–17)

[And then I withdrew. I broke the seal of the letters and opened them properly.][19]

When Rose's beloved returns his letter, it has, in a manner of speaking, been resealed, unable to fulfill its function.

The accumulation of letters within Flos's purse can be seen as a metaphor for the poetic process (1082–85), and the two damsels (from the entourage of his own lady) who purloin it to his embarrassment and take him hostage may represent readers of poetry. He ransoms himself by allowing them to copy the songs sent by Rose and retaining only the prose letters himself; the poems intended for Rose's lady thus reach Flos's beloved (1148–66). Flos then composes another virelay, which he seals in a casket for safekeeping (1215–48).

If the protagonists of *La prison amoureuse* retire to a secluded spot to read poetry, they also need to immure themselves in order to write. The pseudo-Ovidian invention of Pynoteüs and Neptisphelé is written in the safety of Flos's study: "Et j'entrai dedens mon estude, / Qui n'est ne villainne ne rude, / Mes belle pour estudiier" (1290–92) [And I entered into my study, which is neither unpleasant nor uncomfortable, but fine for studying]. The new metamorphosis is, needless to say, folded, sealed, and bound before being sent to Rose: "elle fu ploiee / Et saielee et bien loiie" (2016–17) [it was folded and sealed and well tied]. As he had written a virelay and placed it in a box, Flos now composes three ballades and part of a lay, which he proceeds to place in a leather casket (2029–2203). Rose's next two letters are sent to Flos in exactly the same kind of leather casket in which he had placed his own poems: "un coffin / De cuir bouli, poli et fin" [a casket of treated leather, shiny and fine] (2210–11; cf. 2114–15). The activities of the two protagonists begin to merge into one. Flos retires to his chamber to open his new package (2218–20).

Accompanying letter 7 is Rose's response to the story of Pynoteüs and Neptisphelé, the long allegorical dream episode in which Rose himself is taken prisoner and which is in essence the "prison amoureuse" of the title (2252–3420). This extends the poetic metaphor since it is the result of "ymagination" (VII:20, 22) inspired by Flos's own Ovidian invention. Enclosed in the casket, enclosed "en volume de livret" [in the form of a small book] (VII:27–28) of six leaves (2241), this is to all appearances an independent poem. It begins with the traditional bucolic spring opening, which engenders the dream (2252–317) and ends with the narrator waking up (3393–405). It clearly owes as much to *Le roman de la rose* as Flos's tale does to the *Ovide moralisé*. It is, in a very real sense, Rose's *Rose*. Fourrier has pointed out the structural relationship between the two episodes (pp. 19–20); I would underline that even within these two poems within poems, other pieces are embedded, notably Pynoteüs's prayer (1744–918), Rose's complainte (3010–153), and two virelais (3198–258). Furthermore, Rose's complainte is sealed with a letter in a casket and offered to Souvenir (3160–63). The perspective of Chinese puzzles and multiple *mises en abyme* is profoundly oppressive. There are many more similar images of imprisonment and enclosure in the poem (for example, 3284–85, 3322 ff., 3463–70, 3762–64, 3830–33, 3868–75) that consolidate the argument.

If not exactly his farewell to poetry, *Le joli buisson de Jonece* seems to be Froissart's farewell to love, a retrospective in which the recently appointed curate of Estinnes-au-Mont revisits earlier amorous vicissitudes as he looks toward the spiritual life.[20] There is no reason to doubt that this work reflects a turning point in Froissart's life, and we have seen elsewhere that his poetry, however conventional and contrived it may be, has close links with reality. Many of the devices from his earlier narratives are found in *Le joli buisson de Jonece*.²¹ It is even the release from a casket of the portrait of his lady that inspires the poet-narrator to compose his first virelai and provides the catalyst for the rest of the narrative:

> Et la vins ou ja mis avoie
> Le coffre, en sauf lieu et couvert;
> Si l'ai deffremé et ouvert
> Et l'ymage, que tant desir
> A veoir, voi illuec jesir.
> Je le pris et le desploiai
> De le toille ou ja le ploiai
> Et, si tretost qu'au nu le vi,
> Mon coer entirement ravi
> En un penser fresc et nouviel
> Qui me fist faire, et par reviel,
> Un virelay en ce moment. (550–61)

[And I came where I had placed the casket, concealed in a safe place; and I unsealed and opened it, and there saw lying the image which I so desired to see. I took it and removed it from the cloth in which I had wrapped it, and as soon as I saw it clearly, it filled my heart with a new and fresh thought that then caused me in joy to compose a virelay.]

As in *Le temple d'honneur* and *L'orloge amoureus*, the image is confined until the most propitious moment arrives for its release as a creative force; that moment is here determined by Philozophie. The inspiration of the image leads to the central vision of the poem experienced by Froissart in his chamber ("en la cambre ou je me dormoie") (873) [in the chamber where I slept] on November 30, 1373.

The "buisson" of the title is an odd locus: an apparently spherical object at the center of which the poet-narrator finds himself after having been guided there by Venus (1367–68, 1401). Venus leaves him in the hands of Jeunesse, who, unlike the poet-narrator, seems to perceive the *buisson* as a prison since he asks his charge if he would not prefer to leave:

> "Volés vous point de chi issir
> Et aultres aventures querre,
> Et dieus et deesses requerre
> Qui vous mesissent mieulz a main
> Vostre esbat de soir et demain?" (1821–25)

[Do you wish to leave here and seek other adventures, and ask other gods and goddesses to arrange better evening and morning pleasure for you?]

The poet-narrator, who finds the enclosure of the *buisson* conducive to poetic activity since he has just composed a virelay (1768–99)—"Je sui en vostre prison" [I am in your prison] (1793)—replies in the negative. Within this one enclosure, Jeunesse now leads the protagonist to another: "Chils lieus fu enclos ou Buisson/ Dont je parloie maintenant" (1873–74). [This place was enclosed in the thicket of which I was speaking.] It is here that the lady from the portrait in the casket is found.

As the image had caused the vision, so the sight of the lady draws her erstwhile lover into a long allegorical sequence populated by personifications from *Le roman de la rose* (2306 ff.), preceded by Jeunesse's citing of Ovidian and pseudo-Ovidian faithful lovers (2010–305). As Rose had rewritten Flos's mythography in an allegorical mode in *La prison amoureuse*, so the poet-narrator engages in a dialectic in which Jeunesse and Désir (3154–407) counter myth with allegory. The underlying unity of the workings of love and its literary manifestations is exemplified by the fact that it is precisely the allegorical personifications (Jeunesse and Désir) who are spokesmen for the mythographical tradition. Needless to say, the poet-narrator is a prisoner of love, as Désir suggests to the lady when he delivers the message and the supplicant's accompanying ballad:

"Dame, chi devant
Ai je laissiet vostre servant
Dedens che buissoncel tous seus,
Triste, pensieu et angousseus." (3832–35)

[Lady, I have just left your servant alone in this thicket, sad, pensive, and anguished.]

After repeated refusals, the lady finally consents to open and read the ballad, releasing it to perform its function. Désir then makes the explicit connection between the production of the poem and his friend's captive state:

"Parler voel encor de cheli
Dont elle vient et qui l'envoie.
Qui le muet et le met en voie
De faire ensi? Je di, par m'ame,
Que c'est tout pour vostre amour, dame,

> Dont il est si pris et lachiés
> Qu'il n'en poet estre deslachiés,
> Ne ne sera ja jour ne heure." (4019–26)

> [I still wish to speak of the person who sent it. Who made it and sent it out for this purpose? I say, by my soul, that it is all for love of you, lady, by whom he is thus captured and bound that he cannot be untied, nor ever will be.]

This, too, the lover admits: "Enfremés dedens le Buisson / Tout ensi qu'en une prison" [shut up inside the thicket, just like in a prison] (4368–69).

La prison amoureuse is the key text in this discussion of enclosure and confinement as a structuring principle of Froissart's aesthetic. In letter X, Rose requests Flos to gather together all of their correspondence and accompanying poems:

> Je vous pri chierement que toutes lettres, trettiés, balades, virelais que nous avons envoiiet l'un l'autre, vous voelliés rassambler et mettre en .I. volume par maniere de livret. (10:11–14)

> [I beg you sincerely to compile and put in a single booklet all the letters, treatises, ballads, and virelays we have sent each other.]

Flos undertakes to do this, but in the full knowledge that it is not an easy task:

> Car Rose escript, che me samble,
> Que je remette tout ensamble
> Par ordenance belle et noeve
> Les escriptures que g'i troeve.
> Or en y a de pluiseurs tires,
> Et de rompues et d'entires,
> Dont c'est grant painne au rajouster. (3768–74)

> [For Rose writes, it seems, for me to assemble in a fresh and pleasing order the writings I find there. But there are several sequences, both fragmentary and complete, which will be difficult to put together.]

It seems clear that once imagination has generated visions, lyrics, and other individual components, the art of composition is a matter of *ordonner* and *rajouster*. *La prison amoureuse* is a metaphor for Froissart's poetic activity on all levels as much as it is a finished product of the same.

In *Le dit dou florin* ("Dits" et "Débats," pp. 175–90), a florin, captive in

Froissart's purse (114–16), engages in a dialogue with the poet concerning his life and achievements. As the penultimate poem in fr. 830, this is also in a sense a retrospective assessment of Froissart's career. The florin's pronouncement on posterity is therefore particularly significant:

> "Car fait en avés mainte hystore
> Dont il sera encor memore
> De vous ens ou temps a venir,
> Et ferés les gens souvenir
> De vo sens et de vos doctrines." (203–7)

[For you have written many stories which will cause you to be remembered in time to come, and you will make people remember your wisdom and teachings.]

And when Froissart relates how he indeed wrote *Meliador* and read it to Gaston Fébus, the one characteristic of the romance he singles out for comment relates precisely to the poetics of enclosure:

> "Dedens ce rommanc sont encloses
> Toutes les chançons que jadis,—
> Dont l'ame soit en paradys!—
> Que fist le bon duc de Braibant,
> Wincelaus, dont on parla tant." (300–4)[22]

[In this romance are enclosed all the songs that the good Duke Wenceslas of Brabant, of whom so much was spoken—may his soul be in Paradise—once made.]

The insertion of Wenceslas's lyrics into the narrative of *Meliador*[23] adds a supplemental dimension to what I see as *an*, not *the*, underlying compositional principle of Froissart's narrative oeuvre. What are works attributed to others within the fiction of a narrative (such as the letters and lyrics of Rose in *La prison amoureuse*) are in *Meliador* poems by a real "other" that possess or can possess a separate existence outside of the *récit*. Lyric has quite literally, therefore, been "imprisoned" by Froissart within a structure of narrative. This same principle is visible, moreover, on a material level, namely that of the structure and composition of the two manuscripts, B.N. fr. 831 and 830, where groups of Froissart's own lyrics are inserted in the gaps between longer narratives and dits. In the latter, whose order I have used for the present discussion, clearly demarcated (and rubricated) groups of lais, *pastourelles, chançons royales et ser-*

ventois Nostre Dame, ballades, virelais, and rondeaux are inserted between *La prison amoureuse* and *Le joli buisson de Jonece.* The principle is even clearer in fr. 831, where the lais and pastourelles are to be found between *Le dit de la marguerite* and *La prison amoureuse;* the *Chançons royales et serventois* between *La prison amoureuse* and *L'espinette amoureuse;* and the *balades,* virelais, and rondeaux between *L'espinette amoureuse* and *Le joli buisson de Jonece.* The structuring of the manuscript in this way requires Froissart to *rajouster* and *ordonner* as Rose had asked Flos to do in *La prison amoureuse.* Indeed, the *incipits* and *explicits* of both fr. 830 and fr. 831 suggest that "ordering" is the final step in the process both of composing an individual work and of putting together the codex:

> ... dedens ce livre sont contenu pluisour dittié et traitié amourous et de moralité, les quels sire Jehans Froissars ... a fais, dités et ordonnés a l'alde de Dieu et d'Amours. (fr. 831, f. 1v°a; cf. f. 200v°a; fr. 830, f. 1v°a and f. 219v°a)

> [In this book are contained many poems and treatises of love and morality, which Sir Jean Froissart ... made, composed, and arranged with the help of God and Love.]

The *incipit* and *explicit* of fr. 830 both add "sentement" to "Dieu" and "Amours" as aids in the poetic process. This would seem to mean the kind of discipline that can only be imposed by confinement.

The final poem in both manuscripts of Froissart's poetry is *La plaidoirie de la rose et de la violette* (*"Dits" et "Débats,"* pp. 191–203). As a legally conducted debate between two lawyers arguing the merits and virtues of the two flowers, its own conclusion constitutes a verdict, which is, short of an appeal, the final word. Its very position endows it with a significance beyond its own textual boundaries and with an application to Froissart's poetic corpus as a whole. Throughout Froissart's work runs a fundamental dialectic between poetry and reality, between his lovers and their ladies, between mythography and allegory, between lyric and narrative. If this dialectic is characteristic of the *jeu-parti* or *tenso,* it is also the defining feature of legal discourse. As the concluding work in both codices, *La plaidoirie de la rose et de la violette* seals the material repositories of Froissart's poetic oeuvre. Followed only by the extradiegetic *explicit,* its final verse is Froissart's last. As the covers of the manuscript prepare to confine the parchment that both encloses and is enclosed by the text, this final verse could hardly be more appropriate: "Atant fu la chils procés clos" (342). [Thereupon was this trial closed.]

Notes

1. The best descriptions are probably those in Jean Anthime Fourrier's edition of Froissart's *L'espinette amoureuse* (Paris: Klincksieck, 1963), pp. 7–12. See also Sylvia Huot, *From Song to Book: The Poetics of Writing in Old French Lyric and Lyrical Narrative Poetry* (Ithaca: Cornell University Press, 1987), 302–37.

2. Jean Froissart, *"Le paradis d'amour" and "L'orloge amoureus,"* ed. Peter F. Dembowski (Geneva: Droz, 1986).

3. In what may reflect a wider habit of intimate private reading, Froissart relates in his chronicles that Richard II immediately has the presentation copy of the poems taken to "sa chambre de retraite" by Richard Credon. Quoted by Jacqueline Cerquiglini-Toulet, *La couleur de la mélancolie: la fréquentation des livres aux XIVe siècle* (Paris: Hatier, 1993), 160–61.

4. See, for example, Maureen Barry McCann Boulton, *The Song in the Story: Lyric Insertions in French Narrative Fiction, 1200–1400* (Philadelphia: University of Pennsylvania Press, 1993).

5. In Jean Froissart, *"Dits" et "Débats,"* ed. Anthime Fourrier (Geneva: Droz, 1979), pp. 91–127; see Barbara E. Kurtz, "The *Temple d'onnour* of Jean Froissart," *Modern Philology* 82 (1984): 156–66.

6. Douglas Kelly, *Medieval Imagination: Rhetoric and the Poetry of Courtly Love* (Madison: University of Wisconsin Press, 1978), 248–56.

7. *"Dits" et "Débats,"* p. 44; *Le joli mois de mai* is edited on pp. 129–46.

8. *"Le paradis d'amour" and "L'orloge amoureus,"* ed. Dembowski.

9. This has been ably discussed by Fourrier (*"Dits" et "Débats,"* 46–51), who believes that the marguerite is emblematic of Froissart's first love. On Machaut, see James I. Wimsatt, *The Marguerite Poetry of Guillaume de Machaut* (Chapel Hill: University of North Carolina Press, 1970).

10. See Douglas Kelly, "Les inventions ovidiennes de Froissart," *Littérature* 41 (1981): 82–92.

11. See Normand R. Cartier, "Le bleu chevalier," *Romania* 87 (1966): 289–314. Fourrier (*"Dits" et Débats,"* 60) regards all attempts to identify the Bleu Chevalier with a historical personage as "vain, pour ne pas dire absurde."

12. Cf. Fourrier, ibid., 53.

13. Although its strophic form is unusual (AAAB, BBBC, CCCD, EEEF, etc.), the sequence of three decasyllabic lines followed by a tetrasyllable is exactly that of the complaintes inserted into *Le paradis d'amour, L'espinette amoureuse,* and *La prison amoureuse,* where the sixteen-line strophes are all structured AAAB AAAB BBBA BBBA.

14. *L'espinette amoureuse,* ed. Fourrier, 14; on *L'espinette* generally, see W. W. Kibler, "Self-Delusion in Froissart's *Espinette amoureuse,*" *Romania* 97 (1976):77–98.

15. "Mythological Typology in Froissart's *L'espinette amoureuse,*" *Res Publica Litterarum* 3 (1980):207–21, 213.

16. Jean Froissart, *La prison amoureuse,* ed. Anthime Fourrier (Paris: Klincksieck, 1974), 16. The images of enclosure in *La prison amoureuse* have also been examined

by Laurence de Looze, "From Text to Text and from Tale to Tale: Jean Froissart's *Prison amoureuse*," in *The Centre and Its Compass: Studies in Medieval Literature in Honor of Professor John Leyerle*, ed. Robert A. Taylor et al. (Kalamazoo: Western Michigan University, 1993), 87–110. See also Claude Thiry, "Allégorie et histoire dans la *Prison amoureuse* de Froissart," *Studi Francesi* 61–62 (1977): 15–29, and Claire Nouvet, "Pour une économie de la dé-limitation: la *Prison amoureuse* de Jean Froissart," *Neophilologus* 70 (1986):341–56.

17. The evidence is presented by Fourrier in the introduction to his edition, 20–28.

18. Nearly all of the poems are said to be "clos" in the letters; I will not quote all instances here.

19. Rose also withdraws to read his beloved's response (III:75–76).

20. *La prison*, ed. Fourrier.

21. See Philip E. Bennett, "The Mirage of Fiction: Narration, Narrator, and Narratee in Froissart's Lyrico-Narrative *Dits*," *Modern Language Review* 86 (1991): 288–89.

22. Jacqueline Cerquiglini-Toulet writes of *Le dit dou florin:* "L'image de la prison y revient lancinante" (*La couleur de la mélancolie*, p. 66).

23. See Jeanne Lods, "Les poésies de Wenceslas et le *Méliador* de Froissart," in *Mélanges Charles Foulon* (Rennes: Université de Haute-Bretagne, 1980), 1:205–16.

6

Imitation, Metamorphosis, and Froissart's Use of the Exemplary *Modus tractandi*

Douglas Kelly

Du mußt dein Leben ändern. . . .
Denn Bleiben ist nirgends.
Ranier Maria Rilke[1]

It is generally agreed that late medieval authors like Jean Froissart wrote "treatises" in the special sense this word had for his time.[2] A "treatise" treats its subject matter using specific modes and forms of writing. One of the most common modes of handling a subject matter was the *modus exemplorum positivus*—the use of examples to prove, develop, illustrate, invalidate, or problematize the subject matter and its meaning or meanings. Dante is no doubt the author best known for his use of this and other *modi tractandi*, and it is not difficult to find any number of them in late medieval writing from the *Roman de la rose* on.[3] The composition of the *Ovide moralisé* contributed as well to the use of the exemplary mode, first by making French-speaking publics familiar with a wide range of mythological examples and, second, by illustrating the numerous ways in which such examples may be read and reread on both literal and allegorical levels.[4] The metamorphosis or mutation of examples is what this essay examines in the case of Froissart's *dits* and some of his lyrics.

In a fairly recent study of the use of the word *exemplum*, Peter von Moos identifies two broad kinds of exempla that we find as well in Froissart: the illustration, or deductive exemplum, and the enthymeme, or inductive exemplum.[5] The first is the obvious kind of exemplum, and Froissart offers numerous illustrations of it. For example, in the *Paradis d'amour* he illustrates, in three mythological examples, the eye-heart-arrow metaphor for the amorous *coup de foudre*:

> Sicom Achillés fu jadis
> De belle Polixena pris
> Seulement et par regarder,
> Et Neptunus, li diex de mer,
> Par Eqeulenta la pucelle,
> Et Leander tout pour la belle
> Hero, que telement cheri
> Que pour s'amour en mer peri. (493–500)[6]

[Just as Achilles in olden days fell in love with Polyxena at sight of her, so did Neptune, the sea-god, fall for Eqeulenta and Leander for the beautiful Hero, whom he loved so much that he perished for love of her in the sea.]

Froissart himself is a reflective poet—at least he presents himself in that way. In the *Prison amoureuse*, for instance, he tells how he construed a given poem by means of at least two readings of it.

> Des foelles lisi jusqu'a sis[7]
> Et puis recommenchai mon tour
> A la premiere page, pour
> Mieuls concevoir et cler entendre
> A quoi la matere poet tendre. (2241–45)[8]

[I read up to six folio leaves, then began again on the first page in order better to construe and more clearly comprehend the intention of the work's subject matter.]

Let us apply this mode of reading to the example cited from the *Paradis d'amour*: Let's reread it "pour / Mieuls concevoir et cler entendre / A quoi la matere poet tendre."

A moment's reflection on these lines from the *Paradis d'amour* will suggest that love's arrow not only inflames the heart but also kills. This is explicit in Leander's case, he who "pour s'amour en mer peri." And anyone familiar with Achilles' courtship of Polyxena, as told through the various sources available to late fourteenth-century audiences,[9] would certainly recall the ambush in the temple plotted by Hecuba and executed by Paris. Neptune's alleged love for "Eqeulenta" is more problematic. Unlike the Achilles-Polyxena courtship, there is no record of an affair between Neptune and a maid by this name; in fact, her name is absent from ancient mythology and medieval *poétries* and from catalogues of exempla.[10] What is notable, however, is that Neptune had dominion over the very sea in which Leander perished. The reflective audience would certainly be perplexed and disturbed by the implications of this exemplary love depicted in allegorical chiaroscuro.

In the *Prison amoureuse* Froissart makes an important terminological distinction, a distinction that conforms to practice in his lyric and narrative dits. Froissart uses one exemplum to gloss another exemplum. It follows that a "gloss" is not only to an exposition, or discursive commentary that explains the allegorical meaning of such exempla, but is itself also an example that, in conjunction with the first one, provides a mutually illuminating exposition.[11] In the *Prison amoureuse,* Flos's treatise on Pynoteüs and Neptisphelé prompts Rose's dream about his own imprisonment in the "prison amoureuse" (p. 113, ll. 19–28). The pseudo-Ovidian fable and the dream gloss one another, and they both point to the later gloss as exposition in letters 9 and 12.[12] Similarly, in the passage cited from the *Paradis d'amour,* the fates of Achilles and Polyxena, Neptune and Eqeulenta, and Hero and Leander are glosses on one another, whereas the exposition is the statement that all illustrate the *coup de foudre* with which love begins. Froissart shows this by an explanation of Love's arrows, which thrust beauty into the observer's eyes and ears (*Paradis,* 486–87). What this combination of image and exposition implies is the distinction between what Rosemond Tuve has called two ways or modes of treating a subject matter. Her illustration is helpful in studying Froissart's poetry as "treatise." In discussing the distinction between images (Froissart's "gloss") and the concept that explains them or gives them context (Froissart's "exposition"), Tuve states: "I suppose it is not necessary to underline the fact that the images do not *equate with* [her emphasis] the concepts spoken of (if this were so, no images would be needed)." Such equations are "bad allegory." Tuve goes on to explain that

> "Bad allegory" may use a set of concretions to mean nothing more or less than some set of concepts we could write out, and to which they are "equal," but even this is so hard to work out in practice that it is far scarcer in literature than in critical interpretation. Some statable concept or nameable abstraction is generally a key and an indication; but so is the literal "thing." "Leviathan the sea-beast" and the word "Evil" are, respectively, the closest men have come to the bodies of meaning they refer to. They represent two of the ways we have developed to refer to things too complex to state in full, though experienced by all of us.[13]

Although Froissart treats "love" more than he does "evil," Tuve's generalization holds. When Froissart speaks of love, he has a concept. He may treat it by choosing, for example, the moment of first sight, as in the *Paradis* examples, using both the literal description of the event and the metaphoric one of Love's arrows. This correlates concept and image. But the arrow-of-love image is hackneyed. Therefore he illustrates it further by using images that exemplify the action but that also, on reflection or second reading, point to the ambiguous, even nefarious consequences of love at first sight, as we have seen in the *Paradis d'amour* passage. The various treatments of the idea are so many exemplary glosses in different modes of expression that point to the implications and meaning—the "exposition"—of the original "first sight" and the uncertain happiness of love itself.

These issues are set forth clearly in Froissart's ballade 32: "Amours, vous savés ma pensee." The examples, the poet says, of Daphne and Phebus, Achilles, Helen, and Acteon as well as of Medea and Jason suggest that appearances deceive—as in his own case:

> ... ja dient li envieus
> Que vous me faites des bontés,
> Mais moult bien poés dire a ceuls,
> Que contraires est verités.(7–10)[14]

[The envious say that you show me favors, but you can certainly tell them that the opposite is true.]

The corrective refrain gives to every example, and to every stanza in which it is repeated, a double truth. It informs the lyric poet's own experience and that of the exemplary figures he mentions as well as that of anyone sympathetically identifying with or reflecting on the poem's contraries. As the double truth emerges, the literal illustration points to an opposing and thus "other" or allegorical reading deduced from the examples and—like the texts in many a motet—counterpointing or, as in ballade 32, contradicting or subverting one another's meanings.

Froissart's language in ballade 32 conforms to the double edge of the exemplary mode, which, as proof, may demonstrate or invalidate a proposition—as in the bestiary examples Richard de Fournival reads one way in the *Bestiaire d'amours* and in a different way in the Response to the *Bestiaire* that he or someone else wrote.[15] The response is not a definitive rereading; it is a new exposition of the exemplary evidence, just as in medieval *jeux-partis* the audience, and each individual in the audience, is invited to reread the examples as illustrations and inductively reconsider them.¹⁶ The woman narrator herself in the *Réponse au bestiaire* seems to suggest as much. Thus, in concluding her response to the *Bestiaire* as *salut d'amour*, she sums up her rejection of his offer, a rejection based on her rereading of the beast images she borrows from that work: "Et pour che que j'ai entendu par vous que on ne set qui bons est ne qui mauvais, si couvient que on se gart de tous. Et je si ferai." [And since I heard you say that no one can distinguish who is good from who is bad, then one must watch out for everyone. And I will do that.] Yet the door is not entirely shut: "Et je le ferai, tant que par raison merchis ara son lieu, dont il m'est avis que qui le cose veut faire mout i a de refuis."¹⁷ [And I will do that, until such time as mercy may reasonably be appropriate, in which case I think that anyone who doesn't want to do that has many ways out.] Would not this development oblige the reader to return to the positive context of the *Bestiaire* itself and to reread both it and the *Response* in the light of their *contraires verités*?

Froissart both illustrates and invites such rereading. A lover's sincerity may emerge from careful mutual reconsideration of his and her words and a rational decision to act—or not to act—by seeking those escapes which the lady of the *Response* refers to. The *Paradis d'amour* examples that begin this essay illustrate the pleasurable moment of first sight, the fatal consequences of that moment, and—in the case of Neptune and Eqeulenta—the problematic matter of the exemplum and its mental referent in audience recall, reflection, and induction. They also imply first reading and subsequent readings by the same or different persons, readings that may confirm, alter, or refute the first reading. The modern scholar-critic who is not one of the lovers may freely contemplate all of these potential responses to the poetic example.

Froissart also frequently uses the same examples. But he adapts them too. These contraries and diversities allow for different readings of the same example. As we have observed, the Froissart-narrator tends to delineate a specific reading, then correct it by pointing to the difference between the explicit lesson of his own case and those implied by other exemplary "cases." But he does not necessarily resolve the contraries, being content often to juxtapose them as in a conundrum. The truth as *contraire chose*—a logical operation familiar to readers of the *Roman de la rose*¹⁸—is problematic, not explicit. We find an illustration in the curious example of the Blue Knight—the Bleu Chevalier of one of Froissart's short dits.¹⁹

The Bleu Chevalier alternately sings blithely of his joy and grievously laments his fate while, respectively, walking or sitting. This paradoxical conduct arouses the narrator's curiosity. He therefore follows the odd knight, introduces himself, and learns the reason for the contradictory display of emotion: The knight is in prison far from his beloved. Although he has the deep pleasure of memory and love, his imprisonment prevents his meeting the demands of both arms and love. Could this cause his lady to esteem him less? Such are the effects of Fortune. "Trop est diverse"— but "on ne s'en doit changier,"[20] opines the narrator. [She is too perversely capricious—one mustn't be inconstant.] Yet the paradoxical sequence of opposite emotional outbursts, marvelous as it may be, nonetheless resonates with important intertextual reverberations, and it thereby reveals two distinct truths about conduct. That is to say, we may read this example in two ways: either for its obvious literal lesson or for its intertextual lesson, relying notably on the analogous example of Hector at the Fontaine du Pin in the Prose *Lancelot*,[21] a work perhaps as familiar to Froissart's audiences as the Ovidian examples remembered from school or from the recent success of the *Ovide moralisé*.[22] In the case of both Hector and the Bleu Chevalier, a marriage threatens to separate two lovers, a prospect that leads to joy in love, alternating with grief at the possible loss of the beloved.

The Bleu Chevalier contrasts his lot with that of lovers like Achilles and knights like Hector in ancient and medieval legend. According to the Bleu Chevalier, each was willingly separated from his beloved in order to perform feats of arms that were inspired by their love and that, in turn, made the knights more loveable. The Bleu Chevalier is not so fortunate. Pursuing arms, he has become a prisoner and is therefore unwillingly separated from his beloved. Yet, he is constant—hence, the attribute "Blue." But he is also jealous, fearing that his lady will love him less because he fails to demonstrate his martial prowess. The *Dit du bleu chevalier* thus transmits two messages: that of his joy in love, and thus of his constancy, and that of his jealous sorrow—a double message built on rewriting the Fontaine du Pin episode in the Prose *Lancelot*, in which Lancelot's half brother Hector experiences the same schizophrenia. Perhaps the *pin* also suggests an *aube espine*—that is, an *espinette amoureuse* like that referred to in both the *Bleu chevalier* (69) and the somewhat later *Espinette amoureuse*.[23]

Thus the *Bleu chevalier* also illustrates the two kinds of exempla identified by von Moos: the illustration and the enthymeme. The illustration is complete in its lesson: We know why the Bleu Chevalier, like Hector before him, alternately sings his joys and grieves his loss. But it also raises a question. What does the example prove? The question turns the example into a "case." An enthymeme is an incomplete syllogism in which the conclusion is left to whoever hears and evaluates the work, as in *jeux-partis*. A case such as the one at hand raises issues resolved in the missing conclusion to the enthymeme, when the lady hears the dit that Froissart writes about the Bleu Chevalier.[24] What will that reaction be? The *Dit du bleu chevalier* does not tell us but leaves the question open to multiple potential answers, any one of which might be colored by individual experience and morality. For example, a reader may prefer an optimistic projection of the lady's response, or an ambiguous reading as in the *Response,* or, finally, a flat-out rejection, as in Chartier's *Belle dame sans merci.*

In considering what is happening here, there are two factors to take into account. One is the rewriting of a source and the accompanying reflection on the differences between the first and the second author's versions of the knight who alternately laughs and weeps. The second factor is multiple readings of the same matter—that is, those expositions through which the exemplary illustration becomes, on second or third reading, an enthymeme. We can never know what the potential "Dame" or "Amie" of the Bleu Chevalier may have thought of the dit if she heard it and recognized its source. The knight hopes and the poet confidently assures him that her response will be favorable. This is the optimistic reading. But the courtly habitués would surely realize the possibility of a response such as the one to Fournival's *Bestiaire* or even the response of a "Belle dame sans merci." Was the knight's beloved perhaps his wife? or more than one woman?[25] Do not these possibilities activate, as Michel Zink has suggested, that "réflexion du moi" characteristic of medieval subjectivity and the beginnings of literature in the Middle Ages?[26]

Froissart's treatment of exemplary material in sources has attracted some attention because he in fact invents examples that he attributes to Ovid, although no known text by or attributed to Ovid in the Middle Ages contains them—except Froissart's.[27] One illustration from the *Paradis* is the character Enclinpostair, the son of Morpheus, whom Chaucer adopted in the same role in the *Book of the Duchess.* The consternation these metamorphoses have elicited in some modern scholarship is based on a positivist *petitio principii:* It assumes that Froissart—and medieval writers in general—sought to copy their sources as precisely as possible. However, all evidence points to the new author as *unfaithful*—deliberately unfaithful[28]—transcriber. He or she seeks to rewrite traditional material with originality and new insights into its potential meaning or meanings. (After all, if Ovid illustrated anything for medieval poets, it was surely metamorphosis.) Froissart just happens to push further than most authors his role as "metamorphant," or unfaithful transmitter.[29] For example, although he faithfully relates the traditional Narcissus story in the *Prison amoureuse* with no more adaptations than one finds in Guillaume de Lorris's version, he rewrites the fable in the *Joli buisson de Jonece.* In this dit Narcissus dies because Echo, whom he loves, has herself died (*Joli buisson,* 3252–335). What is the reason for this apparent contradiction or infidelity? What purpose does Froissart's metamorphosis serve? To answer these questions, we must read each example not only as a rather obvious illustration but, more important, as an enthymeme that raises issues when contrasted with the remembered traditional story of Narcissus's death.

We may start by considering how Froissart himself reads poems in the *Prison amoureuse*. Froissart envisages multiple readings, as we have seen. He does so for three possible reasons: the poet's pleasure in original invention, the multiple interlocking meanings possible in allegorical interpretation, and the reader's own private response to the work's lesson as distinguished from its artistry. Examples are therefore part of a larger whole. Froissart's artistry integrates them with other examples that they gloss and with his own discursive exposition of the examples. In this sense, then, Froissart's so-called "Ovidian" example of Pynoteüs and Neptisphelé in the *Prison amoureuse* elicits as gloss a dream that his correspondent Rose reports (*Prison amoureuse,* p. 113, ll. 19–28). The two modes, exemplary and oneiric, permit a lengthy exposition that explains the configuration of elements in example and dream by an analysis of Rose's love (*Prison amoureuse,* letters 9 and 12). It is this treatment that integrates the parts of the work into a polymodal treatise. We are reading Froissart's allegory as Tuve suggested: not as an equation but as a body of meaning to which the examples and expositions refer us.

These different configurations and their integration permit an author to rewrite traditional material in order to illustrate a body of meaning like that referred to by words such as *evil, love, prowess, melancholy*. The fundamental idea provides an interpretive context: It makes the fable exemplary and therefore true in that context—arguably true, provided the reader accepts the conclusion. The locus of truth, it seems to me, will be all the more striking if the audience confronts a new version of familiar material and mentally seeks to explain to itself the rationale for the new version. For example, why did Narcissus love Echo so much that he died of bereavement? As Horace claimed and as medieval writers repeated and practiced after him: "rectius Iliacum carmen deducis in actus, / quam si proferres ignota indictaque primus"[30] [you would do better to relate the song of Troy than be the first to publish things unknown or unheard in verse]. Yet, in the same place, Horace stresses the importance of originality: The new author must not be a *fidus interpres* (*Ars poetica,* 133–34). Is this not precisely Froissart's role as poet (Jung, *Poetria,* 60–62)—an unfaithful interpreter of source material?

In terms of Froissart's rewriting, moreover, we move from the example as illustration to the example as enthymeme. The enthymeme as incomplete syllogism occurs in the *Prison amoureuse* when Rose's beloved makes the objection that the exposition of the Pynoteüs-Neptisphelé fable as gloss on Rose's dream leaves out an exposition of the Phaeton material that Froissart includes in the fable as part of Pynoteüs's prayer to Phebus (see my *Medieval Imagination*, 156–59). Here one fable is brought into conjunction with another to yield a more elaborate exposition of good and bad love. The complex amalgam of images begins when Rose requests a poem from Flos—"un petit dittié amoureus, qui se traitast sus aucune nouvelle matere qu'on n'aroit onques veü ne oÿ mise en rime, tele com, par figure, fu jadis de Piramus et de Tysbé, ou de Eneas et de Dido, ou de Tristran et de Yseus" (*Prison amoureuse*, p. 82, ll. 44–48) [a little poem on love that would be based on some new matter as yet unseen and unheard in rhyme, like the figural representations of Pyramus and Thisbe, Dido and Aeneas, or Tristan and Iseut]. The three exemplary couples, like those in the *Paradis*, fall, however, into a new, different context and, according to Rose's request, represent a different matter, which (as he suggests) combines a number of old matters into a new one.

> Je n'ai cure d'anulliier
> Le matere et le pourpos Rose.
> Adont tournai sus une glose
> Qui nous approeve et nous acorde,[31]
> Si com Ovides le recorde,
> Les oevres de Pynoteüs. (*Prison amoureuse*, 1293–98)

[I don't wish to ignore Rose's matter and intent. I therefore sought a gloss as Ovid reports it in such a way as to demonstrate and harmonize for us Pynoteüs's works.]

It is noteworthy that, in the phrase "Si com Ovides le recorde," the Picard feminine singular "le" does not refer to the plural "oevres" but to the singular "glose"—a gloss found in Ovid. That gloss is, among Rose's examples, the cases of Piramus and Thisbe and of Dido and Aeneas (Ovid does not relate a Tristan and Iseut). The figure that all these examples have in common is the death of the beloved. Although the tale of Pynoteüs and Neptisphelé contains this scheme, it also shows striking differences—differences that those in Froissart's audiences who knew the *Ovide moralisé* or some version of the Tristan legend (probably the Prose *Tristan*) might note and consider, just as they would do on hearing Froissart's new version of Narcissus, in which the fabled young man died pining for his lost Echo. In all these transformations Froissart typifies original allegorical invention in the Middle Ages. The Pynoteüs-Neptisphelé fable is an example of such originality. Scholars have been disturbed by this allegedly Ovidian tale, which is found nowhere in antiquity or in the Middle Ages except in Froissart's dit. However, what Froissart says is that Ovid records the gloss, not the fable. That gloss includes Pyramus and Thisbe, a fable in which the protagonists not only rhyme and form a kind of anagram of Pynoteüs and Neptisphelé but also fold into other fabulous tales through Froissart's new exposition. Neptisphelé resuscitates Thisbe.

What do these metamorphoses imply? That is, what concept or idea comes into constellation, as Tuve puts it, with these exemplary tales of love and death?

The *Prison amoureuse* offers two answers to this question. First, it proposes another gloss, or exemplary image, and then it sets forth an exposition. Let's look at the image first. A message from Rose to Flos contains a letter and a poem that was inspired by Flos's "treatise" (*Prison amoureuse*, p. 112, l. 9) on Pynoteüs and Neptisphelé. Or, as Rose explains it, Flos's "livret" (p. 113, l. 23) on these two lovers caused a dream and inspired the design, or "pourpos" (p. 113, l. 26), to write it down. The dream itself was an "ymagination" (p. 113, l. 22)—that is, a true representation of something: "Devant Ymagination," Froissart writes elsewhere, "on doit par droite action / Mettre memores et escrips."[32] [One should by rights place memoirs and writings before Imagination.] The dream and its meaning, which make the true imagination combining them, is patterned on the Pynoteüs-Neptisphelé story. That is, the dream glosses the pseudo-Ovid fable, just as that tale glossed Ovid's version of Pyramus and Thisbe.

However, each—the dream and the fable—has a different exposition. The fable, which includes Phaeton's ride, is part of a digression set as a prayer that contrasts good and bad love. It also contrasts good and bad conduct in the defeat and capture of Rose, alias Wenceslas de Brabant, in the now largely forgotten battle of Bastweiler, the subject of Rose's dream.[33] The common model of prudent and imprudent conduct in love and in war permits the two expositions to gloss one another because each is modeled on principles of reasonable and unreasonable conduct. This constellation of elements turns the fable and dream into extraordinary imaginations. All these treatments and contexts fit Tuve's analysis of allegorical writing. Parallel images are associated with parallel concepts and analogous models. They all interface and fold together in the reader's mind into a body of meaning—a general understanding of prudent conduct, its varieties in special or private instances, and its contraries. In poetic "montage"—Jacqueline Cerquiglini has found the right word[34]—to dismember is also an original, if roundabout way to remember.

Jacqueline Cerquiglini has also called our attention to the importance of the anagram as a mode of treatment (*modus tractandi*) in late medieval dits. In the dit as in the anagram, "il faut . . . savoir désassembler puis rassembler à nouveau"[35]—dismember in order to remember. The operation applies both to the author and to the reader. The best illustration is perhaps the *Prison amoureuse* and the poem Rose sends to Flos, which was inspired by the Pynoteüs-Neptisphelé invention. The narrator begins to read the poem upon receiving it. He first construes its meaning, then rereads it in the manner I referred to earlier so as to understand it better. Froissart is, I submit, illustrating reading in the same way Rosamond Tuve recommends that we read allegory—that is, by construing and harmonizing bodies of meaning and the matter and modes that communicate that meaning. In the *Prison amoureuse* illustration, we have two distinct exemplary poems linked in imagination but separate in the text. One is Froissart's treatise on Pynoteüs and Neptisphelé; the other is Rose's dream, a kind of psychomachia, which the Pynoteüs story provoked. The pseudo-Ovidian example and the oneiric psychomachia form a constellation. The reader construes the dream by reference to its pseudo-Ovidian model. That model permits the mirroring of the two poems framed in the dit, both in their letter and in the letter's private allegory based on personal amorous experiences and on larger political issues.

Exactly the same kind of montage is operative in the *Espinette amoureuse*. It too introduces an allegedly Ovidian fable, that of Ydoree and Papirus (2668–724). In this fable a mirror allows two lovers to see one another even when they are separated. It is modeled on Froissart's rewriting of the fountain of Narcissus as well as of the magic mirror invented by Vergil, the Roman magician, to show the approach of an enemy (2590–93). Papirus is himself on his way to Sicily, just as Froissart is going overseas, probably to England, in the *Espinette*. Papirus has mirrors made so that he and Ydoree can communicate with one another while separated. The situation is clearly analogous to that in the contemporary *Dit du bleu chevalier* in which the dit itself allows the beloved to hear and mentally see her imprisoned knight. Froissart himself has such a mirror (*Espinette*, 2725–52): It is his own imagination, which reveals his lady in a dream mirror. But the image is ambiguous. Does it betoken good fortune, as in the Papirus-Ydoree exemplum, or a misfortune such as the death or marriage of his beloved, as in Vergil's mirror or the Narcissus story? We do not learn the answer in the *Espinette*. Froissart's dream remains ambiguous, as do all dreams in the Macrobian *insomnium*, which shows lovers gaining their desire or losing their love—but doing so only in "imagination." It is an ambiguous imagination, because good and bad are mutually exclusive and the falsehood of the one must be the truth of the other. But we are not told where truth lies.[36]

The complexity of the anagrammatic treatment of allegorical material appears most vividly, I think, in Froissart's last dit, the *Joli buisson de Jonece*. This poem deserves far more attention than this chapter can give it. It is a truly paradoxical dit that works its way to the palinode rejecting human love that is related and dramatized in its conclusion. For example, two of Froissart's counsellors are Jonece and Philozophie; however, the counsel of each is a reversal of the sense of the noun personified, such that Jonece's morality is closer to Philosophy's in Boethius whereas Froissart's Philozophie teaches a youngish, carpe diem epicureanism worthy of the twelve-year-old Jonece in Guillaume de Lorris.

Froissart's Jonece gives a lesson on the seven ages of life while showing a remarkable awareness for a synecdoche of the six other parts of the whole that he is one part of. Yet, synecdoche may name a part for a whole. He, Jonece—exceptionally Froissart uses the masculine, or syllepsis, for this personification[37]—is mature, a personified *puer senex* who teaches and exemplifies the "vie sobre" (*Joli buisson*, 1534) that the thirty-five-year-old (794) young man Froissart should follow (Dembowski, *Jean Froissart*, 36–41). This is certainly not the carefree twelve-year-old Jonece that Guillaume de Lorris depicts in the *Roman de la rose*. The "younger" role falls, paradoxically, on Philozophie's shoulders. This quite un-Boethian personification of philosophy provides the no longer quite so young Froissart with various arguments in favor of a wish-fulfillment dream of eternal youth, one of the varieties of *insomnium* in Macrobius's scheme, and thus analogous in general, if not in detail, to Jean de Meun's part of the *Rose*.[38] She teaches a philosophy hardly consonant with the waking world of responsibility suggested by Jonece's vision of the seven ages of life. Reversing the ornamental synecdoche paradigm, Froissart's Philozophie seems to express only the epicurean part of her whole name, thus shredding philosophy, like those philosophers who rend Philosophy's garment in Boethius's *Consolation*.[39] Indeed, Froissart's personification even recommends some of the very false goods that Boethius condemns—love, wealth, and fame (see, for example, *Consolatio*, book 3, prose 2, §12)—in the face of the aging poet's awareness that things have changed: "Or voi je cangié mon afaire / En aultre ordenance nouvelle" (*Joli buisson*, 458–59; cf. 374–90). [Now I see that my condition has changed into a different, new pattern of life.] This seems to call as well for new or revised examples, including Narcissus's bereavement because of Echo's death.

This chapter cannot dwell on the quandaries posed by the very interesting, allegorically rich *Joli buisson de Jonece*. Suffice it to note that the contrary morals drawn by Jonece and Philozophie in that work do illustrate a couple of features common to Froissart's allegory and its lessons. First, there are in *Joli buisson* the antitheses typical also of the *Bleu chevalier* and ballade 32. The personifications in *Joli buisson*, moreover, illustrate metonymy, not allegory, functioning by their lessons as allegories. That is, the name of each personification makes a literal statement, but the words each of them speaks make a second, "other" statement. As so often in Froissart's poems, *contraires est verités*. Jonece teaches the wisdom of the ages, while Philozophie mouths the carpe diem of eternal youth. The *modus tractandi* is not dissimilar to Jean de Meun's: The *Rose*'s literal lesson—how to pluck roses—is refracted through various voices that question, revise, or refute the literal lesson. Similarly, Froissart's juxtaposition of Philozophie and Jonece, each speaking out of character, produces an implicit allegory by antiphrasis, or a statement implying the opposite of its literal meaning.[40] We hear Philozophie teach the lessons of a literal Jonece and of Venus herself, just as we know that Jonece's morality is Philosophy's traditional lesson, one that Jonece remembers hearing in school (*Joli buisson*, 1559). For we are, as in the *Rose*, interfacing with a Boethian view of the universe.[41] This becomes perfectly obvious in the *Joli buisson*'s "bush" as "metamorph." Froissart is greying. The *espinette amoureuse* becomes therefore the Tree of Life before appearing as the Burning Bush (*Joli buisson*, 5376–411).[42] Froissart has come to know that life brings change and that the status quo will not abide. Metamorphosis is a constant of both life and art in Froissart's world. His examples prove it.

Notes

1. "You must change your life. . . . For one may abide nowhere." Rilke, *Werke*, vol. 1 (Frankfurt: Insel, 1966), pp. 313 ("Archäischer Torso Apollos") and 443 ("Die erste Duineser Elegie").

2. See my "Assimilation et montage dans l'amplification descriptive: La démarche du poète dans le Dit du XIVe siècle," in *Mittelalterbilder aus neuer Perspektive: Diskussionsanstöße zu amour courtois, Subjektivität in der Dichtung und Strategien des Erzählens*, Kolloquium Würzburg 1984, ed. Ernstpeter Ruhe and Rudolf Behrens (Munich: Fink, 1985), 289–302; Jacqueline Cerquiglini, "Le dit," in *La littérature française aux XIVe et XVe siècles*, ed. Daniel Poirion, vol. 8.1 of

Grundriß der romanischen Literaturen des Mittelalters: (Heidelberg: Winter, 1988), 86–94. Both articles contain additional bibliography on the treatise.

3. See my *Internal Difference and Meanings in the "Roman de la Rose"* (Madison: University of Wisconsin Press, 1995), chaps. 3 and 4. On the *modus tractandi* in medieval literature and the *accessus ad auctores* traditions to which it belongs, see Bruno Sandkühler, *Die frühen Dantekommentare und ihr Verhältnis zur mittelalterlichen Kommentartradition* (Munich: Hueber, 1967), and A. J. Minnis, *Medieval Theory of Authorship: Scholastic Literary Attitudes in the Later Middle Ages* (London: Scolar Press, 1984).

4. See Paul Demats, *Fabula: Trois études de mythographie antique et médiévale* (Geneva: Droz, 1973).

5. Peter von Moos, *Geschichte als Topik: Das rhetorische Exemplum von der Antike zur Neuzeit und die "historiae" im "Policraticus" Johanns von Salisbury* (Hildesheim: Olms, 1988), 26–39.

6. Jean Froissart, *Le paradis d'amour*, ed. Peter F. Dembowski (Geneva: Droz, 1986).

7. That is, for an hour or so. Froissart read about the same number of "foeilles" a night to Gaston Fébus, comte de Foix. Fourrier estimates on evidence from the *Chroniques* that each reading lasted about one hour; see *Le dit dou florin*, 368–69 and 367, note (p. 235) in Jean Froissart, *"Dits" et "Débats,"* ed. Anthime Fourrier (Geneva: Droz, 1979).

8. Jean Froissart, *La prison amoureuse*, ed. Anthime Fourrier (Paris: Klincksieck, 1974). For a discussion of this passage, see my *Internal Difference*, 30–32.

9. Demats, 81–103; Brian Woledge, *Bibliographie des romans et nouvelles en prose française antérieurs à 1500* (Geneva: Droz, 1954) and *Supplément 1954–1973* (Geneva: Droz, 1975), §§171–85 in each volume; Frantiÿek Graus, "Troja und trojanische Herkunftssage im Mittelalter," in *Kontinuität und Transformation der Antike im Mittelalter* (Sigmaringen: Thorbecke, 1989), 25–43; and Marc-René Jung, *La légende de Troie en France au moyen âge: analyse des versions françaises et bibliographie raisonnée des manuscrits* (Basel: Francke, 1996).

10. I have searched Ernest Langlois, *Recueil d'arts de Seconde Rhétorique*, Collection de Documents inédits sur l'histoire de France, no. 85 (Paris: Imprimerie Nationale, 1902); Jacques Legrand, *Archiloge sophie; Livre de bonnes meurs*, ed. Evencio Beltran (Paris: Champion, 1986). On *poétries* see Marc-René Jung, "*Poetria*: zur Dichtungstheorie des ausgehenden Mittelalters in Frankreich," *Vox Romanica* 30 (1971), especially pp. 57–64. Dembowski asks if "Eqeulenta" might not be an incorrect form of "Leucothoé," as in the *Ovide moralisé*; see Dembowski, *Paradis*, p. 129, s.v. Eqeulenta. But "Lencote," as Leucothoé is spelled in the *Prison amoureuse*, 1763 (as Dembowski notes), is loved by Apollo, not by Neptune. The name seems to be another Froissart invention or adaptation. I do not find Neptune's name anywhere else in Froissart's poetry.

11. See "glose" in the following passage from Jean Froissart, *Le joli buisson de Jonece*, ed. Anthime Fourrier (Geneva: Droz, 1975): "une figure avons / Par la quele

moult bien savons / Que de vraie amour c'est grant cose. / Li poëtes tret une glose / De deus amans . . . " (2010–14). [We have an example that teaches us quite well that true love is an important thing. The poet draws a gloss with two lovers.] It is the story of Ydrophus and Neptiphoras. A sequence of a dozen or so such "interglossing" examples appears in *Joli buisson*, 3132–381. Among them are traditional examples that are reconfigured to fit a new exposition they collectively serve to explicate, including Narcissus dying of love for Echo, Orpheus in love with Proserpina, and Hero in love with Cepheus after Leander; others, like Achilles and Polyxena and Helen and Paris, conform to their traditional plots.

12. See my *Medieval Imagination: Rhetoric and the Poetry of Courtly Love* (Madison: University of Wisconsin Press, 1978), 160–69, and Laurence de Looze, "From Text to Text and from Tale to Tale: Jean Froissart's *Prison amoureuse*," in *The Centre and Its Compass: Studies in Medieval Literature in Honor of Professor John Leyerle*, ed. Robert A. Taylor et al. (Kalamazoo: Western Michigan University, 1993), 96–107.

13. Rosemond Tuve, *Allegorical Imagery: Some Mediaeval Books and Their Posterity* (Princeton: Princeton University Press, 1966), 21–22.

14. Quoted from Rob Roy McGregor Jr., ed., *The Lyric Poems of Jean Froissart*, Studies in the Romance Languages and Literatures no. 143 (Chapel Hill: University of North Carolina Press, 1975); I have also consulted Jean Froissart, *Ballades et rondeaux*, ed. Rae S. Baudouin (Geneva: Droz, 1978), which numbers the poems in the same way that McGregor's edition does.

15. See most recently Helen Solterer, *The Master and Minerva: Disputing Women in French Medieval Culture* (Berkeley: University of California Press, 1995), chaps. 3–4. Solterer sets forth clearly the lady's role as corrector (8–9).

16. See the *Recueil général des jeux-partis français*, ed. Arthur Långfors, with A. Jeanroy and L. Brandin, 2 vols. (Paris: Champion, 1926), 1:vii. Cf. Jacqueline Cerquiglini-Toulet, *La couleur de la mélancolie: La fréquentation des livres au XIVe siècle 1300–1415* (Paris: Hatier, 1993), 52–53; on *jeu* and its mimetic implications for medieval audiences, see Michel Stanesco, *Jeux d'errance du chevalier médiéval: Aspects ludiques de la fonction guerrière dans la littérature du moyen âge flamboyant* (Leiden: Brill, 1988), especially chap. 6, "La perspective de la *mimesis*," and chap. 8, "Le cérémonial du jeu." Peter F. Dembowski also treats these paradoxical features in Froissart's writings; see Dembowski, *Jean Froissart and His "Meliador": Context, Craft, and Sense* (Lexington, Ky.: French Forum, 1983), especially chap. 2, "Sense."

17. *Li bestiaires d'amours di Maistre Richart de Fornival e li response du bestiaire*, ed. Cesare Segre (Milan: Ricciardi, 1957), 136, ll. 15–18. Such an open ending is typical of courtly dialogues, as in Andreas Capellanus, *De amore*, ed. E. Trojel (Copenhagen: Gadiana, 1892), 80: "Si, ut verbis assertive proponis, facto curaveris adimplere, facile non posset accidere, quin a me vel alia retributionem susciperes abundanter." [If you strive to accomplish what you claim to do, you can hardly fail to be abundantly rewarded by me or some other woman.] Note that the addition of "some other woman" is as subtly provocative and open-ended as the words of the *Response* lady.

18. See Nancy Freeman Regalado, "'Des contraires choses': La fonction poétique de la citation et des *exempla* dans le 'Roman de la Rose' de Jean de Meun," *Littérature* 41 (1981): 62–81.

19. The possible original of Froissart's knight cannot be identified except as a very young knight in captivity. See 54–60 in Fourrier, *"Dits" et "Débats."* Fourrier argues that the *Bleu chevalier* was written in 1364 during time Froissart spent in England. It is perhaps worth recalling here that the knight is "blue" because he is faithful, not because he has the "blues."

20. *Le dit dou bleu chevalier* in *"Dits" et "Débats,"* 134. On the meaning of *changier*, see 193, 256.

21. This episode is also found in the precyclic or noncyclic *Lancelot*. See Elspeth Kennedy, ed., *Lancelot do lac*, 2 vols. (Oxford: Clarendon Press, 1980), vol. 1, pp. 367–78; and Alexandre Micha, ed., *Lancelot* (Geneva: Droz, 1982), vol. 8, §§LVa.4–LVIa.18. Regarding the episode, see Philippe Ménard, *Le rire et le sourire dans le roman courtois en France au moyen âge (1150–1250)* (Geneva: Droz, 1969), 385–86. The motif is common not only in the *Lancelot-Graal* prose cycle but elsewhere as well; see Valeria Bertolucci Pizzorusso, "Il motivo del 'lieto e dolente' nella prosa del Lancelot," *Medioevo Romanzo* 12 (1987): 329–36. However, Hector in the Prose *Lancelot* is the closest analogue to Froissart's Blue Knight.

22. In the writings of authors like Froissart, one tends to find a common body of exemplary figures, which assures rapid recognition and easy identification of significant differences. However, in Froissart, Hector appears only as the Trojan, never as Lancelot's half brother. Tristan and Iseut are especially common figures in Froissart, but he also includes a generous sampling of Greek and Arthurian knights (based on consultation of the glossaries of names in the standard Froissart editions). Of course, there is the wide selection of old and new names in *Meliador*. See as well Peter F. Dembowski, "La position de Froissart-poète dans l'histoire littéraire: bilan provisoire," *Travaux de Linguistique et de Littérature* 16 (1978): 134, 136, 141–42.

23. On Froissart's knowledge of earlier French writing, see Fourrier, ed., *L'espinette amoureuse* (Paris: Klincksieck, 1963), 33–37 and 175, v. 385, note.

24. On "case" in this sense, see Matilda Tomaryn Bruckner, "An Interpreter's Dilemma: Why Are There So Many Interpretations of Chrétien's *Chevalier de la charrette?*" *Romance Philology* 40 (1986): 159–80; and my *Internal Difference*, 145–51. The "case" as rhetorical *casus* produces a *causa*. When the *causa* is represented by an example, the example may be explicit, as von Moos points out. But it may also be inductive, as an enthymeme when the conclusion of the argument is left to the reader or public (*inductio*); on such examples, see Heinrich Lausberg, *Handbuch der literarischen Rhetorik: Eine Grundlegung der Literaturwissenschaft* (Munich: Hueber, 1960), vol. 1 §§419–20; see §421 on the relation between the *exemplum*, which has its own meaning, and allegory, which bestows on it a more serious relation to the *causa* it serves to exemplify. An enthymeme is not necessarily only a form of syllogism, although it was usually taken in this sense in the Middle Ages; see Manfred

Kraus, "Enthymem," in the *Historisches Wörterbuch der Rhetorik* (Tübingen: Niemeyer, 1994), vol. 2, columns 1197–202 and 1210–12; Thomas M. Conley, "The Enthymeme in Perspective," *Quarterly Journal of Speech* 70 (1984): 168–87. On the enthymeme in medieval literature, see as well SunHee Kim Gertz, *Poetic Prologues: Medieval Conversations with the Literary Past* (Frankfurt: Klostermann, 1996).

25. See Fourrier, *"Dits" et "Débats,"* p. 54. These not impossible readings open the dit to a whole new set of potential responses. Probable audience response includes, but does not limit readings to, recent feminist interpretations of both high and late medieval literature. See, notably, Roberta L. Krueger, *Women Readers and the Ideology of Gender in Old French Verse Romance* (Cambridge: Cambridge University Press, 1993); Solterer, *Master;* and Simon Gaunt, *Gender and Genre in Medieval French Literature* (Cambridge: Cambridge University Press, 1995). It remains to be determined to what extent the feminist academic mentality that informs these readings actually existed among aristocratic women in the Middle Ages.

26. See Michel Zink, *La subjectivité littéraire: Autour du siècle de saint Louis* (Paris: Presses Universitaires de France, 1985), 21.

27. See my "Les inventions ovidiennes de Froissart: Réflexions intertextuelles comme imagination," *Littérature* 41 (1981): 82–92.

28. See Rita Copeland, *Rhetorics, Hermeneutics, and Translation in the Middle Ages: Academic Traditions and Vernacular Texts* (Cambridge: Cambridge University Press, 1991), especially pp. 158–78.

29. Perhaps we have here the distinction between *imitatio* as rewriting based on the anterior work and *aemulatio* as rewriting that vies with or seeks to outstrip the achievement of the earlier work. On such *Nachahmung* and *Nacheifern*, and on *imitatio* in general, see the now essential study by Alexandru N. Cizek, *Imitatio et tractatio: Die literarisch-rhetorischen Grundlagen der Nachahmung in Antike und Mittelalter* (Tübingen: Niemeyer, 1994). Cizek identifies three kinds of imitation: translation or paraphrase, material or stylistic imitation, and transformation of the source (*interpretatio, imitatio, aemulatio*), 44. Cf. 37: "Dies kann als ein mehrstufiger Prozeßerfolgen, der bis zur Auflösung der Vorlage und zu ihrer Ausbeutung als stofflichem Steinbruch geführt werden kann. Dieser komplexe, die formal-stilistische Umsetzung miteinschließende Imitationsvorgang" is imitation as *aemulatio*. On the relationship between such imitation and the *modus tractandi*, see Cizek 49–50.

30. *Ars poetica*, 129–30, in *Q. Horati Flacci opera*, ed. Edward C. Wickham, 2nd ed. rev. by H. W. Garrod, (Oxford: Clarendon Press, 1901). Cf. n.28.

31. "Mettre en harmonie" (trans. Fourrier, *Prison amoureuse*, 201, glossary, s.v. *acorder*). My translation of this passage—"a gloss that would validate and fit for us"—in *Medieval Imagination*, 157, should be corrected accordingly; see also de Looze, "From Text to Text," 95–97.

32. See "La plaidoirie de la rose et de la violette," 1–3, in *"Dits" et "Débats"*; on this passage, see my *Medieval Imagination*, 289, n.2.

33. See Fourrier, *Prison amoureuse*, 20–27 and 187–92 notes; William W. Kibler, "Poet and Patron: Froissart's *Prison amoureuse*," *L'Esprit Créateur* 18.1 (1978): 32–46; Dembowski, *Jean Froissart*, 52; de Looze, "From Text to Text," 107–10.

34. Jacqueline Cerquiglini, "Le clerc et l'écriture: le *voir dit* de Guillaume de Machaut et la définition du *dit*," in *Literatur in der Gesellschaft des Spätmittelalters*, ed. Hans Ulrich Gumbrecht, Begleitreihe zum Grundriß der romanischen Literaturen des Mittelalters, no. 1 (Heidelberg: Winter, 1980), 151–68.

35. Cerquiglini, "Dit," 94. See also her *Couleur*, 140, and de Looze, "From Text to Text," 98–99.

36. See William W. Kibler, "Self-Delusion in Froissart's *Espinette amoureuse*," *Romania* 97 (1976): 77–98.

37. On syllepsis in personification and the *sexus* topos, see my *Internal Difference*, 107–10. Froissart appears to use the masculine *jovent* more often than the feminine *jonece*; for an example of *jonece*, see *Espinette*, 348. Perhaps he uses the masculine personification in the *Joli buisson* because he identifies himself with it.

38. It is also analogous to the false *visum*, which, according to Macrobius, occurs while the dreamer believes he or she is still awake—*dorveille* in Old French. On *dorveille* in the *Joli buisson*, see Stanesco, *Jeux d'errance*, esp. 161 and 169, but also more generally chap. 11, "'Entre sommeillant et esveillé'—d'une technique chevaleresque à une expérience poétique." On the *insomnium* and the *visum*, see Macrobius, *Commentarii in Somnium Scipionis*, ed. Jacobus Willis (Leipzig: Teubner, 1963), 9–10; and Steven F. Kruger, *Dreaming in the Middle Ages* (Cambridge: Cambridge University Press, 1992), 21–22.

39. Boethius, *Philosophiae consolatio*, ed. Ludovicus Bieler, Corpus Christianorum: series latina no. 44 (Turnhout: Brepols, 1984), book 1, prose 1, §§4–5.

40. Christine de Pizan thought that misogynist treatises might be read in this way; see Pizan's *Livre de la cité des Dames*, ed. Maureen Cheney Curnow, Ph.D. diss., Vanderbilt University, 1975, 624–25. She herself practiced antiphrasis by rewriting the *Rose* in the *Dit de la rose* and the *Epistre au dieu d'amours*.

41. Fourrier, *Joli buisson*, v. 30.

42. On the poem in which this image appears, see Alice Planche, "Du *Joli buisson de jeunesse* ou *buisson ardent*: Le lai de Notre Dame dans les *Dits* de Froissart," in *La prière au moyen-âge (littérature et civilisation)*, Senefiance 10 (Aix-en-Provence: CUER MA; Paris: Champion: 1981), 395–413.

7

History and Narration in Froissart's *Dits*

The Case of the *Bleu chevalier*

RUPERT T. PICKENS

Jean Froissart's *Dit dou bleu chevalier* has generally suffered from benign and not-so-benign neglect from critics. One of Froissart's first modern champions, Baron Kervyn de Lettenhove, found it completely unworthy of attention.[1] In F. S. Shears's chapter on Froissart's poetry, the *Bleu chevalier* is one of two *dits* not mentioned.[2] B. J. Whiting, in his pioneering article "Froissart as Poet," devotes a plot summary but little else to the *Bleu chevalier*; he remarks that it is "an engaging piece" with "the infinite merit of being short,"[3] thereby implying that it grows infinitely tedious. More recently, two scholars who have written article-length studies on the *Bleu chevalier*, Normand Cartier[4] and James Wimsatt,[5] have been concerned with identifying the historical personage whom Froissart depicts as the Blue Knight and with deciding whether Froissart's poem influenced (Cartier) or was influenced by (Wimsatt) Chaucer's *Book of the Duchess*. Only the poem's most recent editor, Anthime Fourrier, shows concern for the *Bleu chevalier*'s literary qualities.[6] Meanwhile, Douglas Kelly,[7] Peter Ainsworth,[8] and Peter Dembowski[9] show that they have read the poem with awareness and understanding, but they mention it only in passing in studies of Froissart's literary enterprise as a whole.

This chapter is intended to demonstrate that despite its neglect, the *Bleu chevalier* merits attention in its own right as a richly complex work, an ambiguous, plurivalent, culturally relevant text. It is a text that is deliberately structured to call attention to its own composition, to its own status as literary discourse, and to its own place in the Froissartian canon. As such, the *Bleu chevalier* not only demands but also rewards our efforts to come to grips with it, and it stands as exemplary of the Froissartian dit as a genre.

The narrator of the 504-line poem says that one springtime toward the end of April, as he was walking in a wood, he saw a knight all dressed in blue; he then describes the knight's arms. (The "I" functioning as character is subsequently referred to here as the clerk or, occasionally, the poet-clerk.) The clerk observes the knight making his way through the wood singing joyfully of his lady and their love. Without warning, the knight begins to weep, grieving because his lady is not with him. But then, suddenly, he begins singing again—*chansons* and *virelais*—to make him forget Fortune's fickleness, and he is once again filled with the joy of love. But again his joy turns to grief. The violent mood swings continue as the clerk follows the knight along a path to a spring, where he faints in a spasm of grief. The clerk and the knight recognize each other. The knight asks for counsel, and much of the rest of the poem is taken up with the clerk's advice and its consequences.

The text is quasiautobiographical—not truly autobiographical, of course, because we notice its very conventionality, a conventionality that Froissart in fact celebrates.[10] How like Machaut, how like Froissart to imagine a poet-clerk hiding in the bushes—or in his room—to eavesdrop on a noble personage lamenting about love and then to follow him as he wanders through a *locus amoenus*, a garden or a wood. How like Machaut, how like Froissart to create a knight or a prince in his own image, singing virelais as well as *complaintes*. How like Machaut, how like Froissart to depict the poet-clerk as willing and able to offer *confort d'ami* to his noble acquaintance. The *Bleu chevalier* is a quasiautobiographical—pseudoautobiographical—text.

Aside from its status as autobiography and aside from its conventionality, two features in particular stand out: the emphasis on heraldry, as in the poem's very title, and the Blue Knight's lovesickness. Scholars have taken note of these two features at one time or another but never in relationship to each other. In fact they are profoundly linked, and the one is the key to the other.

The heraldic details are a siren's song that has lured readers into a preoccupation with historical referentiality; this siren's song has haunted much commentary on the *Bleu chevalier* by instilling a desire to discover the "real," historical identity of the Blue Knight and the nature of his relationship with the "real" Froissart. Two candidates have been proposed. Normand Cartier makes a case for Louis I, duke of Anjou, son of John the Good, therefore younger brother of Charles V, and eventual pretender to the throne of Naples. He was sent to England as a hostage for his father after the treaty of Brétigny in 1360 ("Le bleu chevalier"). He won notoriety two years later by breaking his solemn oath when the royal hostages were transferred to Calais and then escaping to his own lands. Cartier's arguments depend upon the traditional dating of the poem in the early 1360s, when Froissart first joined the court of Philippa de Hainaut in England. Cartier surmises that Louis d'Anjou must have rejected Froissart's dedication because the text depicts its hero as mentally unstable. James Wimsatt, who convincingly dates the *Bleu chevalier* after Queen Philippa's death in 1369, puts forward another well-known figure as the Blue Knight's model: none other than Wenceslas of Luxembourg and Brabant ("The *Dit dou Bleu chevalier*"). Wimsatt thus associates the *Bleu chevalier* with the same presumed occasion as the *Prison amoureuse*, the duke's capture and imprisonment in 1371. According to Wimsatt, Froissart's *Bleu chevalier* constitutes an appeal for ransom to the duke's brother, the emperor Charles IV.

These identifications are both supported by heraldic evidence. Both dukes could have been called "blue knights" because the field of their shields—the basic background color—was azure, although both shields bore additional charges or superimposed images: the royal fleur-de-lis on one, the golden lion of Luxembourg on the other. The azure shield of Froissart's *Meliador* bears a golden sunburst and thus reflects the colors of the duchy of Luxembourg; Meliador dubs himself *li bleus errans* and is known alternately as *le chevalier bleu* and, more often, *le chevalier au soleil d'or*.[11]

Like Cartier, Anthime Fourrier assumes that the Blue Knight "manifestly" represents one of John the Good's hostages, but he argues, from Froissart's self-conscious efforts to conceal his hero's identity, that the text's meaning and intent cannot depend upon historical reference.[12] On the contrary, continues Fourrier, the reader should be concerned with the overriding symbolic value of the knight's "blueness," which for him is above all a sign of his steadfast loyalty to his lady. Among other texts, Fourrier cites in support of his thesis a ballade by Machaut, which concludes (as quoted by Fourrier, introduction, pp. 57–58):

Si vueil amer l'azur et tenir chier
Et moy parer de li, en ramembrance
De loyauté qui ne saroit trichier,
Et li porter honneur et reverence,
 Car, en bonne verité,

> Riens ne vaut chose ou il n'a verité
> N'il n'est amans qui ne tesmongne et die
> Que fin azur loyauté signefie.
>
> Si l'ameray de fin cuer et entier
> Et porteray sans nulle difference,[13]
> Car moult me puet valoir et avancier
> Et donner pais, joie et bonne esperance;
>   Et mes amis, qui bonté
> Ha dessus tous, m'en sera tresbon gré,
> Car il scet bien entre amy et amie
> Que fin azur loyauté signefie. (ll. 11–24)

[And so I intend to love azure and hold it dear and deck myself with it, in memory of loyalty that does not deceive, and bear it honor and reverence, for in very truth nothing is worthy where there is no truth, and there is no lover who does not attest and say that rare azure signifies loyalty.

[And so I shall love it with a full and noble heart and shall wear it without any difference, for it can prove valuable to me and advance my cause and give me peace, joy, and worthy hope; and my friend, whose merit is above all others, will indeed be grateful to me, for he knows well that between lovers rare azure signifies loyalty.] (translations mine unless otherwise indicated)

The lady in whose voice the poem is written wishes to wear blue to honor loyalty (1–3), while in the refrain the signification is made explicit. Countless other texts from the period support this symbolic meaning, including Machaut's *Remede de fortune*, which is called in one manuscript *L'ecu bleu*. The God of Love's shield has a blue field bearing a charge, a red heart pierced by a black arrow with silver tips. Esperance tells the Lover that these blue arms are appropriate for the *fin amant*; the azure field, she continues, signifies loyalty.[14]

A technical point in medieval heraldry further substantiates Fourrier's argument that the Blue Knight's arms are not those of a "real" nobleman. Froissart's narrator says that the knight was dressed all in blue and that the clerk did not see any "differentiation" in his coat of arms: "perçoi .I. chevalier venir / Tout bleu vesti, sans differensce vir" (26–27) [I caught sight of a knight coming all dressed in blue, and I saw no difference]. This means that the knight's arms are "plain," that is, of solid azure without a charge (see n.13). The lady in Machaut's ballade pledges to wear "undifferentiated" blue, that is, nothing but blue (l. 20). If the Blue Knight's arms are plain, undifferentiated, then his shield cannot be that of either Louis of Anjou or Wenceslas of Luxembourg. As further guarantee of the knight's anonymity, Gerard J. Brault confirms that very few historical personages have plain arms, but they are very common in literature (29–37). The impossibility—or the unlikelihood—of biographical referentiality in the *Bleu chevalier* forces a shift in critical attention to other textual features.

For Fourrier the knight's blue arms unequivocally signify his loyalty to his lady. There can be no questioning that faithfulness. But other possible significations must also be accounted for. Equally as meaningful from many standpoints is a passage from another of Froissart's dits, the *Plaidoirie de la rose et de la violette*.[15] As the violet's lawyer argues,

> Mais je les [les violettes] voel nommer les filles
> Dou firmament qui est reons
> Sicom par l'apparant veons,
> Car elles ont sa coulour propre,
> Sans blanc, noir, vermel ne sinopre;
> Et quant dou chiel furent venues
> Avoecques la vapeur des nues,
> La terre la semence en but
> Dont les violettes conchut;
> Si les tieng en tres grant chierté.
> Bleu segnefie estableté
> Et chils ou chelle, sans doubtance,
> Qui le porte par ordenance,
> —De moi retiengne ce notable—,
> Doit avoir coer ferme et estable
> Et conforté sans nul moiien. (202–17)

[But I mean to call them (violets) the daughters of the firmament, which is round just as we see by the way it looks. For they are of its very color, unspotted by white, black, scarlet, or green. And when they had come down from heaven with vapor from the clouds, the earth drank in the seed with which she conceived violets, and so I consider them to be of the highest worth. Blue signifies firmness, and men and women who wear it as a rule—let them take this axiom from me—must have a strong and stable heart, one that is always comforted.]

Here Froissart conveys the conventional association of blue, the violet's color, with loyalty by means of a series of synonyms. Blue signifies "estabilité" (212), and the one who wears blue "doit avoir coer *ferme et estable et conforté*" (216; my emphasis). Fourrier glosses "conforté" here as "affermi, confirmé, résolu" (glossary, p. 256), but these same terms have denotations far broader than steadfast faithfulness alone. The other acceptations are equally as important in reading the *Bleu chevalier* and have implications in the poem's preoccupations with mental and physical health as opposed to acute emotional instability, with clear-headed resolve over and against the vicissitudes of Fortune, and with consolation—*confort d'ami*—as therapy for lovesickness. Indeed, in his argument's opening lines, the violet's lawyer points to a common link that ties color symbolism to heraldry and both to science and medicine. Azure-blue violets are "daughters of the firmament" (202-3); the seed that engendered them (209–10) was borne to earth in vapor from the clouds. Thus blue is also associated with air (the firmament of heaven), with moisture, and with insemination.

In late medieval heraldic treatises, tinctures—that is, metals, colors, and furs—are linked with the natural world: with the four elements, with the humors, with the seasons, with precious stones, with the cosmos, thus with the forces that govern human destiny and the human condition. According to one early fifteenth-century treatise written in France, azure "connotes the sapphire, praise, beauty, hauteur, the sanguine temperament, the planet Venus, Gemini, Libra, and Aquarius, air, fine silver (because this was used in the manufacture of a number of fine blue pigments) and Friday."[16] In mid-century, Sicily Herald makes somewhat different associations. John Gage observes that "he agree[s] about sapphire, air and the sanguine temperament but his moral associations for azur [are] with loyalty, [learning] and justice; he introduce[s] childhood but also autumn; his blue planet [is] Jupiter and his blue day Tuesday" (83).[17] For our purposes, it suffices to concentrate on the connotations these two treatises have in common: sapphire, air, and the sanguine temperament. An important political work written in Froissart's own day for Charles V contains important supplementary evidence. The *Somnium viridarii* was completed by 1376 and translated into French by 1378 as *Le songe du vergier*. In terms recalling the speech by the violet's lawyer, the *Songe* associates armorial blue with the element air:

> L'autre couleur plus noble, après [third in order after gold and purple], si est assur, laquelle couleur represente l'aër, lequel est corps tres soutif et est recevable de lumiere, et est le element plus

noble aprés le feu. Et les couleurs cy dessus nonmees sont dittes nobles, pour lez choses qu'elles representent.[18]

[The next most noble color after that is azure, which represents the air, which is a very light substance capable of receiving light, and it is the noblest element after fire. And the colors mentioned above are said to be noble because of the things they represent.]

So the sapphire, the sanguine temperament, and the element air.

Léopold Pannier notes a revival of interest in the early medieval lapidary tradition under Philip VI, that is, in the 1330s and 1340s, when the king ordered a new prose translation of the eleventh-century *Liber lapidum seu de gemmis* of Marbode of Rennes.[19] According to Marbode, the purest sapphire resembles a cloudless sky. No stone has greater powers, none is more beautiful. Among its many properties, the following are especially pertinent to the *Bleu chevalier*: It has curative powers and restores wholeness and strength to injured limbs; it brings harmony and peace; it keeps its owner safe from capture or, if he is caught unprotected, it releases him from prison; it is especially powerful as a medicine and can reduce fevers and cool down those who are overheated (cf. Pannier, 39–41). If the sapphire has significance for Froissart's text, the properties conventionally attributed to this bluest and noblest of gems have the most ironic implications for the knight who claims blue as his heraldic color. He does not enjoy its protection: He is weakened, not whole; he lives in a world of precarious instability, not peace and harmony; he is in prison, not free; he is sick, not healthy; his temperament is hot, not cool.

The Blue Knight's predicament, which is not alleviated by the health-giving effects of the sapphire, is directly associated with two overriding qualities signified by heraldic blue: the element air and the sanguine complexion. Maurice Wilmotte[20] and Normand Cartier ("Le bleu chevalier," 306) both observe that, despite all else, the Blue Knight is obviously mentally deranged. In their wake Anthime Fourrier diagnoses him as manic-depressive, and he goes on to characterize the main body of the dit as an instance of psychoanalysis (introduction, esp. 52–53). The Blue Knight's psychosis stems from a triple complex, according to Fourrier: claustration (he is imprisoned), frustration (he is isolated from his lover), and inferiority (he is not free to go out and prove his prowess as a knight); in this Froissart shows his originality with respect to his primary source, Machaut's *Fontaine amoureuse*. Such commentary is charming and insightful, but it misses the mark in both historical and literary terms. On the one hand, it describes the knight's condition in modern, not medieval, medical language. In fact, medieval medicine provides a more meaningful—a more poetically meaningful—context for understanding lovesickness. On the other hand, Froissart's narrator does not function in the text like a physician; although he proves himself to be familiar with moral dimensions in standard treatments for certain mental disorders, he attempts to help his lovesick companion by offering him the talents, the abilities, and the training he has as a poet-clerk.

As already suggested, air and the sanguine temperament conjoined are highly significant. According to the Galenic model of humors and elements, air is associated with blood, the sanguine complexion, and springtime; all four—air, blood, sanguinity, and springtime—are among the significations of heraldic blue, and all are warm and moist.[21] As for the Blue Knight's pathology, Fourrier is right to mention sexual frustration, but a medieval physician would have described the knight's condition in different terms, as being a mental derangement of which the ultimate cause lay not in his psyche but in his physical condition.

According to medieval medicine, in the words of the widely disseminated *Liber de coitu* by the late eleventh-century translator Constantinus Africanus of Monte Cassino, sexual arousal involves three elements:

> Tria vero sunt in coitu: appetitus ex cogitatione fantastica ortus, spiritus et humor. Appetitus ab epate, spiritus ab corde, humor a cerebro: nam cum delectabilis motus sit in coitu, per motum omnia membra corporis coalescunt et per calorem eliquatur humor qui est in cerebro, et eliquatus attrahitur per venas que post aures ducuntur ad testiculos, et inde per virgam in vulvam iacitur.[22]

> [Three things are involved in intercourse: appetite (created by the fancy), spirit, and the humor from the brain. The delightful movements of intercourse give warmth to all the members, and hence to the humor which is in the brain; this liquid is drawn through the veins which lead from behind the ears to the testicles and from them it is squirted by the penis into the vulva.][23]

As the Salernitan Question "Queritur quare tanta delectatio sit in coitu?" elaborates in greater detail, the *cogitatio fantastica* is activated by visual stimulation (Love's arrows shot through the eyes):[24] "Love is nothing more than a feeling of pleasure accompanied by joy, and every pleasure springs either from ... the soul or from ... nature. Each of these two kinds of pleasure begins its operation through ... the eyes. The spirit which the optical nerve transmits ... apprehend[s] external things ... and [then] represents them to the higher soul."²⁵ There the thing perceived is impressed in the memory. Moreover, continues the Salernitan Question, one's ability later to imagine a renewal of pleasure sets into motion the appropriate physiological mechanisms. A psychic virtue emanating from the soul stimulates the natural virtues by causing the blood contained in the liver to grow hot. The blood vaporizes, and the spirit thus produced moves from the liver to the heart, the seat of emotions. From the heart the hot spirit moves through the arteries to make the reproductive organs ready for copulation (Jacquart and Thomasset, 115–16).²⁶ Thus human copulation depends upon heat and moisture.

This process occurs in all human beings. In the sanguine individual, we recall, heat and moisture dominate. This is how a thirteenth-century English copyist in the tradition of the prose Salernitan Question summarizes the conventional wisdom regarding the relationship of temperament and sexual prowess: Those who are sanguine, who are warm and moist, desire greatly and accomplish much; the choleric, warm and dry, desire much and accomplish little; the phlegmatic, cold and moist, desire little and accomplish much; the melancholic, cold and dry, desire little and accomplish little.²⁷ Hildegard of Bingen (1098–1179) notes of healthy sanguine men:

> Alii autem masculi [sanguinei] sunt, qui calidum cerebrum habent et amabilem colorem faciei candore et rubedine permixtum ac pingues venas sanguine plenas atque spissum sanguinem recti et rubei coloris. Sed ei delectabilem humorem in se habent, qui nec tristitia nec acerbitate oppressus est, et quem acerbitas melancoliae fugit et devitat. Et quoniam calidum cerebrum et rectum sanguinem habent, et quoniam humores eorum oppressi non sunt, pingues carnes in corporibus suis habent.²⁸ (72)

[There are other males (the sanguine) whose brain is hot and who have in their face a lovely color, a mixture of white and red, and they have fat veins full of blood that is thick and of a healthy red color. Furthermore, they have a delightful disposition, not troubled by sadness or acrimony, which the moroseness of melancholy flees and avoids. And because they have a hot brain and healthy blood, and because their humors are not depressed, they have solid flesh on their bodies.]

According to Constantinus Africanus, men of sanguine complexion are the most virile and produce the most sperm:

[D]icemus in primis de illis hominibus qui fortes sont et prevalentes ad emittendum semen. Hiis nimirum testiculi sunt calidi et humidi temperate, verbi gracia, si fuerint homnes multum vinum bibentes, habundant in appetitu et semine; similiter, si fuerit vernum tempus, quod est calidum et humidum temperate. Calor enim auget appetitum velut masculinum, frigiditas autem diminuit appetitum et femininum reddit. Si ergo natura testium fuerit calida, multus erit appetitus luxurie. (*De coitu*, 96–98)

[We will first discuss those men who are strong and excel in producing semen. Their testicles (are of course hot and moist)[29] in the right proportion; for example, men who are great wine-drinkers will have plenty of desire and of semen. This will also be the case if the season is spring, when warmth and moisture are well mixed. Warmth increases desire and masculinity, whereas cold reduces desire and renders effeminate. If a man has warm testicles, therefore, he will be very lecherous.] (Delany, 57)

We shall come back to the question of wine drinking, which is regarded as especially characteristic of the sanguine nature.[30]

Severe physical disorders can result when heat and moisture are excessive. In medieval medicine sexual abstinence is generally regarded as harmful to the health, but its ill effects are exaggerated in sanguine men, who are the most potent sexually and who produce the most semen; their spermatic vessels can become gorged with an excess of fluids. One result is satyriasis, which is distinguished from priapism by the disappearance of the symptoms upon satisfactory copulation (Jacquart and Thomasset, 202–3).[31] To avoid satyriasis, or to relieve it, monks of sanguine complexion were urged to drink calming herbal teas, to eat salt fish to reduce moisture, to wash themselves in cold water, to sit on cold rocks (*Brevarium practice*, cited by Jacquart and Thomasset, 203).

Abstinence can also produce particularly grave psychological effects in the sanguine. Semen retained in excess can vaporize, and the spirit produced affects the heart, first resulting in mental anguish and sadness, then endangering other bodily functions (Jacquart and Thomasset, 204–5). One specific disorder that has severe psychic implications for sanguine men is clearly related to the Blue Knight's condition: "heroic love," *amor (h)eros, hereos*, or *heroicus* (Jacquart and Thomasset, 116–18).[32] We may well wonder whether or not the concept of heroic love grew in a confusion of the Latin words *heros* (hero, heroic) and *eros*. In any case, medieval medicine associates it generally with the noble class and compares it especially with excessive zeal in feudal service (cf. Wack, 324, 336–38). According to Constantinus Africanus, "quidam philosophi dicunt: heros est nomen maxime delectationis designatiuum. Sicut autem fidelitas est dilectionis ultimitas, ita et heros delectationis quedam est extremitas" (Wack, 330) [certain philosophers say that the word *heros* designates the greatest love. Just as loyalty is the height of love, so *heros* is an extreme form of some kind of love]. Johannes Afflacius is more explicit: "quidam philosophi diffinierunt herum esse amorem immoderatum. Sicut enim fidelitas est immoderatus amor erga dominos, ita et heros amor est intemperatus erga habendos" (Wack, 327) [certain philosophers defined *heros* as immoderate love. Just as loyalty is immoderate love toward lords, so also *heros* is intemperate love toward those to be possessed [sexually] (*sic*)] (Wack, 328).

Melancholy (cold and dry) is not the cause of the disease, but heroic love manifests some of the same symptoms as melancholy.[33] Johannes Afflacius, citing Rufus of Ephesus, compares the effects of heroic love to melancholy: "quidam Rufus dixisse perhibetur: Coitus, inquid, est iuuantinus quibus colera nigra nel mania dominantur, per quem sensus reuocantur et superfluitates heroicorum similiter adiuuantur" (Wack, 327). [A certain Rufus is said to have remarked: Intercourse aids those who suffer from black bile or mania; through it they are brought back to their senses, and the superfluities of those suffering *heros* are similarly relieved] (Wack, 328).[34] Even if melancholy is not a cause, in extreme cases patients eventually fall into melancholy. According to Constantinus Africanus, for example, "si non eriosis succurantur ut cogitatio eorum auferatur et anima leuigetur in passione melancolica necesse est incidant" (Wack, 330)[35] [unless sufferers of heroic love are helped so that their excessive thoughts are removed and their soul relieved, of necessity they fall into melancholic passion] (translation mine).

The disease develops as the process of sexual arousal described earlier is set into motion, either by perception of the beloved or by memory of her impressed upon the imagination. According to Johannes Afflacius, "Huius autem herois causa aliquando est rationalis anime oblectatio in aliqua re pulcra. Quam pulcritudinem si in sibi simili conspexerit forma furor accenditur ut ei se uniat. . . . ergo hanc huius morbi pessimitatem pessima anime comitantur accidentia, id est cogitationum assiduarum incendia" (Wack, 327). [Sometimes the cause of this disease *heros* is the delight of the rational soul in a beautiful object. For if it contemplates beauty in a form similar to itself, a rage to unite with it is kindled. . . . therefore grave psychological symptoms accompany this serious disease, that is, the kindling of incessant thoughts] (Wack, 328). Arousal assumes pathological dimensions when one's judgment, acting in concert with memory and imagination, deems that the pleasure associated with the beloved surpasses all other pleasures and constitutes the only goal worth pursuing. For Arnald of Villanova, as for most medieval physicians, the heart is the source of vaporous humors that impair judgment (Jacquart and Thomasset, 117). The heart, we recall, transmits to the genitalia heat generated by blood in the liver; it also transmits to the brain the noxious spirit of vaporized semen. The effects of heroic love are compounded when intercourse with the beloved does not take place to alleviate the syndrome. Symptoms include dark circles under the eyes, lividity, weight loss, accelerated pulse, incoherent speech, abrupt gestures, and, in extreme cases, loss of self-control, disinterest in living, complete insanity (Jacquart and Thomasset, 117–18).[36]

From much the same causes—the Blue Knight's sanguine temperament, his forced sexual abstinence, and the consequent production and retention of excessive amounts of semen—stem two diseases, or perhaps two forms of the same disease, that afflict him in combination. Satyriasis is born in the memory of joy and pleasure and in anticipation of *jouissance*, hence the knight joyfully sings of his lady and celebrates her beauty. (An irrepressible urge to smile is also a symptom of heroic love; see n.36.) But desire too long unfulfilled leads to mental derangement and despair: the "depression" of heroic love.

The clerk does not approach the Blue Knight as a physician, as noted earlier. Instinctively, perhaps, the knight bathes his face in the cool water of the spring, and the clerk splashes water on him to bring him out of his swoon. But the clerk does not advise the knight to sit on cold rocks, eat salted fish—or drink wine. Drinking wine is generally the preferred remedy for heroic love. In Johannes Afflacius's words,

> Est autem maior auferendarum cogitationum heroicorum causa temperatum in quanitate et qualitate bibere uinum. . . . Inde Rufus dixit: Vinum fortis medicina timidis, tristibus, et heroicis. Similiter et Galenus: Quicumque, inquit, uinum de uite educere allaborauit ex quo tristicia sedatur et leticia reuocatur maxime fuit et sapientissinum. Zenon dixit: Sicut amaritudines lup[in]orum [sic] dulcorat aqua, ita et uinum aninum meum oblectat ut tristiciam eius auferat. (Wack, 327)

> [Drinking wine that is temperate in quantity and quality is one of the better ways of removing the thoughts of patients of *heros*. . . . Rufus said: Wine is a strong medicine for the timid, the sad, and the heroic. Similarly, Galen: Whoever took pains to bring forth wine from the

vine, which calms sorrow and calls forth joy, was greatest and most
wise. Zeno said: Just as water sweetens the bitterness of lupines, so
wine gives pleasure to my soul, relieving its sorrow.] (Wack, 329)

There is no wine in the Blue Knight's forest; moreover, as we shall see,
drinking might well prove detrimental in the knight's case. Temperate
baths and music, also sanctioned treatments,[37] are likewise unavailable in
the knight's prison.

The clerk does apply, however, one of the prescribed therapies in a
setting, also recommended by the treatises, that is provided by the forest.
In the words of Johannes Afflacius:

> Sed tamen duobis his [music and wine] pulcras et delicatas ami-
> corum facies amisceri conuenit. Unde quidam dixerunt iocundum
> est bibere uinum et audire colloquia amicorum. Galenus: Colloqui,
> inquit, dilectissimis laborem a membris subtrahit. Si autem hec
> omnia—bibere uinum, scilicet, musica et amicorum colloquia—
> hortos habeant atque prata et aquarum fluenta, insimul omnia sunt
> delectabiliora. (Wack, 328)

> [Nonetheless, it is fitting to add to these two (music and wine) the
> beautiful and tender faces of friends. Thus some have said that it is
> cheering to drink wine and to listen to the conversation of friends.
> Galen said: Talking with intimates removes a burden from the
> shoulders. If all these things—namely, drinking wine, music, and
> talking with friends—take place in gardens and meadows with
> flowing water, everything is altogether more delightful.] (Wack,
> 329)

Constantinus Africanus's *Viaticum* in fact recommends the ministrations
of friends in gardens or orchards as the most beneficial treatment of all:

> Quod perfectissimum sibi esse dinoscitur si boni consocii aggre-
> gentur qui et in pulchritudine ualeant scientia uel moribus. Dictum
> est enim quia maxima est delectatio ut uinum bibatur et colloqui
> sapientibus. Galenus: Colloqui se amantibus laborem eicit ex mem-
> bris interioribus. Quod si fiat in ortis lucentibus et odoriferis seu
> fructiferis obtimum et iocundissimum fit. (Wack, 331)

> [The thing that is distinguished as the most perfect for oneself is
> when good companions who are worthy in beauty, in knowledge,
> and in their habits gather together. This has indeed been said be-

cause it is the greatest pleasure to drink wine and to have conversation with learned people. Galen: Conversing with people who love one another relieves distress from the innermost parts. Whenever this is done in sunny, sweet-smelling or fruitful gardens, it is done in the best and in the most cheerful way.]

As a friend, the clerk offers therapy of a peculiarly learned and literary kind.

Treatment for mental disorders brought on by heroic love is, therefore, moral as well as physical. Danielle Jacquart observes that some techniques derive from Ovid's *Remedia amoris:* anything to erase the beloved's image from the patient's memory and imagination—or anything at least to deface that image—by turning desire into revulsion, by seeing or imagining the beloved in disgusting, obscene circumstances.[38] Avicenna recommends invective (Jacquart and Thomasset, 118).

Froissart's clerk does not resort to misogyny, but he serves the knight in the capacity for which he is professionally equipped: as a learned writer who is familiar with a literary tradition of consolation that goes back to Boethius and embraces the work of his contemporaries Machaut and Chaucer. This is one way *clergie* serves *chevalerie*. Among Froissart's obvious models, works that he consciously and self-consciously imitates, are Machaut's *Confort d'ami* and *Remede de fortune* and their analogues in the *Roman de la rose*, particularly Reason's appeal to the Lover. Another model is Machaut's *Fontaine amoureuse*, yet another his *Jugement du roy de Behaigne*, whose intricate verse form Froissart imitates: the monorhymed quatrain consisting of an introductory half line followed by three complete decasyllables (*Le jugement*, introduction, p. 10).

The second part of the *Bleu chevalier* is taken up with a dialogue between the Blue Knight and the clerk. We recall that the clerk has observed several recurrent episodes of the knight's obsessive behavior. Near the poem's midpoint the knight faints, and the clerk fears that he has died, but, taking him in his arms, he sees that he is alive. He recognizes physical symptoms of the knight's illness, how his color changes and how he sweats, and he knows its cause: love for a lady (229–30). To relieve him from his physical and mental distress, "anoi" and "penser" (225), the clerk prescribes the therapy that is appropriate for him to give: *confort d'ami*. But the knight believes his case is hopeless: "How can I stop behaving the way my heart makes me?" (233–34). Besides, he is not even sure he wants to be cured (235–36).

The clerk's *confort d'ami* begins with classical examples of negative and positive behaviors. The knight should not imitate Pyramus, who killed himself for love of Thisbe, or Leander, who drowned while swimming to an assignation with Hero (242–47). But if Fortune is fickle and cruel toward him, he should take Socrates as his model (248–53). As "Ovid the Perfect" says (254), according to the clerk, Socrates was so just and so true that he never "changed" in anything he ever did (255–56). Here Socrates's moral resoluteness, which the Blue Knight shares in his loyalty to his lady, becomes a metaphor for physical health and psychological balance, which the knight lacks.

Pyramus and Thisbe and especially Hero and Leander are among Froissart's favorite Ovidian or, to use Douglas Kelly's very apt expression, "pseudo-Ovidian" references.[39] For example, in the *Espinette amoureuse*,[40] an important intertext for the *Bleu chevalier*, the clerk, in despair after his lady's cruel rejection of his love poem, would follow Leander in seeking a glorious death for the sake of love (1313–15). Later, in her "Reconforte," the lady's image says she loves the clerk more than Hero did Leander (2831–32). The Blue Knight, however, like Pyramus and like Leander, is headed toward death.

More prominent is the clerk's reference to Socrates. Socrates as a model of courage and steadfastness in the face of adverse fortune is a commonplace in consolation literature. In the *Chronique de Flandre*, for example, Froissart draws the lesson from Count Louis II's misfortunes that God does not abandon His steadfast friends, for He did not fail Job, Boethius, or Socrates:

> Ches merveilleuses aventures ou fortunes adonnent grant exemple à tous prinches et à toutes aultres gens que les dons de fortune mondaine ne sont point estables, et que nul ne s'i doit fyer, ne asseurer, . . . dont chascuns doibt prendre en patienche les fortunes que Dieux luy envoie, car au besoings Dieux ne fault point à son amy, comme il ne fist à Job, Boesce et Socrate et plusieurs aultres, et fait et fera.[41]

> [These wondrous adventures or fortunes provide all princes and everyone else with the great lesson that the gifts of worldly fortune do not endure and that no one should trust them or count on them, . . . this is why people should accept with resignation the fortunes God sends them, for God does not abandon His friends in need. He did not fail Job, Boethius or Socrates and many others; He does not now nor will He.]

A reference to Socrates as a model of stability in adversity and in good fortune occurs near the midpoint of Machaut's *Confort d'ami*.[42] Socrates in the *Bleu chevalier* is all the more prominent because his name falls exactly at the midpoint of Froissart's composition: line 252 of 504 lines.

Here is the full account: Do not pay attention to the vicissitudes of Fortune, the clerk says,

> ... mes prendés la rancune
> De Socratés,
> Qui fu tous jours si justes et si vres,
> Ensi que dist Ovides li parfés,
> Qu'on ne le vit onques en tous ses fes
> Changier une heure. (251–56)

[... but take the bitterness of Socrates, who was always so just and true, as Ovid the Perfect says, that no one ever saw him waver for a minute in his deeds.]

The clerk's prescription is to take the "rancune"—the rancor, the bitterness—of Socrates. I cannot say that I fully comprehend this striking image. I have found no instances when the Latin *rancor* and its French derivatives—*rancour, rancoeur, rancune*—have positive meanings, nor have I found references specifically to Socrates' "bitterness." So I must—tentatively—recommend accepting this as an ironic reference to stoic behavior generally; thus "to take Socrates' bitterness," meaning perhaps "to drink bitter hemlock," is a metaphor for adopting stoic behavior.

To compound the difficulty, the clerk names "Ovid the Perfect" as his authority (254), but this turns out to be a false citation—a "pseudo-Ovidian" reference. Socrates is not mentioned in the *Metamorphoses* or for that matter, insofar as I can tell, in the *Ovide moralisé*,[43] which was certainly Machaut's source of Ovidian material[44] and perhaps also Froissart's. In fact, I have found but a single instance in Ovid that might have relevance here, in the *Ibis*, where the poet curses his enemy with ironic invective: "Sollicitoque bibas, Anyti doctissimus olim / Imperturbato, quod bibit ore reus."[45] [And you shall drink with shaking lips what that most learned man accused by Anytos once drank in steady calm.] We may well doubt that Froissart knew this obscure text with its highly indirect reference to Socrates, "Anyti doctissimus reus." Ovid is nevertheless a most appropriate authority to mention at this point. Not only does Socrates stand, as the unswerving philosopher, in stark contrast with the mutability and instability that characterize the *Metamorphoses*, but the clerk also means, as a cure for heroic love, to find a "remedy for love" in the literal sense of the term, by making implicit reference to Ovid's *Remedia amoris*.

The clerk's source is not Ovid, but the *Roman de la rose*, specifically a passage in Reason's speech that the clerk in fact abbreviates. Reason pleads with the Lover to abandon the God of Love, to whom he has paid homage, and to become "li miens loiaus amis" (5813)[46] [my loyal friend]. Although this is indeed a *remedium amoris*, Jean de Meun cites not Ovid, but Solinus:

> Le dieu leras qui ci t'a mis,
> et ne priseras une prune
> toute la roe de Fortune.
> A Socratés seras semblables,
> qui tant fu fors et tant estables
> qu'il n'iert liez en prosperitez
> ne tristes en adversitez.
> Tout metoit en une balance,
> bone aventure et meschaance,
> et les fesoit egal peser,
> sanz esjoïr et sanz peser,
> car de chose, quel qu'ele soit,
> n'iert joieus ne ne l'en pesoit.
> Ce fu cil, le dit Solin,
> qui par le respons Apolin
> fu jugiez du mont li plus sages;
> ce fu cil a cui li visages
> de tout quan que li avenoit
> toujours en un point se tenoit,
> n'onc cil mué ne le troverent
> qui par cegüe le tuerent. (5814–34)

[You will abandon the god who has put you here, and you will not value one whit the whole of Fortune's wheel. You will be like Socrates who was so strong and steadfast that he was neither joyful in prosperity nor sad in adversity. He put everything in a balance, good luck and ill, and made them weigh out the same, without rejoicing or grieving, for he was neither happy nor unhappy about anything, no matter what. It is he, according to Solinus, who was judged the wisest man in the world by Apollo's oracle. It is he whose face, regardless of what happened to him, was always composed in the same way, and they who killed him with hemlock did not find him changed.]

Like Boethius's Philosophy, Reason claims Socrates as her friend (*Rose*, 6856–57). The Lover, of course, specifically rejects Socrates as a model

(6879–80). Through Jean de Meun's Reason, Froissart's clerk prescribes exactly the same remedy, that is, to forswear love.

Imbalance, inconstancy, change, wild swings in mood—joyful anticipation giving way to debilitating, sorrowful heroic love—are precisely the Blue Knight's problem—his "blue" loyalty to his lady giving way to a "blue" instability. In imitation of Socrates, the clerk prescribes that

> ... en lïece, en joie et en solas
>   Devés manoir
> Et prendre en vous coer, confort et espoir,
> Qu'encor porés, s'il plaist Dieu, moult valoir.
> Il m'est avis que je vous die voir. (*Bleu chavalier,* 263–67)

> [... you should live in happiness, in joy and in solace and take comfort and hope into your heart, for you can yet be most worthy, if it pleases God. I think I am telling you the truth.]

So the knight should, like the man who wears blue, according to the violet's lawyer, "avoir coer ferme et estable / Et conforté" (*Plaidoirie,* 216–17) [have a strong and stable heart, one that is always comforted]. But the knight does not and cannot, precisely because he "wears blue" in other senses.

A condition not directly related to the Blue Knight's love disease complicates his case still further, what Fourrier characterizes as his inferiority complex (introduction, 53). He is a young man, and young knights ought to be out in the world making a name for themselves, but his imprisonment in the wood makes it impossible to exercise chivalry. He confesses that he does not know which is worse, his worry about inactivity or his obsession with love.[47]

The clerk does not understand the implications of this new concern, however, and here his limitations as a literary healer come to the fore. He turns to the *matière de Bretagne* for examples to complement his Socratic model of appropriate behavior, and he cites knights who have been in love and yet have been separated from their ladies for many years: Tristan, Yvain, Guiron le Courtois, Perceval. The knight will find in their stories that they loved loyally and well. Explicitly, these heroes "think well on their ladies," and thereby redouble their strength,[48] while the Blue Knight's thoughts are misdirected and his strength is sapped in sickness.

But the clerk has missed the point of the knight's newer complaint, and he is deservedly reproached: "Amis, vous n'avés nullement / Solu vos mos" (331–32) [Friend, you haven't made your words fit]. For they do not apply to the knight's situation. Those knights so renowned for love sought adventure and practiced chivalry for their ladies' sake as much as for their own glory (333–40). But the Blue Knight cannot be compared with them, for he is imprisoned in the wood as though in a tower and cannot be freed or ransomed (341–64). Thus he is in despair because he cannot have what he wills (367), to win honor in chivalric exploits, or what he desires (368), his lady. And so, however much he suffers pain and grief, he honors his lady and maintains his own honor by directing all his thoughts toward her and loving her with steadfast faith (396–404). This is all he can do.[49]

In response to this almost tragic confession, the clerk further undermines his role as comforter-therapist as he shifts his moral position from one of learned objectivity to one of sympathetic identification with his disconsolate patient: "Que poet on plus en bonne amour eslire / Que foi garder et honnour? Qui desire / El, il vault mains" (406-8) [What better thing can one do in choosing true love than keep faith and honor? Whoever desires anything else is less than worthy]. And so the clerk's project of therapeutic consolation collapses: The love disease must continue unabated if its very cause is admitted as a transcendent value. In this light the clerk's concluding recapitulation seems little more than a summary of empty platitudes. The knight should be filled with comfort and take Socrates as his companion, and so he will pass his time easily and live a cheerful life:

> Or vous suppli, ciers sires, jointes mains
> Que vous voeilliés estre de confors plains
> Et si soiés a Socratés compains,
>   Qui tant fu fors
> Contre Fortune et si plains de confors
> Qu'ains ne mua, non plus que fist Hectors,
> De hardement jusqu'a tant qu'il fu mors.
> Par tel couvent
> Passerés vous le temps legierement
> Et viverés tres envoisiement. (409–18)

[So now I pray you, dear sir, my hands joined together, please be filled with comfort, and be a companion to Socrates, who was so strong against Fortune and so full of comfort that he never wavered in his courage, no more than ever did Hector, until the day he died. This is a guarantee that you will pass your time easily and you will live most cheerfully.]

Responds the knight, not without irony: "Certes, amis, / Je vous crerai, car vos consaus m'a mis / En grant confort, et s'en soiiés tous fis" (420–22) [Indeed, friend, I'll believe you. Your advice has been a great comfort to me, you can be sure of that]. Thus Froissart subverts the *confort d'ami* model. But the Blue Knight himself intervenes to propose another solution—another, purely literary alternative to the *confort d'ami:* The clerk must write a poem.

It is at this point that we must return to the question of the *Bleu chevalier*'s status as quasiautobiography or pseudoautobiography. The therapy session concludes in failure, but not the poem, for *clergie* will find another way to serve *chevalerie*. Laurence de Looze has recently attempted a definition of pseudoautobiography as a distinct literary genre that has its own structures and its own concerns and values.[50] We all recognize in general what pseudoautobiography involves: the use of conventional quasiautobiographical discourse to portray events that are obviously fictional or fanciful. Peter Dembowski remarks that Froissart's *Espinette amoureuse* "offers a long pseudo-autobiographical introduction describing his [the clerk-narrator's] childhood and stressing the precocity of his love inclination" (376). Most if not all of Froissart's dits are pseudo-autobiographical in this sense. When William Kibler argues that the *Espinette amoureuse* should be read "as literature (and not as autobiography)," he means, as I understand him, that the text does not pretend to be a sincere account of events lived by the narrator; thus he proposes pseudoautobiographical reading in the same sense.[51] And, as Michel Zink has recently remarked of the highly personal, highly "realistic" *Dit du florin,* "C'est un poème autobiographique. . . . Mais il y a plus."[52]

De Looze goes even further and suggests that, as a genre, pseudoautobiography invariably—and overtly—draws attention to itself as fiction, to its own fictionality and to its own textuality, and it ultimately calls into question its own status as autobiographical narrative. Any shreds of apparent reference to external historical reality are utterly subsumed within the fiction and eventually come to serve that fiction ("Pseudo-autobiography," 76). De Looze makes a strong case, for example, for reading Froissart's *Prison amoureuse* as a text concerned primarily with its own poetics and only secondarily, if at all, with the actual imprisonment of Wenceslas of Luxembourg (*"Corpus poetae,"* chap. 5). The prison is one of Love's making, not one of stone and mortar. Kibler has already said as much,[53] but the *Prison amoureuse* need not necessarily be appraised as the record of an exchange of texts between Froissart and Wenceslas, as Kibler goes on to assert. The dit celebrates not Wenceslas and his servant and friend, or not just those men and that relationship, but the fictional Flos-as-poet, the fictional Rose-as-correspondent, Froissart-as-writer, and the texts produced by all three.

This view of pseudoautobiography is appropriate in discussion of the *Bleu chevalier* for a number of reasons—for example, in laying to rest the question of the Blue Knight's historical identity. And what about the relationship between Froissart and the Blue Knight?

When the clerk and the knight simultaneously recognize each other, the clerk is dumbfounded—"esbahis" (214)—perhaps repulsed or frightened, for he gets up and leaves.[54] But the knight calls him back with words of conciliation.[55] It is at this point that the clerk diagnoses the knight's condition and begins his therapeutic consolation. This scene, coming just before the key midpoint naming of Socrates, is highly charged with meaningful, yet ambiguous references. One involves the clerk's identification of himself with the knight as lover. When, before the recognition, the clerk first takes the semiconscious knight in his arms and addresses him, the knight opens his eyes and heaves a deep sigh.[56] And at that moment the clerk is reminded of a time when he too was subject to "changes," that is, deranged by lovesickness, but, thank God, he then received "un brief confort" [a timely comfort], which served as a remedy that has lasted to this day.[57]

In the *Espinette amoureuse*, Froissart's clerk-poet is in despair after the lady he loves pointedly returns to him unopened the book in which he concealed a ballade written for her. He comes down with a virulent fever that we recognize as a symptom of lovesickness, and he is put under the care of a physician "qui bien savoit / Quel maladie avoie ou corps" (1727–28) [who well understood what disease I had in my body]. The treatment prescribed is to reduce the fever by withholding drink:

> Pour moi traire de caleur hors
> Avoit a mes gardes bien dit
> Qu'on ne laissast entour mon lit
> Nul buvrage, ne pot ne voirre,
> Car trop contraires m'estoit boire;
> Et on m'en garda bien ossi. (1529–34)

[In order to draw me out of the heat, he had well instructed my keepers not to leave any drink about my bed, neither pot nor glass, for it was very harmful for me to drink; and so they succeeded in keeping me from it.]

This particular cure is not found in the medical texts cited earlier (on the contrary), but we understand the physician's reasoning: to decrease the influence of sanguinity (blood is hot and moist), and consequently to reduce an excess of semen, by drying the patient out. Thus Froissart's physician must perceive the preferred treatment of administering wine as counterindicated, for drinking wine, which is characteristic of the sanguine, would only compound the effects of a disease that is exacerbated by the patient's heat and moisture.

At one point in the *Espinette amoureuse* the clerk's suffering from fever and thirst is so great that he feels he can be cured only by drinking, that is, by feeding the disease—as lovers are wont to do:

> Dont une fois avint ensi
> Que j'avoie calours si grans
> Que de riens je n'estoie engrans
> Fors de tant que beü euïsse,
> Et me sambloit, se je peüisse
> Boire, que j'estoie garis. (1535–40)

[Then one time I happened to be so hot that I craved nothing more than to have something to drink, and it seemed to me that if I could drink, I would be cured.]

Then he composes a complainte, *La complainte del amant,* in which he details the causes of his lovesickness (memory of his lady, his blood) and its effects (his abandonment to fickle Fortune, his feeling of being in prison). Thus Froissart documents another case of heroic love. The opening line of the complainte is emphatic in its medically significant reference to a burning heart: "A boire! A boire! Li coers m'art" (*Espinette*, 1556) [Give me drink! My heart is on fire!]. This remarkable lyric, which is fifty stanzas and eight hundred lines long, falls at the dit's midpoint.

The clerk's "complainte," however, eventually turns itself into a poem of self-consolation. At its own midpoint (the beginning of stanza 25), the clerk expresses his need for counsel and consolation, but there is no one who can help him. He wrestles with the problem of who can give him comfort and counsel and who is worthy of doing so. Simultaneously he discovers that what he thirsts for is not wine but words (*Espinette*, 2020–34). He finally concludes that there is only he who can console himself, and with words: self-reflective, self-reflexive autobiographical writing that comes from his heart and that he intends to address to his lady (*Espinette*, 2068–85, 2088–94).

So the clerk consoles himself in the act of composing the very complainte that has as its subject his disease and how it can be cured, not by abstaining from drink but by drinking—words. And the very words he drinks are the complainte itself. The clerk's "complaint" ("Mes complains," *Espinette*, 2357), that is, his sickness, gradually abates, and all the while, throughout his "treatment," he recites his "complaint" ("Ce complainte," *Espinette*, 2359),[58] that is, his poem, at least once a day. After three months of this self-imposed therapy, his fever breaks (*Espinette*, 2366–67).

In the *Bleu chevalier*, it is to the *Espinette's* multifaceted, self-reflexive *Complainte del amant* that the clerk refers as he gazes into the face of his stricken companion and remembers a time when he, too, suffered from instability and received "un brief confort" (194) [a timely comfort]. If we consider the knight's joyful songs to be a similar attempt at self-healing, self-consolation, we see that his enterprise fails as he is continuously overwhelmed by melancholy. Among the knight's first words to the clerk is an expression of his hope that the clerk will in fact succeed in bringing him "consauls et proufis" (219) [counsel and improvement]. This is a profound and highly charged moment of sympathetic identification between knight and clerk. A previous such moment, which we can now regard with renewed understanding, is the collapse of the clerk's project of therapeutic consolation as he adopts the knight's viewpoint: that his is the worthiest of loves, the only worthy love—which is the very foundation of *La complainte del amant*.

Of course Froissart's text does not intend a total assimilation of clerk and knight. Froissart, like Machaut, delights in creating noble figures who are reflections of himself, yet he maintains a certain, necessary distance. For example, the Blue Knight is a singer of songs—chansons, virelais, complaintes—and thus is perhaps a poet in his own right.[59] But Froissart's narrator never quotes the knight's texts as individual poems, as the narrator does elsewhere his own lyric poems or those of the privileged Wenceslas. When he does cite words the knight sings, the verse form does not shift to that of a *forme fixe* but continues in the narrative quatrain Froissart borrows from Machaut to represent his narrator's style. Thus the clerk-narrator of the *Bleu chevalier* assimilates the other's lyric texts into his own verse. The distance between clerk and knight is marked even more explicitly at a moment of mutual recognition.

The clerk recalls his own lovesickness, which resembles that of the knight, as we have seen. When the knight awakens from his swoon, the clerk looks into the knight's eyes, and each simultaneously identifies the other. In that intensely dramatic moment the knight names the clerk (212), but the narrator does not report that name. The clerk is dumbfounded to see that the knight is "a certain lord, *that* lord"—"ce seignour la" (213)—whom the narrator also refrains from naming. The power of this recognition is so great that scholars again hear the siren's song of historical reference inspired by heraldry and the Blue Knight's arms. What knight of his acquaintance, one he dares not name, could strike such terror in the heart of Froissart—perhaps the notorious Louis d'Anjou? Or else, what knight of his acquaintance, one he dares not name, could provoke such astonishment that he could be subject to lovesickness—perhaps the noble Wenceslas of Luxembourg? Much more significantly, however, this passage serves Froissart by reestablishing an appropriate distance between his clerk and his knight, whose identities are threatening to merge. Such a distance is necessary in order to bring back into focus an overriding principle in Froissart's poetry as well as in his *Chroniques:* that *clergie* serves *chevalerie* in natural harmony but that *chevalerie* cannot exist, cannot live in memory, without *clergie.*

At the end of the tale, when the clerk's therapeutic project collapses, the knight prescribes the only possible cure for literary lovesickness. In symbiotic imitation of the clerk of the *Espinette amoureuse,* he asks his clerical interlocutor to compose a poem, a *dittier* (425), a dit. We have seen how Froissart from the outset projects the knight in terms of lyric textuality: In imitation of the clerk he sings love songs and complaintes. Eventually, as the knight's dialogue with the clerk draws to its conclusion, the knight also begins conceiving of his own self in terms of narrative as well as lyric textuality. In despair, like the clerk of the *Espinette amoureuse,* the knight longs to establish communication with his lady:

A tout le mains, se peüisse veïr
Ma droite dame et a tres grant loisir
Parler a lui, ce saciés sans mentir,
    A eüreus
Je me tenroie .IIII. ans ou .III. ou .II.,
Et doucement par beaus mos amoureus
Li compteroie en disant, coers joieus:
    "Aiiés de mi,
"Par vo douçour, et pité et merci,
"Car je vous jur, et si le cres ensi,
"Ensus de vous languis et me murdri.
    "Il n'est pas doubte,
"Vous m'oubliiés, ma dame, je m'en doubte,
"Et bien saciés qu'en la mer n'avra goutte
"Quant ma pensee a vous ne sera toute
    "De coer entier.
"Dame, pour Dieu, veci vo chevalier

"Qui n'a bon jour ne esté ne yvier,
"Tant fort le tient vos coers en son dangier
    "Et le tenra
"Jusques adont que vos frans coers l'avra
"Reconforté: en ce point le laira
"Et, s'il vous plaist, en cel estat morra." (369–91)

[At the very least, if I could see my rightful lady and talk with her at leisure, you can be truly certain that I would consider myself happy enough to last me four years or three or two, and, my heart rejoicing, I would say to her tenderly with fine, loving words: "In your kindness, take pity on me and have mercy, for I swear to you, and I believe it to be true, that far away from you I languish and die. There is no doubt that you forget me, my lady, and I am sure of it, and you must know that not a drop will be left in the sea when my thought is not devoted to you alone with my whole heart. Lady, for God's sake, here is your knight who has not a good day in summer or winter, so strongly does your heart hold him under its dominion and shall hold him so until your noble heart has comforted him: at that moment it will set him free and, if it pleases you, thus will he die."]

It is not the *confort d'ami* he would seek from her, but her *reconforte de l'amant* (389–91). Here the Blue Knight, like the clerk of the *Espinette amoureuse*, reveals the transcendent nature of his incarceration in the wood where we discover him: The knight is held prisoner under the dominion of his lady's heart (387). And also like the clerk of the *Espinette amoureuse*, the Blue Knight formulates a self-justification he would utter in his lady's presence. Here also, starting with line 385, the Blue Knight begins speaking of himself in the third person, as the object of another's gaze (385–91) and of another's discourse.

Indeed, the only way to realize that level of textual representation is by means of a dit:

Mais au partir, avec .V. cens mercis,
    Je vous requier
Que vous voeilliés ordonner .I. dittier
Com d'aventure avés, et sans cerchier,
Dedens ce bois trouvé un chevalier
    De bleu vesti
(Et de la dame ordonnés ent aussi)
Dont vous avés hui maint regret oÿ,
Une heure en joie, et puis l'autre en soussi

> Et en esmai,
> Car en tous temps, soit marc, avril ou may,
> Le chevalier a la painne que j'ai. (423–34)

[But in parting, with five hundred thanks, I beg you please to compose a dit about how, by apparent chance, you have found within this wood, without looking for him, a knight dressed in blue—and write therein about the lady as well—a knight whose many laments you have heard today, at one moment rejoicing, then the next worried and dismayed, for in all seasons, whether in March, April, or May, the knight suffers the sorrow I feel.]

The knight, who earlier conceives of himself as the third-person object of his own discourse, is thus already in the process of becoming the object of another's narrative discourse, one he imagines the clerk will organize on his behalf. His response is consciously to turn himself into a literary character. As the knight continues projecting the clerk's dit, it is clear that he is composing the very text we are in the process of reading.

Just as the knight provides the matter for what is to be the narrator's poem,[60] so he also plants the seed of the narrator's prologue, which is about discovery and literary invention:

> On cerche bien ce qu'on ne poet trouver,
> Si troeve l'en souvent sans demander
> Ce qu'on ne cuide veoir ne encontrer.
>   Pour moi le dit,
> Car il m'avint, n'a pas grant temps, ensi
> Que sans cerchier je trouvai devant mi
> Une aventure.... (1–7)

[People look hard for what they cannot find, and often they find, without asking for it, something they do not expect to see or encounter. I am speaking from my own experience, for so it happened to me, not very long ago, that without looking for it I found before me an adventure.]

The knight also foreordains the narrator's epilogue when he bids the clerk to write about his lady as well. As the narrator says:

> Or pensai tant au dit de puissedi
>   Que je le fis.
> Or me couvient, ensi li ai prommis,

Qu'en plusieurs lieus soit recordés et dis:
S'il pooit ja de la dame estre oÿs,
    Je le verroie
Moult volentiers, car lor je li diroie
Dou chevalier comment il vit sans joie
Pour son amour qui l'arguë et mestroie
    Si ardanment,
Et s'en ferai mon devoir plainnement.
Or me lait Diex esploitier telement
Que je trouver le puisse temprement,
    Ou qu'elle soit. (479–92)

[Now I pondered about the dit after that day until I composed it. Now it is right, for so I have promised him, for me to have it inscribed and performed in many places: if it could ever be heard by the lady, I would very gladly see her, for then I would tell her about the knight, how he lives without joy because of his love which wounds him and so ardently overpowers him. And thus I shall fulfill my duty. And God grant me that I succeed soon, wherever she may be.]

Thus the clerk, having failed in his *confort d'ami*, undertakes a new therapeutic project that replicates the experiment of the *Espinette amoureuse*, but at the knight's behest and in a new context, as the clerk is transformed into Froissart's narrator. His/their text bears the words of an imprisoned, lovesick knight seeking to establish contact with the distant lady who is the cause of his imprisonment and of his disease, which are one and the same thing, aggravated by his "blue" complexion and temperament.

It is difficult to perceive how the new text, its inscription, and its performance will prove salutary for the Blue Knight in the same way that the Lover's complainte in the *Espinette amoureuse* is the drink that eventually heals him—that is to say, how the new text will produce a *reconforte de l'amant*. Doubtless, as in the *Espinette*, the cure lies in the words themselves and in the way they engender hope—hope for the establishment of communication with the lady, hope for the *reconforte* that only she can give but that in fact, in the *Espinette*, proves literally to be an illusion and, in the *Bleu chevalier*, appears impossible. The key lies in the knight's injunction to write about the lady in her turn, an event that depends upon Froissart's eventual discovery or invention of her, which has yet to take place. In other words, the dit has not been completed. Meanwhile, the clerk-made-narrator can but pray that "Bonne Amour" (494; cf. 406) will bring to the knight—and to all courteous lovers (498–99)—the comfort he has not thus far been able to provide.

The *Bleu chevalier* proves itself, as pseudoautobiography, to be fully text-centered and self-centered, and the narcissistic mirror-play among Froissart, his narrator, the clerk, and the Blue Knight sparkles. But, true to the genre, the dit calls into question its own status as text, as apparently autobiographical writing, because the knight, a protagonist who is the object of the clerk-narrator's gaze and his/their narrative discourse, is the one who seems to invent everything and everyone—himself, his lady, the clerk-as-poet, the narrator, their texts. Quite literally, the lunatic is in charge of the asylum.

Such textual play is paramount in the *Bleu chevalier*, and it proves worthwhile to approach the whole of the Froissartian dit in much the same light. Yet, although pseudoautobiography is a useful generic concept in exploring the textual limits of the dit, it is not self-sufficient. Heraldry and related fields such as science and medicine serve poetry and poetics both independently of pseudoautobiography and in conjunction with it. In addition to the generic features that may help define the Froissartian dit, each work has its own idiosyncratic characteristics, and some works require digging into seemingly extraliterary areas of fourteenth-century culture in order to bring fully to light the cultural literacy in terms of which the works must be read. Contemporaneous events may be one such area. This is one way that history relates to narration in Froissart's dits. In his major dits, among which we should now count the *Bleu chevalier*, Froissart exploits a serious contemporary problem of history-shaping and epoch-making dimensions—the imprisonment of princes—and turns it into a powerful metaphor for exploring the affairs of the heart and, more important, the affairs of literature.

Notes

1. Baron Kervyn de Lettenhove, *Etude littéraire sur le XIVe siècle* (Brussels, 1857), cited by Normand R. Cartier, "Le Bleu chevalier," *Romania* 87 (1966): 289–314; here p. 289.

2. F. S. Shears, *Froissart: Chronicler and Poet* (London: Routledge, 1930), pp. 193–220. The other not mentioned is *Plaidoirie de la rose et de la violette*.

3. B. J. Whiting, "Froissart as Poet," *Mediaeval Studies* 8 (1946): 189–216; here p. 201.

4. Normand Cartier, "Le Bleu chevalier" and "*Le Bleu chevalier* et le *Livre de la Duchesse*," *Romania* 88 (1967): 232–52.

5. James I. Wimsatt, "The *Dit dou Bleu Chevalier*: Froissart's Imitation of Chaucer," *Mediaeval Studies* 34 (1972): 388–400.

6. Anthime Fourrier, ed., *"Dits" et "Débats,"* by Jean Froissart (Geneva: Droz, 1979); introduction to *Le bleu chevalier,* pp. 52–62; text, pp. 155–70. This is the edition cited throughout. All translations are my own.

7. Douglas Kelly, *Medieval Imagination: Rhetoric and the Poetry of Courtly Love* (Madison: University of Wisconsin Press, 1978), pp. 182, 186.

8. Peter Ainsworth, *Jean Froissart and the Fabric of History: Truth, Myth, and Fiction in the Chroniques* (Oxford: Clarendon Press, 1990), pp. 244–45, 303.

9. Peter F. Dembowski, "Froissart," in *Medieval France: An Encyclopedia,* eds. William W. Kibler and Grover A. Zinn (New York and London: Garland, 1995), p. 376.

10. See Philip E. Bennett, "The Mirage of Fiction: Narration, Narrator, and Narrative in Froissart's Lyrico-Narrative *Dits,*" *Modern Language Review* 86 (1991): 285–97.

11. Jean Froissart, *Meliador,* ed. Auguste Longnon, 3 vols. (Paris: Firmin Didot, 1895–99): "Pour l'amour de la blewe dame / Serai li bleus errans, par m'ame" (3294–95) [For love of the Blue Lady I shall be the Blue Knight Errant, by my soul]; "On l'appelle le chevalier / Bleu, armé au cler solel d'or" (7066-67) [He is called the Blue Knight, armed with the bright golden sun] (cf. 3289–93, 3326–27, 3581, 10800). Much more frequently, however, he is known as "li chevalier au soleil d'or" (3418, 3817, ss.) ("the knight of the golden sun"). All translations mine.

12. Fourrier, *Le bleu chevalier,* introduction, 54–55. In this Fourrier was anticipated by Whiting: "We may assume that the poem was written for one of Froissart's noble friends or patrons, but there is little likelihood that the blue knight can be identified" (201).

13. Gerard J. Brault, in *Early Blazon: Heraldic Terminology in the Twelfth and Thirteenth Centuries with Special Reference to Arthurian Literature* (Oxford: Clarendon Press, 1972), defines difference as "a variation in a coat [of arms] assuring distinctiveness from related armorial bearings" (168a). This is the heraldic sense of modern French *brisure.* Significantly, the Blue Knight's arms are "sans differensce" *(Bleu chevalier,* 27) [without any difference], which Fourrier takes as meaning that they are solid blue without distinguishing marks or charges *(Bleu chevalier,* introduction, 56–57). I shall return to this matter below.

14. Guillaume de Machaut, *Le jugement du roy de Behaigne and Remede de Fortune,* ed. James I. Wimsatt and William W. Kibler (Athens: University of Georgia Press, 1988), 1863–78, 1903–4.

15. In Fourrier, *"Dits" et "Débats,"* 191–203; translations mine.

16. See John Gage, *Color and Culture: Practice and Meaning from Antiquity to Abstraction* (Boston: Little, Brown and Co., 1993), p. 83; Gage cites Louis Douët d'Arcq, "Un Traité du blazon du XVe siècle," *Revue Archéologique* 15 (1858): 324.

17. Gage cites Cicille (herald of Alphonso V, king of Aragon), *Le Blason des couleurs en armes, livrees et devises,* ed. Hippolytte-François-Jules-Marie Cocheris (Paris: A. Aubry, 1860), pp. 38ff., 56ff.

18. *Le Songe du vergier,* ed. Marion Schnerb-Lièvre, 2 vols. (Paris: Editions du C.N.R.S., 1982), bk. 1, chap. 148, §15 (vol. 1, p. 292); translation mine. Cf. *Philothei*

Achillini consiliarii regii, Somnium Viridarii, de ivrisdictione regia & Sacertodali, in Melchior Goldast, *Monarchia S. Romani Imperii siue Tractatvs de ivrisdictione imperiali* . . ., vol. 1 (Hanover: Conrad Biermann, 1611; rpt. Graz: Akademische Druck-U. Verlagsanstalt, 1960): "The next color [the third in order of nobility after gold and purple] is azure: by it is signified air, which is a diaphanous body that is very receptive to light; and it is the next noblest element after fire. The aforementioned colors are thus called more noble because of what they are opposed to [*sic*]" (chap. 133, p. 105); translation mine. Goldast wrongly attributes the 1376 Latin text to Philoteus Achillinus; it is probably by Evrart de Trémaugon (Schnerb-Lièvre, lxxxv-lxxxviii).

19. Léopold Pannier, *Les Lapidaires français du moyen âge des XIIe, XIIIe et XIVe siècles* (Paris, 1882; rpt. Geneva: Slatkine, 1973), p. 287.

20. Maurice Wilmotte, *Froissart* (1942; rpt. Brussels: Coll. Notre Passé, 1948), p. 41.

21. Danielle Jacquart and Claude Thomasset, *Sexualité et savoir médical au Moyen Age* (Paris: P.U.F, 1985), p. 68, cited hereafter as Jacquart and Thomasset.

22. *Constantini Africani Liber de coitu: El libro de andrología de Constantino el Africano,* ed. and trans. E. Montero Cartelle (Santiago de Compostella: Universitad de Santiago de Compostella, 1983), chap. 1, p. 80.

23. The translation used throughout is Paul Delany, "Constantinus Africanus' *De Coitu:* A Translation," *Chaucer Review* 4 (1970): 55–65; here p. 56.

24. Hildegard of Bingen takes up the conventional metaphor in discussing the attraction of women to sanguine men, whose eyes are like arrows: "oculi aliorum . . . velut sagittae sunt" (*Hildegardis causae et curae,* ed. Paulus Kaiser [Leipzig: B. G. Teubner, 1903], p. 72). All translations of Hildegard's text are my own.

25. "Queritur quare tanta delectatio sit in coitu?" in *The Prose Salernitan Questions,* ed. Brian R. Lawn (Oxford: Oxford University Press, 1979), pp. 10–11, cited by Jacquart and Thomasset, who translate (p. 115): "L'amour n'est rien d'autre qu'un plaisir accompagné de joie et tout plaisir surgit soit de l'extérieur, c'est-à-dire de l'âme, soit de l'intérieur, c'est-à-dire de la nature. Chacun de ces deux types de plaisir opère grâce à des instruments appropriés et au moyen de certaines parties du corps, à savoir les yeux. L'esprit que transmet le nerf optique est émis au dehors pour appréhender les choses extérieures; après avoir saisi celles-ci, il les embrasse et les représente à la partie supérieure de l'âme."

26. Cf. Constantinus Africanus, *De coitu,* chap. 2, p. 82: "When appetite arises in the liver (as we mentioned), the heart generates a spirit which descends through the arteries, fills the hollow of the penis (like a womb being filled) and makes it hard and stiff" (Delany, 56).

27. Lawn, 6, cited by Jacquart and Thomasset (197): "—les sanguins (chauds et humides) 'désirent beaucoup et peuvent beaucoup';—les cholériques (chauds et secs) 'désirent beaucoup et peuvent peu';—les flegmatiques (froids et humides) 'désirent peu et peuvent beaucoup';—les mélancoliques (froids et humides) 'désirent peu et peuvent peu'."

28. Elsewhere Hildegard discusses corresponding traits in sanguine women: "they are of a plump nature and have soft, delightful flesh and thin veins and healthy blood without impurity.... And they have clear, white faces and are under the sway of love; they are loving and adept in the arts..." (87).

29. Delany's translation is more tentative and, indeed, ambiguous. On the one hand, he reads *nimirum* as introducing an element of doubt: "must have warmth and moisture" (p. 57); this translation also implies a need. According to Lewis and Short, *A Latin Dictionary* (1879; rpt. Oxford: Clarendon Press, 1962), *nimirum* is used "to introduce an assertion as indisputable" (p. 1208a); I have not found opinions to the contrary in medieval glossaries.

30. The conventional association of the sanguine complexion with wine drinking as well as with lovemaking is summarized in the thirteenth-century verse *Regimen sanitatis salernitanum:* "By nature they [the sanguine] are plump and jolly, / they always like hearing gossip nonstop, / they like mounds of food and laughter; Venus and Bacchus love them / and make them mirthful and speakers of sweet words;" *Regola sanitaria salernitana: Regimen sanitatis salernitanum,* ed. and trans. Fulvio Gherli (Rome: Sedac, n.d.), chap. 90, p. 73; my translation.

31. The condition is described by Galen and Avicenna (Jacquart and Thomasset, 202, n.1). Jacquart and Thomasset particularly cite the *Brevarium practice,* erroneously attributed to Arnald of Villanova (1235–1313), from *Opera Arnaldi de Villanova* (Lyons: F. Fradin, 1504), f. 176v. Constantinus Africanus, citing Galen and Rufus of Ephesus in *De coitu,* mentions a particular form of madness (cf. *furia,* Jacquart and Thomasset, 202): "Rufus's opinion is that intercourse relieves harmful bodily conditions and calms madness. It is good for melancholiacs, recalls madmen to their senses, and frees lovers of their passion (provided they can lie with some other whom they desire). Thus Galen says that every wild animal is fierce before it has intercourse, but is tamer afterwards" (*De coitu,* chap. 10, pp. 126–28; Delany, 60); "Galen said that this is the cause of eunuchs' longevity. For the same reason they seem mad to anyone who talks to them, because every disturbance of the mind is calmed by the emission of semen (as we quoted Rufus), and the nature of their agitation makes their faces disordered, like their condition. Therefore we find animals to be wild before intercourse and tame afterwards" (chap. 11, p. 134; Delany, 61).

32. Two important treatises address heroic love specifically: Arnald of Villanova's *Tractatus de amore heroico* or *Epistola de amore qui dicitus heroicus,* in *Arnaldi opera,* which serves as Jacquart and Thomasset's source in *Sexualité et savoir* (also in *Opera Arnaldi omnia,* ed. Michael R. McVaugh, vol. 3 [Grenada and Barcelona: Seminarium historiae medicae granatensis, 1985], pp. 50–51), and Constantinus Africanus's *Viaticum.* See Danielle Jacquart and Claude Thomasset, "L'Amour 'héroïque' à travers le traité d'Arnaud de Villeneuve," in *La Folie et le corps,* ed. Jean Céard (Paris: Publications de l'Ecole Normale Supérieure, 1985), pp. 143–58. Constantinus's student Johannes Afflacius translated the same Arabic handbook as his master; see Mary Frances Wack, "The *Liber de heros morbo* of Johannes Afflacius and

Its Implications for Medieval Love Conventions," *Speculum* 62 (1987): 324–44, which contains a critical edition and English translation of Johannes's text (327–29), as well as an edition of the *Viaticum* (329–31). Translations from Constantinus Africanus's *Viaticum* are my own.

33. The disease is "voisin de la mélancolie" (Jacquart and Thomasset, 117).

34. In Constantinus Africanus's *Viaticum*, the association of heroic love with melancholy is much closer: "As Rufus said: Intercourse seems to help those who suffer from black bile or mania. Their sanity is restored and the heroic disturbance is removed" (Wack, 330).

35. Cf. Johannes Afflacius: "If therefore the obsessive thoughts of the patients of *heros* are not removed, they necessarily fall into melancholy" (*De coitu*; Wack, 329).

36. According to Johannes Afflacius, "their eyes are necessarily hollow and rapidly moving because of thoughts of intercourse and of the beloved; there is a great desire to smile. Their eyelids are swollen, their skin is yellow from the admixture of red bile generated by excessive wakefulness; their pulse is strong without a natural [beat] [sic]. The more the soul plunges into these sorts of thoughts, the more its actions and the body's are damaged. The body follows the soul's actions, while the soul follows the body's passions. Whence Galen said: The powers of the soul follow the complexions of the body. If therefore the excessive thoughts of the patients of *heros* are not removed, they necessarily fall into melancholy. For just as the body is seriously fatigued by hard work, so these people fall into mania from the soul's labor" (Wack, 328–29).

37. Thus Johannes Afflacius: "Rufus likewise: Wine is not the only thing that diminishes the soul's sorrow, but also temperate baths. Wherefore certain people who take temperate baths desire to hear the sweet tones of songs. Certain philosophers thus approved these tones: Music, they say, resembles the spirit, wine the body; when they are joined together sorrow must necessarily depart" (Wack, 329). In this light the knight's periodic joyful singing could be regarded as an attempt at self-healing.

38. See Danielle Jacquart, "La Maladie et le remède d'amour dans quelques écrits médicaux du Moyen Age," in *Amour, mariage et transgresions au Moyen Age: Actes du colloque des 24, 25, 26, 27 mars 1983* (Gröppingen: Kümmerle Verlag, 1984), pp. 93–101. According to certain treatises, however, patients suffering from heroic love should be shielded from that which is repulsive. Johannes Afflacius: "Nor should anything approach them that might cause revulsion" (Wack, 328); Constantinus Africanus concurs (Wack, 331).

39. Douglas Kelly, "Les Inventions ovidiennes de Froissart: Réflexions intertextuelles comme imagination," *Littérature* 41 (1981): 82–103.

40. Jean Froissart, *L'Espinette amoureuse*, ed. Anthime Fourrier (Paris: Klincksieck, 1963); subsequent translations mine.

41. Baron Kervyn de Lettenhove, ed., *Oeuvres de Froissart*, 25 vols. (1867–77; rpt. Osnabrück: Biblio Verlag, 1967), vol. 10, p. 41; translation mine.

42. Guillaume de Machaut, *Le Confort d'ami (Comfort for a Friend)*, ed. and trans.

R. Barton Palmer (New York and London: Garland, 1992), l. 1758 (of 3978, excluding the closing "Explicit").

43. Cornelis de Boer, ed., *Ovide moralisé, poème du commencement du quatorzième siècle*, Verhandelingen der Koninklijke Akademie van Wetseschappen, n.s., vols. 15.3, 21.3, 30, 37, 43 (Amsterdam, 1915–1938). At the end of book 6 (vol. 21.3), de Boer prints a virtually complete index of proper names up through that point; the list contains very few errors (see Joseph Engels, *Etudes sur l'Ovide moralisé* [Groningen: Batavia, 1945]).

44. See de Boer's introduction to vol. 1 (= 15.3) of the *Ovide moralisé* and Engels, *Etudes*, passim.

45. Ovid, *Contre Ibis*, ed. Jacques André (Paris: Les Belles Lettres, 1963), 557–58; translations mine. My thanks to Jane Phillips and Robert J. Rabel, my colleagues in the Department of Classics at the University of Kentucky, for this reference.

46. Guillaume de Lorris and Jean de Meun, *Le roman de la rose*, ed. Félix Lecoy (Paris: Champion, 1968); translations mine.

47. "... au dire voir, / Tant a li uns et l'autre de pooir / Ne sçai dou quel me puis le plus doloir" (*Bleu chevalier*, 292–94) [To tell the truth, both are so powerful that I do not know which one I can grieve about more].

48. "Qui bien regarde la matere et les fes / ... / Certainnement / En leurs vies trouvera plainnement / Que par amours amerent loyalment / Et doubloient en euls leur hardement / Par bien penser / A leurs dames de coer et de penser" (*Bleu chevalier*, 303, 310–13) [Whoever looks well into the matter and deeds (of such Arthurian knights) will surely find it amply demonstrated in their lives that they loved deeply and loyally and that they doubled their knightly valor by meditating about their ladies in their hearts and minds].

49. Similarly, the clerk fails to perceive—perhaps because the knight does not pursue the matter—the implication that the knight is imprisoned in the forest out of some sense of feudal obligation: "Et se je prenc ores ci mon sejour, / C'est en gardant ma foy et mon honnour, / Et si est pour mon naturel signour; / Si le doi faire" (121–24) [And if I now have my dwelling here, it is because I keep my faith and my honor; indeed, it is for my natural lord that I must do it]. We recall from the definitions of heroic love cited previously that lovesickness is comparable in its own way to excessive devotion to one's overlord.

50. Laurence de Looze, "'Pseudo-autobiography' and the Body of Poetry in Guillaume de Machaut's *Remede de Fortune*," *L'Esprit Créateur* 33 (1993): 73–86; Laurence de Looze, *"Corpus Poetae": A Study of the Pseudo-Autobiography in the Fourteenth Century* (Gainesville: University Press of Florida, 1997).

51. William W. Kibler, "Self-Delusion in Froissart's *Espinette amoureuse*," *Romania* 97 (1976): 77–98; here p. 82.

52. Michel Zink, "Le temps, c'est l'argent: remarques sur le *Dit du florin* de Jean Froissart," in *"Et c'est la fin pour quoy sommes ensemble": Hommage à Jean Dufournet*, ed. Jean-Claude Aubailly et al., vol. 3 (Paris: Champion, 1993), 1455–64; here p. 1455.

53. William W. Kibler, "Poet and Patron: Froissart's *Prison amoureuse*," *L'Esprit Créateur* 18 (1978): 32–46.

54. "Lors me cognut et aussi fis je li, / Si me nomma. / Et quant je vi que c'ert ce seignour la, / Esbahis fui; . . . / Partir me voc" (211–15) [Then he recognized me and I did him, and he named me. And when I saw that it was *that* lord, I was dumbfounded; . . . I made to leave].

55. ". . . Amis, / Li bien venus soiiés, car je sui fis, / Puis qu'aventure et Dieux vous ont ci mis, / Qu'il m'avendront et consauls et proufis / De vo venue" (216–20) [Friend, you are welcome, for I am sure, since chance and God have brought you here, that counsel and benefit will come to me from your coming].

56. "Li chevaliers, qui en tres grant anoi / Avoit esté, / Ouvri ses yex, s'a .I. souspir jetté, / En souspirant m'a .I. peu regardé" [The knight, who had been in very great distress, opened his eyes, let out a sigh and, sighing, looked at me for a while](187–90).

57. "En ce regart pris je si grant pité / Qu'il me souvint / Dou temps passé dont changier me couvint. / Mes, Dieu merci, .I. brief confort me vint, / Qui de monstrer toutes doulours m'abstint / Tant qu'en present" [And in that look, such great pity overcame me that I remembered the time past when I was subject to change. But, thanks be to God, a timely comfort came to me which made me to stop showing signs of all kinds of grief down to the present day] (191–96).

58. Here masculine (but "une complainte," feminine [1554]).

59. To introduce poems composed by the knight, Froissart uses the same verbs that introduce texts that his clerk-poets compose and sing in the *Paradis amoureus* and the *Espinette amoureuse:* "faire" (45), "dire" (70). Cf. "dire" (*Paradis amoureus*, 74, 845, 1417, 1626); "faire" (*Paradis amoureus*, 886, 1078; *Espinette*, 919–26, 1019, 2435).

60. "Or vous prommec, chiers sire, loyalment / Que je ferai le dittié ensement / Comme j'en ai matere et sentement / Et pourpos vrai" (461–64) [Now I promise you faithfully, dear sir, that I will make the dit, according to how I have the matter, the sentiment, and the true subject]. On love as the poetic *sentement* par excellence, the inspiration for singing and writing, see Kelly, *Medieval Imagination*, 245–48.

III

Verse Romance and Poetic Renewal

8

Meliador and the Inception of a New Poetic Sensibility

MICHEL ZINK

Why did Froissart write *Meliador*?[1] Why compose an Arthurian verse romance when none had been written for a century? That question remains open, and the more we learn about Froissart, the less sufficient seems the traditional, apparently convincing answer we are tempted to give. Regardless of how we formulate it, that answer is based, more or less explicitly, on an analysis of Froissart's character, opinions, tastes, and the company he kept. He was conservative minded, given to nostalgia, a rather bedazzled admirer of the splendor, glory, and values of chivalry; he was a man of letters trained at the English court. That milieu over the course of the thirteenth century had ceased to launch or even to follow literary trends and, having become conservative in that regard, had remained faithful, much longer than did the Continent, precisely to the tradition of Arthurian verse romance, as Beate Schmolke-Hasselmann has shown.[2] Elsewhere I have suggested that Froissart's *Chroniques* are inspired by the model of romance and that they appropriate that genre's mode of creating meaning and its outlook on prowess and chivalric values.[3] Yet the *Chroniques* are in prose, and their immediate model in terms of romance is the prose romance. This suggests a kind of translation of the significance of verse romance into that of prose romance and thence to that of history, at which point the verse romance would be no more than an empty shell, devoid of significance. Of course Froissart envisaged no such development; it simply comes to mind from the way in which he conceptualizes literary forms and the relations among them. Hence *Meliador*'s relative *insignificance* in the wake of the *Chroniques*. So why retrieve that empty shell? Why would Froissart have wanted to renew a tradition that he himself had done so much to render obsolete?

There are other possible objections to the hypothesis that *Meliador* is a product of nostalgic conservatism. It was written in the 1380s and perhaps revised later on if, as I suggest elsewhere, Camel de Camois's somnambulism was inspired by that of Pierre de Béarn and was absent from the version read before Gaston Phébus in 1388.[4] By that time, Froissart is no longer the young newcomer to England from his native Hainaut, fascinated by the court of his compatriot Queen Philippa and by the flattering stories he heard from veterans of the Franco-English wars. He no longer really believes that these wars mark the advent of chivalry and its opportunity to act out the dream of romance. With growing lucidity, he sees through the chivalric posturing. His *Chroniques* display an outlook that is increasingly analytic, critical, free of illusions. As an early work, *Meliador* would harmonize with what we can guess about Froissart's attitudes during those years. As a work of his later maturity or early old age, the romance is more dissonant.

Rather, it would seem so were it not for the research that has put it into perspective. Years ago, Armel Diverres's articles demonstrated how *Meliador*'s geography grew from Froissart's personal recollections, its world being an imaginary elaboration based on them rather than being a transposition of contemporary political events—which are by no means absent, however—or a resurrection of the traditional Arthurian world.[5] This view agrees with the state of mind of an aging Froissart during the decade between 1385 and 1395, as well as with the prologue to book 4 of the *Chroniques* and the last journey to England. In addition, the valuable and enlightening study by Peter Dembowski, the first monograph devoted to *Meliador*, brings out the role of the crusades, and especially of the Prussian Crusade, as a justification of chivalry.[6] That too corresponds to Froissart's broadening political and strategic outlook at the end of his career. But none of this explains why *Meliador* is a verse Arthurian romance.

The paradox has its limits: While it would indeed be difficult to deny that *Meliador* is a verse romance, I would like to suggest here that it is not an Arthurian romance. At the very least, the nature of this work is such that we cannot perceive it as an anachronistic resurrection of the Arthurian verse romance. Rather than launch out in search of some elusive organizational scheme, let me begin with a look at the prologue—or rather the double prologue. On the one hand, Dembowski has observed that the first forty-three lines comprise a prologue, in the conventional sense of that term, that had not been identified as such because it is not set apart by the manuscript's majuscules and because Lognon's dense, lengthy analysis of the romance makes no mention of it. On the other hand, the first twenty-four hundred–odd verses could be considered a kind of vast prologue, in the same way that Calogrenant's adventure serves as a prologue to Yvain's exploits, the principal subject of the *Chevalier au lion*. Camel de Camois's importunate love for Hermondine, which provides the subject matter of the initial *Meliador* episode, prompts Florée, Hermondine's cousin, to conceive the stratagem of asking King Arthur to organize a five-year quest whose victor will win the hand of the princess of Scotland. This quest is the very subject of the romance. Camel plays hardly any role in it at all, as he reappears only to be immediately killed, and that occurs among the earliest episodes. In addition, the real opening of the romance—one in the tradition of Arthurian romance—occurs not in the initial verses but rather when King Arthur holds his spring court and projects a tournament at Pentecost at which the young Meliador will be awarded knighthood. While holding court, King Arthur receives the Scottish ambassadors and grants their king's request to organize the quest conceived by Florée:

> Li rois Artus, qui fu toutdis
> En fais, en oevres et en dis
> Larges, courtois, et tres vaillans,
> Et en festes tenir poissans,
> En volt une en ce temps tenir. (2452–56)

[King Arthur, who was ever generous, courtly and most worthy, in deeds, works, and speech, and well accoutred to hold festive assemblies, wished to sponsor one on that occasion.] (translations by D. Maddox unless otherwise indicated)

Here we have an Arthurian opening, though as late as l. 2452. Let us return to the first line, where we do indeed find an Arthurian reference, though in a less traditional setting. We learn that the action takes place at the beginning of Arthur's reign:

> En ce temps que li rois Artus
> Qui tant fu plains de grans vertus,
> De sens, d'onneur et de larghece,
> Regnoit au point de sa jonece,
> Et qu'il commençoit a tenir
> Grans festes et a retenir
> Chevaliers pour emplir ses sales. (1–7)

[At that time, when King Arthur, who was well endowed with noble qualities—discernment, honor and largesse—still reigned in the prime of his youth and was beginning to mount lavish festivities and retain knights to swell his assemblies.]

There is nothing particularly extraordinary here. A common device in the late romances is to renew the Arthurian material by returning to its origins: to its prehistory in *Perceforest;* to King Arthur's youth in *Le Chevalier au papegau.* At the opening of *Meliador,* set ten years prior to the illustrious exploits of the classical Arthurian heroes, Froissart says there was even then no dearth of handsome feats of chivalry:

Environ ou .IX. ans ou .X.,
Avant que li preus Lanselos,
Melyadus, ne li rois Los,
Guirons, Tristrans ne Galehaus,
Gauwains, Yewains, ne Perchevaus,
Ne chil de la Table Reonde
Fuissent cogneü en ce monde,
Ne que de Merlin on euist
Cognoissance, ne c'on seuist
Nulle riens de ses prophesies,
Plusieurs belles chevaleries
Avinrent en la Grant Bretaigne. (28–39)

[Around nine or ten years before the bold Lancelot, Melyadus, or King Lot, Guiron, Tristran, or Galehaut, Gauvain, Yvain, or Perceval and they of the Round Table were known to the world, and ere anyone had heard of Merlin or any of his prophecies, many handsome feats of chivalry occurred in Great Britain.]

Yet these notations frame something quite different. They merely indicate that the inception of the Arthurian era coincides with the events that are about to be related. We cited from the first sentence only the subordinate, temporal clause that opens it. Let us look at the succeeding lines:

En ce temps que li rois Artus
. . . .
Avoit en le marce de Galles,
Entre Escoce et Northombrelande,
Priés dou lac c'on dist de Berlande,
.I. chastiel moult fort et moult cointe

Seant doucement sus le point[e]
D'un hault rocier et d'un grant bois.
Chils castiaus fu nommés Camois
Et le sire qui le tenoit
Messires Camelz se nommoit. (1–16)

[At that time, when King Arthur. . . . In the Welsh borderlands, between Scotland and Northumberland, near the lake known as Berlande, there was a well fortified, very charming castle, poised gently atop a craggy summit flanked by dense woods. This castle was called Camois and the lord who held it was named Sir Camel.]

Likewise, further on in the second passage cited, the inventory of future Arthurian heroes provides only a temporal reference. Ten years before they earn renown, Great Britain has already witnessed *plusieurs belles chevaleries* (38). To this Froissart adds:

En ce temps avoit en Escoce
.I. roy qui fu moult vaillans homs.
Chilz rois fu appellés Hermons. (44–46)

[At that time in Scotland there was a king, a most worthy man. The name of this monarch was Hermond.]

These verses lead us from the prologue into the narrative proper. In reality, however, they relate to the evocation of Arthurian heroes in a way that is symmetrical with the earlier presentation of Camel de Camois in relation to the youth of King Arthur. That reference to the great monarch is mere window dressing that conceals a sudden shift of emphasis. Arthur is mentioned from the very first verse, but only in order to assert that our story takes place at a time when he was not yet established and the universe to which he lent his name had yet to be constructed. This projection into a past even more remote than the great Arthurian era is reinforced by an interesting remark in lines 20–27, truly the observation of a historian, concerning the progress of agriculture and living conditions since that remote age. *Meliador* thus purports to be an Arthurian romance, yet boasts not a single Arthurian character, except for Sagremor, whose *enfances* comprise a lengthy parenthesis within the romance—a long "entr'acte," according to Peter Dembowski's apposite formulation.

Furthermore, the opening context is not that of the court of Arthur, not even of his kingdom; we find ourselves in Scotland and "in the Welsh borderlands, between Scotland and Northumberland." Here again, we find nothing particularly new: the *Conte du Graal* opens in Wales, *Lancelot* in Gaul, *Escanor* in Northumbria. In this case, however, remoteness from the Arthurian hearth will endure; indeed, it will never cease. In addition, as noted, the opening verses introduce the character of Camel, yet the story begins thirty lines later on, with the presentation of the king of Scotland, Hermond. Moreover, Hermond disappears immediately, at least temporarily, eclipsed by his brother-in-law, his daughter, and his niece. In what ensues, Camel and the young ladies are brought together in a long curtain-raiser of some twenty-five hundred lines preceding the anticipated scene at the court of King Arthur. At the outset, then, we find a sort of mystification concerning the true subject and the real heroes of the romance, a drift, an uncertainty about what should be the center of attention, a blurring of the focal point.

As for the opening episode itself, it clearly has nothing of the Arthurian about it. In no way does it resemble the type of narrative we are accustomed to reading in the Breton romances, having no young knight whose character takes shape and who makes a name for himself through feats of arms, no itinerance, not even any adventures that could be called chivalrous. No hero either, rather an antihero, who—yet another bit of window dressing—initially elicits the reader's sympathy, then quickly becomes a negative character. Yet the same thing could be said about the opening of the Prose *Lancelot*. Claudas is like Camel, an ambiguous character who vanishes early in the romance.

In contrast, it is very striking that in *Meliador* this first episode, or long prologue, is close in situations and style to those found elsewhere in Froissart's poetry, for example, in the way he portrays a man alone and tormented by two young ladies. Camel de Camois is perhaps in the wrong for his somnambulism, and then he certainly undermines his case seriously by attempting to conquer Hermondine by force, while taking umbrage at Florée's father and odiously resorting to blackmail. Be that as it may, how can we not feel sorry, initially at least, for this poor soul, who is at first so well received, to his utter delight, by two ravishing maidens; who then falls madly in love with one of them, yet is embarrassed by the inadmissible infirmity that compels him to decline their invitation to spend the night in their castle. And then, the minute he turns his back, one of his hostesses, who is not in the least deceived by his excuse, rushes off to reveal his secret to the one he loves and warn her against him.

The poet Froissart returns often to this sort of situation, one that is simultaneously so troubling and yet so exciting, gratifying though frustrating, and finally so humiliating, when the attentions of a group of young ladies focus on the male narrator, though in such a way as to give him the impression that he is the object of their carefully premeditated ridicule. In Froissart's first major narrative *dit, Le paradis d'amour*, we find the narrator at odds with the two charming women he encountered in his dream, Plaisance and Esperance, who chastise him so severely that he is compelled to apologize.[7] The best examples, perhaps, are those in *La prison amoureuse*.[8] During a celebration where ladies are taking turns singing, the narrator is distraught to hear the *virelai* he composed for his beloved, who had learned it by heart, being sung, quite well in fact, by a young woman in whom he has no interest, while the one he adores prefers to sing something else (273–534). Farther on we find a remarkable anecdote. Here I invoke Anthime Fourrier's analysis of this passage, which is admirably discussed from another perspective by Jacqueline Cerquiglini-Toulet.[9]

> Un jour que, pour se détendre, le poète chevauche à proximité du manoir où réside la dame de ses pensées, il apprend qu'elle est allée en promenade avec d'autres "damoiselles." Il porte dans une petite sacoche de soie blanche attachée à sa ceinture les lettres et les poésies que lui a envoyées Rose. Arrivé à l'endroit où se délassent les jeunes filles, il est accueilli fort aimablement: on l'installe dans le groupe, on rit, on badine, et l'une d'elles, d'accord avec les autres, lui dérobe adroitement le contenu de son "aloiiere." Leurs rires étouffés et leurs conciliabules les dénoncent, Froissart s'aperçoit du larcin, supplie qu'on lui rende son bien et finit par le ravoir à condition qu'en guise de rançon, elles aient les chansons pour en prendre copie, tandis qu'on lui laissera les lettres. En souvenir de ce bon moment passé auprès de sa belle, le poète compose un virelai, qu'il serre dans un coffret fabriqué de ses mains.[10]

> [One day when, for relaxation, the poet is riding near the manor where the lady of his musings resides, he learns that she has gone for an outing with other "damsels." In a little white silk hunter's sack fastened to his belt, he is carrying the letters and poems Rose sent to him. When he arrives at the place where the young ladies are enjoying themselves, he is welcomed most warmly: they take him into the group; they laugh, make small talk, and, with the others' consent, one of the tittering ladies deftly relieves him of the contents of his hunting sack ("aloiiere"). Their stifled laughter and whispered asides give them away. Froissart becomes aware of the theft, begs

them to return his possessions and finally gets them back, on condition that, as a ransom, they may have the *chansons* to copy, while leaving him the letters. To commemorate this fine moment spent in the company of his lady, the poet composes a virelai that he encloses in a coffer he made with his own hands.]

A fine moment indeed,[11] but only because the poet, overjoyed at having seen his fair lady, and in such a pleasant mood, chooses to perceive it as such. The joke is nonetheless indiscreet, rather cruel, and the high humor is at his expense.

Similar scenes are found in the other dits. In an example from *L'espinette amoureuse*,[12] the narrator repeatedly encounters his lady in public and tries to arrange a private conversation that would further his suit. Or, especially illustrative, near the end of *Le joli buisson de Jonece*, during the game of *pince merine*, the narrator is "it" ("s'y colle")—to use an infantile and outmoded expression so appropriate for this game—and thus finds himself in the situation of both hero and victim, target and whipping boy: He is unable to resign himself to being led inside the circle of players, his lady among them, but finally agrees and, in keeping with the rules of the game, is pushed, pulled, and shoved every which way, by all of the lads—and ladies—much to his delight.[13]

In the opening of *Meliador*, other details recall Froissart's poetry. The hunt, for example, is a motif that certainly belongs to the world of romance, wherein the sylvan pursuit and encounter with an animal that draws the hunter toward his destiny—notably his amorous destiny (for not all hunters are Saint Eustache)—figures frequently. Likewise, the motif occurs later in *Meliador*, even among the adventures of Sagremor, where in a surprising variant Sagremor is riding the stag (28412–68). As for the association of hunting and somnambulism that links *Meliador* and book 3 of the *Chroniques*, I discuss this elsewhere.[14] The treatment of the motif nonetheless recalls Froissart's poetry, via the mythological reminiscences that proliferate in his works, in this instance via the myth of Acteon: The stag leads the hunter to the fateful discovery of feminine beauty. The story of Acteon is either evoked or developed at length several times in Froissart's works: in the *Chroniques*, where Froissart assumes that the speaking bear encountered by Pierre de Béarn might have been a knight victimized by a metamorphosis similar to Acteon's; in *Le joli buisson de Jonece* (2242–60); in *L'espinette amoureuse* (2807–21), where the transformation is curiously confused with that of Cephalus and Procris.[15] In terms of stylistic affinities, occasionally close, the story of Camel's hunt at the beginning of *Meliador* is related to the hunt of Acteon in *Le joli buisson de Jonece*. For example:

Meliador, ll. 127–32	*Buisson*, ll. 2248–53
Li cers s'en fuit, Camelz le cace,	Li cers fuit, Acteon apriés,
Qui onques n'en perdi la trace.	Qui le sieuoit bien et de priés.
Les bois passe, et apriés la lande	Il a passé les bois menus,
Et les plains de Northombrelande.	Ens es landes s'en est venus.
Courant s'en vient Camelz apr[i]és	Acteons le sieuoit encor,
Jusques a l'estanc de Montgriés.	Qui d'ivore portoit un cor.

[*Meliador:* The stag takes flight. Camel pursues, never losing its trail. It passes through the woods, then the heath, and onto the plains of Northumbria. Camel comes running after, as far as the pond at Montgriés.] [*Buisson:* The stag flees before Acteon, in hot pursuit. It crosses the dense woods, comes onto the heath, Acteon still in pursuit, carrying an ivory horn.]

Froissart is a remarkable versifier. He writes with a rapidity and a density surprising in such a prolix author, with fluidity and precision, yet without apparent effort or padding. His style is elegant, easily capturing a sight or sound in a fleeting detail, without becoming entangled in descriptive complexities, as in his evocation of Camel's castle, "Seant doucement sus le pointe / D'un hault rocier et d'un grant bois." [Poised gently atop a craggy summit flanked by dense woods.]

Further on, Meliador, concerned with preserving his anonymity in the tournament at La Garde, sets up his quarters: "En .I. bois desous le chastiel / Ou vert faisoit, ombru et biel" (6565–66). [In the woods below the castle, where it was verdant, shady and fair.] There is certainly nothing new about this sort of locus in medieval poetry, but who else could say that "il faisait vert et ombreux" [it was verdant and shady]? Then, too, this style has a certain elegiac quality that, even in strictly narrative passages, differs noticeably from the habitual manner of romance, the more so in the depictions of Camel's pathetic bantering ("marivaudage") with the two cousins. This style finds its precursors and models in Machaut, and before that in Jean de Condé or Watriquet de Couvin, much more than among the authors of romance. In sum, it is a style, not surprisingly, of its own age, typical of the verse produced by good writers during the fourteenth century.

From Froissart's own travels, there are the geographic, topographic, and toponymic details (like the very name of Camel's castle) with which he sprinkles—indeed, nourishes—his romance, blending them with an imaginary, specifically literary, toponymy, like the two castles where Hermondine and Florée live in turn, Montgriés (Montgrief), where they are in danger, and Montségur, where they are secure, not to mention Montrose, whose charming lady Meliador rescues. These recollections harmonize Froissart's fictive universe with his own sensibility; they make it an outgrowth of his own life, so that it partakes of the autobiographical tendencies that recur throughout his historical writings and poetry and ultimately lend them all a kind of unity.

These sentimental subtleties and stylistic traits are not confined to the first episode; they emerge throughout the romance. In fact, the mention of Montségur and Montrose occurs well beyond the opening. Such observations pertain to the work as a unified whole, and as Peter Dembowski has clearly demonstrated, they are confirmed by its comprehensive organization. He calls it a composition in four "acts" separated by "entr'actes." Each act is centered by one of the four tournaments that comprise the ordeals of the quest, in which the victor is to receive the hand of Hermondine: the tournament at La Garde organized by King Arthur; the one at Tarbonne organized by the duke of Cornwall, Patris, Meliador's father (which Meliador is prevented from attending); the one at Sigaudon organized by Hermond, the king of Scotland, Hermondine's father; and the one at Monchus, jointly sponsored by Arthur and Hermond. The first entr'acte is made up essentially of Meliador's exploits while rescuing the lady of Montrose, a mission interrupted by the tournament of Tarbonne and his visit, disguised as a merchant, to Hermondine and Florée at the castle of Montségur. The second entr'acte follows the progress of Agamanor's love for Phénonée and of Hermondine's for Meliador. In the third we find Agamanor painting Phénonée's portrait. Framing these entr'actes are the opening prologue, detailing Camel's problems with Hermondine and her cousin, and Sagremor's adventures at the end of the work.

This construction, though generally simple despite a welter of details that can be confusing, offers one quite remarkable feature: The entr'actes, far from being simple interludes between the acts, are in fact what is essential, while the acts themselves serve as little more than the thread that ties them together. The "quest" launched by King Arthur at the suggestion of the king of Scotland is not in fact a quest. In no way does it exact the commitment of the whole being, since not one of the questers except Agamanor has the least sentimental inclination toward Hermondine.

This quest has nothing of the unexpected or mysterious; its objective is clearly designated, its phases and ordeals well defined. It is a championship based on a point system, the goal being to determine a winner at the end of a series of four tournaments. Judging by these standards, the world championship of Formula One racers or the Davis Cup could just as well be called a quest. We find nothing really exciting here, nor anything that corresponds to the spirit of Arthurian romance.

Is this the sign of the genre's impoverishment? Of Froissart's inability to breathe back into it the life it had two centuries earlier? Is it a sign that the "romanesque" has lost its meaning, as suggested earlier? If so, such impoverishment and loss result from Froissart's lack of real interest in the genre of romance. He chooses a minimal plot that seems insipidly transparent when reduced to its essential features, and he develops it with a mechanical kind of clarity: The characters make their entries one after another, while interlacing allows movement from one to the other according to a rigid kind of automatism. Each character advances meekly to take his appointed place within an utterly predictable hierarchy and conveniently falls in love with the woman of his destiny, while carefully avoiding any amorous connection with the woman reserved for his predecessor or follower. Froissart describes combat with an applied virtuosity in which sense of duty and knowledge of set pieces are more in evidence than inspiration. He renews combat scenes simply by showing the hero, after the traditional battle to a draw, winning bare-handed at fisticuffs, seizing his opponent and strangling him, flattening him on his horse in a deft and savage maneuver—in short, by turning him into a championship wrestler or sumo star.[16] This quality—perhaps merely the result of striving for varied and precise accounts of combat, a tendency observable from the thirteenth century on—is apparent in other contemporary romances, though less consistently. Rarely noted in traditional romance is yet another detail in *Meliador*, concerning security measures during tournaments: Froissart specifies that at La Garde the ladies summoned a large number of peasants to lift up the fallen knights.[17] This is all very amusing, and we know that it was of the utmost interest to readers during this period.[18] Yet it all hardly suffices to break the monotony of an excessively symmetrical structure. With a skill that is rather mechanical, Froissart applies the laws and formulas of the genre, touching them up here and there with minute innovations. His rather arid technical mastery and excessively tidy and predictable framework would, if the work were restricted to them alone, justify seeing it as merely a stylistic anachronism based entirely on its apparent model, the Arthurian romance.

However, such is not the case with the entr'actes, in which Froissart's talent and originality come to the fore. *Meliador* acquires renewed depth when we change perspective and bring the entr'actes out of the shadows and into the foreground. We then realize that the central plot, far from being essential, has no other purpose than to introduce and coordinate them, just as the main theme of a variety show or music hall extravaganza is merely a pretext and a unifying thread. While the acts are but necessary transitions and sutures, the entr'actes are the vital moments. In other words, the acts are in fact the entr'actes, and vice-versa.

To a reader who approaches this work without preconceived notions and who allows its dense overgrowth to conceal—fortunately, all things considered—its extremely simple construction, it appears to be an accumulation of stories, each based on a sentimental problem. All Arthurian romances are certainly made of an assortment of stories. But in *Meliador* it is as if all were like the adventure of Gauvain and the maid of Escalot: the tale of Camel, his obscure affliction, his violent and inept love, brutal and doomed; of Meliador the merchant and Hermondine's ring; of Agamanor the artist and Phénonée's portrait; of the latter's passionate and ambiguous infatuation for this hero in whom she thinks she sees her brother, an attraction that is the beginning of something inadmissible.[19] The same is true of Meliador's interrupted itinerary, the happenstances and delays that prevent him from achieving banal renown in the tournament of Tarbonne while ensuring him the excitement and spice of a visit incognito to Hermondine. Then there is the oneiric and marvelous encounter of Sagremor and Sibylle, whose outcome we will never know, alas! By virtue of these episodes—whose worth is in the nuances of sentiment, the bittersweet savor of light-hearted gallantry ("marivaudage"), and the distractions of heart and mind—*Meliador* becomes a collection of dits. It is not analogous to the Arthurian romances of the twelfth and thirteenth centuries but rather is a romance in the spirit of verse narratives of the fourteenth century, a sentimental narration whose fine thread produces a rather loosely woven succession of generic scenes. In sum, beneath its apparent anachronism, it is a work perfectly in the spirit of its time.

The unifying factor is certainly Arthurian, not autobiographical. The episodes do pertain to various characters, not to the author. Otherwise, however, echoes of Froissart's poetry are everywhere in evidence, not merely in the prologue. The wretched Camel is not the only one who must cope with the machinations of two young ladies. Florée never leaves Hermondine, nor Lucienne Phénonée. Meliador and Agamanor, too, although under more favorable circumstances, are always dealing with two cousins, with their complicity, their little ruses, their scheming. Sagremor's dream (ll. 28605–754), in the part of the romance undoubtedly closest to Arthurian models, is characteristic of the poetry of that period and contains analogies with several passages in Froissart's dits.

Sagremor is mounted on a stag that carries him through the forest to a lake. There is a lacuna in the manuscript at this point. When the text resumes, Sagremor is lost in a dream, in which Sibylle, we are given to understand, has just sung him a virelai that condemns gossips. Sagremor seizes the moment in order to emphasize his amatory discretion, and his move allows the literary conversation to drift into amatory topics. At the young man's insistence, Sibylle sings a rondeau, and she begs him to sing one of his own virelais, which she praises. Then she disappears. Sagremor is so overwhelmed that he awakens and finds himself alone in an unknown place.

There is no question of taking up the erotic dream in general here, for in doing so we would have to consider all the poetry of that period. Be it noted, however, that throughout the account of this dream, not merely at the beginning (which is in fact missing) and the end, the author is careful to remind us that this is only a dream and an illusion. He does this implicitly, by systematic usage of the imperfect (the tense for narrating dreams), and explicitly, by recourse at intervals to formulae like *En dormant, ce li estoit vis* [While sleeping, it seemed to him] (l. 28605); *Ce li estoit avis encor* [Again it seemed to him] (l. 28692); *Or sambloit il a Saigremor* [Then it seemed to Sagremor] (l. 28734). Awakened, Sagremor wonders: "Et n'ay jou veü Sebilete / Et oÿ canter la doucete? / Oïl voir, mais en dormant fu" (28752–54). [And have I not seen Sebilete and heard that sweet little one sing? Yea, in truth, but while sleeping 'twas.]

Emphasis on a dream that is gratifying, yet also painful precisely because it is a dream, is what we find in *L'espinette amoureuse*, through the momentary magic of the recovered portrait. Banished, betrayed, exiled, the lover dreams of his cruel lady as if she were so loving, consoling, and warm that upon awakening he decides to return to her, where of course only disappointment awaits him. This is also the essential plot of *Le joli buisson de Jonece*, where the elderly poet becomes young again in his dream and finds his cherished lady just as she had been a decade earlier. Though she is as yet indecisive, her inclinations are evidently more favorable and more auspicious than ever before. But dreams seldom keep their promises, and they last but a single night. Though this motif is shopworn, only Froissart can capture that sense of illusory, wrenching euphoria found in dreams.

In Sagremor's dream, moreover, poems and chansons play a role often attributed to them in Foissart's poetry, that of the sentimental prelude and pretext for a conversation that one hopes will turn to love. Both *L'espinette amoureuse* and *La prison amoureuse* provide numerous examples. In addition, poems and chansons are objects, though not simply in terms of the materiality of writing and transcription, as Jacqueline Cerquiglini has in fact shown.[20] They have a reality and a tension by which they become, literally, sentimental relics. Thus, upon awakening, Sagremor remembers the chansons of his dream; they hold him momentarily before an imaginary landscape. With reference to the *Chroniques,* Lucien Foulet has shown that in Froissart the imagination is not tinged with unreality but that it has the precision of intellectual projections and constructs based on reality and in conformity with it.[21] The chansons do not extend dream into daydream. On the contrary, they allow Sagremor to renew contact with reality, to locate its continuity and remember it, to recognize for what it is the illusion he has just experienced. The chansons help to construct a life:

> Et Saigremor, a son depart,
> Estoit tellement krouciés
> Que dou courous est esvilliés.
> Adont regarde autour de li,
> Ne nul ne nulle n'i oÿ;
> Se ne scet qu'il die ne face,
> Ne apriés quoi il se solace.
> Adont au devant li reviennent
> Les cançons, qui .I. temps le tiennent
> En imagination grande.
> A par soy devise e demande:
> "Et n'ay jou veü Sebilete
> Et oÿ canter la doucete?
> Oïl voir, mais en dormant fu.
> Maintenant ne sceit mies u
> Un cers m'a mis et aporté" (28741–56)

[And Sagremor, upon leaving, was so distraught that his distress awakened him. Glancing all around, he heard neither lad nor lady, knew not what to say or do, nor from what he might take comfort. Then, there before him, the chansons returned and for awhile held him spellbound. To himself he muses, wondering: "And have I not seen Sebilete and heard that sweet little one sing? Yea, in truth, but while sleeping 'twas. Now who knows where this stag has led and left me?]

By choosing to insert into *Meliador* the mediocre poems of Wenceslas of Luxembourg rather than others—rather than his own—Froissart was clearly behaving in courtly fashion. Yet in principle, the insertion of lyrics into a work is not a superfluous kind of ornamentation. As objects, poems lend poise to a romance by providing it with the very core of sentimental life. They indicate that the amatory imagination, that is, the mind's dynamic engagement with love, is its authentic subject, and that if *Meliador* is a romance, it is a romance of amatory situations. They make of *Meliador* a vast dit invested with lyrics.

I can anticipate the objection that might be raised here. The kind of analysis I have sketched could be applied just as well to certain poems inserted into the Prose *Tristan* and elsewhere, so commonplace was the procedure during that period. As for rapprochements with the motifs and situations in the poetry of the period, they can be found also in *Ysaÿe le Triste* and *Perceforest*, for example. In this regard, *Meliador* is linked with a tradition that belongs to Arthurian (as well as to pre- or post-Arthurian) prose romance, as it survives, indeed thrives, at the end of the Middle Ages. But *Meliador* is in verse. Froissart, who certainly was not loath to writing in prose, chose for *Meliador* a medium of expression that immediately makes us aware of his indebtedness to contemporary poetry, one that, moreover, constitutes a full-fledged exemplar of that poetry.

To emphasize what *Meliador* owes to the tradition of Breton romance would mean underlining its kinship with its closest Arthurian precursor, though older by a century, the *Escanor* of Girart d'Amiens. We find there not merely the mellifluous names, with their identical endings, of the two eponymous heroes, not merely lyric insertions, though *Escanor* contains fewer in number than *Meliador*, but more significant affinities as well. First, in the spirit of Beate Schmolke Hasselmann's book and the article she devoted to the two romances,[22] one thinks of the "pro-English" type of political significance that Arthurian romance in both cases assumes. As for *Escanor*, dedicated to Eleanor of Castille, queen of Edward I, this aspect has been well covered by Richard Trachsler.[23] *Meliador* certainly dates from a period in which Froissart's ties with the English court had weakened, but the heart of Queen Philippa's former protégé always remained in the land of his auspicious beginnings, both in the world itself and in the world of letters. Then, too, that he was mindful in writing it for an English public is evident from the praise he lavishes on English noblewomen.[24]

This is nonetheless a very general point. Others, finer, are all the more telling. Consider the role played by Northumbria. Or the taste for anachronistic writing, or the special way in which the romance places itself on the margins of the Arthurian universe—just as Northumbria lies at the extremities of Arthurian geography. Camel de Camois, who appears first, will not be the hero in *Meliador* and will in fact be an adversary of the heroes, who are not knights of the Round Table, for the action takes place before its foundation. Escanor, who lends his name to that romance, is nonetheless not really the hero (that would be Kay, rather)—and is an enemy of Arthur. A tournament will decide who is to marry Andrivete, as the tournaments determine who wins the hand of Hermondine. Although Froissart is a much better poet than Girart d'Amiens, the two romances share a common predilection for amatory dialogues. They also display a similar taste for sentimental intrigues and treat them with an elegiac kind of indulgence that brings them into prominence and makes them stand out, to the detriment of the rather pedestrian military and chivalric skirmishes.

Yet these characteristics suggest that the lyric propensities of verse romance, so apparent in *Meliador*, are already present in *Escanor*. However, the resemblances between the two works suggest that *Meliador* is less related to the old tradition of Arthurian verse romance, to which *Escanor* remains more faithful, than it is merely associated with the general evolution of that tradition. Here, as is the case of its affinities with contemporary poetry—particularly with the poetry of its author—*Meliador* is less eccentric than it appears to be at first blush, provided that we not perceive it primarily as a Breton romance.

Initially, Froissart presents the subject matter of his *Chroniques* as an extension into contemporaneous reality of the chivalrous exploits of yore that provide the subject matter of romance. From this perspective, *Meliador* would seem to maintain a kind of continuity with the *Chroniques*, that of chivalric narrative. This is indeed the case, up to a certain point: Consistent geographical and topographical references cause the Arthurian world to resonate with the expeditions of Edward III and Richard II in Scotland or Ireland; the chronicler habitually quotes addresses to the army and pays homage to the deeds of the most stalwart, which, when transposed by the romancer in his laborious descriptions of the tournaments, produce such formulas as "Ce n'est pas drois que je me taise / Des proeces Melyador" (6688–89). [It is not fitting that I keep silent about Meliador's mighty deeds.] Or again:

> D'autre part est Agamanor
> ....
> De lui doient bien escriptures
> Estre faites et recordees. (6715–21)

[Over there is Agamanor. . . . Writings must be composed and set down about him.]

But if this continuity had been foremost in Froissart's mind, *Meliador* would be a prose romance. As a poem, much more than being aligned with the *Chroniques*, the work resonates with Froissart's personal poetry; it is more suggestive of narrated personal emotions than of chivalric narrative. Whether the self sponsors the "I" of the poem or that of a character, the resonance obviously changes very little. The effusiveness of the Bleu Chevalier in the dit by that title, or of the Bleu Chevalier who is Meliador, is no different from that of the narrator of the major personal dits. The geography itself partakes of the inner world and of memory as much as it does of historical events, in a kind of nostalgic, autobiographic outpouring that, it must be said, overwhelms the end of the *Chroniques* just as it does the dits. The Froissartian self is invasive and never ceases to permeate the world.

The fact remains that if there is a major break in this work, which is more coherent than it would appear, the break sets into opposition, banally but emphatically, prose and verse, world and self. When he presents himself to a prince whose favor he seeks, and who knows him as a chronicler, Froissart gives him not his *Chroniques* but his verse, as a way both of offering his services and of revealing himself; thus did he give *Meliador* to Gaston Fébus in 1388, and his collected poetry to Richard II in 1395: "What does this book speak of?" "Love."[25]

Is that opposition in fact so banal in the fourteenth century? On the contrary, it is brand-new, still in the process of finding its niche. For the first time verse, as such—not merely when associated with song in various lyric forms—is felt as the natural mode of effusiveness, of self-expression, and of a subjective outlook on the world. The notion of poetry as the modern world will know it begins to take shape.[26] In the eyes of an author who writes the history of his own time in prose and his own inward and dreamt personal history in verse, the verse romance begins to be caught up, by the very fact of its being in verse, in the *mouvance* of this new conceptualization of poetry. *Meliador* is part of a tendency illustrated still more clearly around the same period by the *Roman de la dame à la Licorne et du beau chavalier au lion*.²⁷

In other words, *Meliador* embodies only in appearance the end of a genre, the Arthurian verse romance. It is much closer to a beginning: the inception of a new poetic sensibility and the association of that sensibility with verse. This is merely a beginning, this poem of more than thirty thousand lines, for the prologue sets the tone from the outset and, far from being the anomaly it first appears, captures that sensibility and represents it fully in its very marginality. This is only a beginning, for the string of sentimental dits that comprise it could continue endlessly, and they all ratify the position taken in the prologue: amorous gratification measured on the scale of social well-being. This is merely a beginning in the history of poetry. But the rest of the slogan would not in this case be "Let us continue the struggle," for the poem strays insidiously far from that universe of adventure and knightly combat that it feigns to perpetuate. So lengthy and in appearance so weighty, this romance is concerned only with the impalpable, and if Peter Dembowski, with his acts and entr'actes, can serve Froissart and Virginia Woolf as the improbable go-between, it is because the true nature of *Meliador* must be sought "between the acts."

Translated by Donald Maddox

Notes

1. Jean Froissart, *Meliador*, ed. A. Lognon, 3 vols. (Paris: Didot, 1895–99).

2. Beate Schmolke-Hasselmann, *Der arthurische Versroman von Chrestien bis Froissart. Zur Geschichte einer Gattung* (Tübingen: Niemeyer, 1980).

3. Michel Zink, "Les Chroniques médiévales et le modèle romanesque," *Mesure* 1 (1989): 33–45.

4. Michel Zink, "Froissart et la nuit du chasseur," *Poétique* 41 (1980): 60–77, reprinted in Michel Zink, *Les Voix de la conscience: Parole du poète et parole de Dieu dans la littérature médiévale* (Caen: Paradigme, 1992), pp. 117–34.

5. Armel Diverres, "Jean Froissart's Journey to Scotland," *Forum for Modern Language Studies* 1 (1965): 54–63; idem, "The Geography of Froissart's *Meliador*," in *Medieval Miscellany Presented to Eugene Vinaver, by Pupils, Colleagues, and Friends*, ed. F. Whitehead et al. (Manchester: Manchester University Press; New York: Barnes & Noble, 1965), 97–112; idem, "Froissart's *Meliador* and Edward III's Policy toward Scotland," in *Mélanges Rita Lejeune*, vol. 2 (Gembloux: Duculot, 1969), 1399–1409; idem, "The Irish Adventure in Froissart's *Meliador*," in *Mélanges Jean Frappier*, vol. 1 (Geneva: Droz, 1970), 235–51. See also Emmanuèle Baumgartner, "Ecosse et Ecossais: L'entrelacs de la fiction et de l'histoire dans les *Chroniques* et le

Meliador de Froissart," in *L'Image de l'autre européen, XVe-XVIIe siècle*, ed. J. Dufournet et al. (Paris: Presses de la Sorbonne Nouvelle, 1992), 11–21; and, based on the *Chroniques*, the splendid article by Philippe Contamine, "Froissart et l'Ecosse," in *"Des Chardons et des lys": Souvenir et présence en Berry de la vieille alliance franco-écosaise* (Bourges: Conseil Général de l'Indre, 1992), 30–44.

6. Peter Dembowski, *Jean Froissart and His "Meliador": Context, Craft, and Sense* (Lexington. Ky.: French Forum, 1983). Note the assimilation of Scotland into Prussia, a remote, desolate and forbidding country, by the knights that Jean de Vienne led there in 1385: "En quel Prusce nous a chis amenés li amiraus?" [Into what Prussia has the Emir led us here?]

7. Jean Froissart, *Le paradis d'amour*, ed. P. Dembowski (Geneva: Droz, 1986). At the end of this poem, among the heroes of romance the narrator sees dancing on the heath are those from *Meliador*: Meliador himself, Tanghis, and Camel de Camois (985–88). As Dembowski has shown (*Jean Froissart and His "Meliador,"* pp. 57–59), and as G. L. Kittredge long ago maintained, these verses are surely interpolations. *Le paradis d'amour* was written between 1361 and 1363, whereas *Meliador* could not have been begun before the following decade. In addition, a slight break in syntax gives away the interpolation. If Froissart himself is responsible for this (we know that one of the two manuscripts could be the one he gave to Richard II), the presence of Camel (whereas Agamanor is not mentioned, oddly enough) might be indicative of at least a temptation on the poet's part to identify with this mistreated character, who is in a situation so like the one in which he willingly places himself in his poems.

8. Jean Froissart, *La prison amoureuse*, ed. A. Fourrier (Paris: Klincksieck, 1974).

9. Jacqueline Cerquiglini-Toulet, "Fullness and Emptiness: Shortages and Storehouses of Lyric Treasures in the Fourteenth and Fifteenth Centuries," in *Contexts: Style and Values in Medieval Art and Literature*, eds. D. Poirion and N. F. Regalado, *Yale French Studies* (1991), 224–39. See also, by Cerquiglini-Toulet, *La Couleur de la mélancolie* (Paris: Hatier, 1994).

10. Fourrier, ed., *La prison amoureuse*, pp. 9–10. Cf. 1053–1256.

11. " . . . et je,
Esleeciés en coer de ce
Que j'avoie a tres bon loisir
Ceste, qui est tout mon plaisir,
Veü et avoec li esté
Et joliement aresté
En solas et en esbanoi,
Onques depuis si bon tamps n'oi." (*Prison amoureuse*, 1201–8)

[And I was glad at heart that I had seen and lingered with the lady who so delights me, gaily dallying in contented playfulness. Never since have I had such a fine time.]

12. Jean Froissart, *L'espinette amoureuse*, ed. A. Fourrier (Paris: Klincksieck, 1972).

13. Jean Froissart, *Le joli buisson de Jonece*, ed. A. Fourrier (Geneva: Droz, 1975), 2926–4426.

14. In "Froissart et la nuit du chasseur."

15. See Fourrier, *Espinette,* p. 185.

16. Thus, in order to defeat Agamanor, Meliador grabs him around the waist and squeezes him until he suffocates (3987–4009). Or again, below Montrose, when he takes on Griffamon, the first of the four brothers who besiege the castle, he begins by eluding a blow of the lance ("fait tour de Cournaille / Et se lance en tournant sans faille / Dessus le chevalier galois" [executes a Cornish turn and leaps unflaggingly onto the Welsh knight] (10590–92). Then Meliador seizes his opponent's neck in his arm and drubs his chest with the hilt of his sword until his opponent begs for mercy (10593–614).

17. Mais les dames, pour ordener
Le tournoi mieus a sa maniere,
Avoient sus la sabloniere
Fait la venir grant quantité
De paysans, pour verité,
Tout a piet et pour redrecier
Aucun mesaisiet chevalier,
Se cheüs estoit en peril. (6608–15)

[But the women, the better to conduct the tournament according to its conventions, had summoned a large number of peasants onto the esplanade, on foot, to raise up knights in disarray, when they were at risk.]

18. See Dembowski, *Jean Froissart and His "Meliador,"* p. 88, on the views of B. J. Whiting, "Proverbs in the Writings of Jean Froissart," *Speculum* 10 (1935): 294, and Whiting, "Froissart as Poet," *Medieval Studies* 8 (1946): 216.

19. See the sensitive evocation by Félix Lecoy in the summary of his course: *Annuaire du Collège de France* (1970–71), pp. 514–15.

20. See note 9.

21. Lucien Foulet, "Imaginer," *Romania* 68 (1944–45): 255–72.

22. Beate Schmolke-Hasselmann, "Ausklang der altfranzösischen Artusepik: Escanor und Meliador," in *Spätmittelalterliche Artusliteratur: ein Symposion der neusprachlichen Philologien auf der Generalversammlung der Görres-Gesellschaft Bonn,* ed. K.-H. Göller (Paderborn: Schoningh, 1984), p. 42.

23. Girart d'Amiens, *Escanor, roman arthurien en vers de la fin du XIIIe siècle: Edition critique,* ed., Richard Trachsler, 2 vols. (Geneva: Droz, 1994), vol. 1, pp. 56–67.

24. Car li affaires biaus et gens
Estoit lors tels, et li usages,
Que les dames vaillans et sages
Faisoient a estragniiers
Honneur et a tous chevaliers,
Et plus en .I. paÿs qu'en aultre;
Et principaulment ne voel d'autre
Paÿs parler que d'Engleterre.
Car, qui en vorroit bien enquerre,

> La son les dames gracïeuses,
> Lies, plaisans et amoureuses,
> Et qui sevent gens honnourer
> Trop mieulz c'ailleurs, au vrai parler;
> En ce point sont elles nouries,
> Escolees et ensegnies. (9552–66)

[For the event was so fine and noble, and the customs such, that these women, worthy and wise, honored foreigners and all knights, the more so in one country than in another, and in particular I wish to speak of no country other than England, for, to whomever might care to look into the matter, the women there are gracious, joyful, agreeable and amorous; and they know, better than elsewhere, in truth, how to honor people. On this point they are well bred, schooled and cultivated.]

25. "Donc me demanda le roi de quoi il [i.e., le livre que lui offre Froissart] traitoit, et je lui dis: 'D'amours!' De ceste response fut-il tous resjouys." [Then the king asked me what it [the book Froissart was giving him] was about, and I said, 'Love!' He was thoroughly delighted with that answer.] (*Chroniques*, book 4, chap. 41, ed. Buchon, vol. 3, p. 207).

26. See Michel Zink, *La Subjectivité littéraire: Autour du siecle de Saint Louis* (Paris: Presses Universitaires de France, 1985).

27. See Michel Zink, "Le Roman," in *La Littérature française aux XIVe et XVe siècles*, ed. Daniel Poirion, *Grundriss der Romanischen Literaturen des Mittelalters*, 8 vols. (Heidelberg: Winter, 1988), vol. 1, p. 206.

IV

Froissart and His Contemporaries

9

Theory and Practice
The Portrayal of Chivalry in the Prose *Lancelot*, Geoffroy de Charny, and Froissart

ELSPETH KENNEDY

The terms *fact* and *fiction*, which I had originally intended to put in the title of this essay, might lead, I realized, into a series of false oppositions in relation to the works discussed here. I have only recently put a toe into the fourteenth century, through my work on the editing and translating of the *Livre de chevalerie* of Geoffroy de Charny.[1] Having been interested for some time, however, in the reception of the great thirteenth-century Arthurian prose romances, I have examined "The Knight as Reader of Arthurian Romance" for the interplay between the literary works of three thirteenth-century knights and the Prose *Lancelot*.[2] The first is Philippe de Novare, who in *Les quatre âges de l'homme* quotes and paraphrases advice given in the Prose *Lancelot* concerning the conduct suitable in a young knight, stressing the need not only to show courage in battle but also to listen to the counsel of his elders;[3] one of the passages emphasizes the duty of a knight to be loyal to his lord. The other two authors, Philippe de Beaumanoir, who wrote *Les coutumes de Beauvaisis*,[4] and Ramon Llull,[5] draw on the Prose *Lancelot* for their accounts of the origin of chivalry or kings and emphasize the role of knight and king in the maintenance of justice. While none of these three knight-authors mentions the role of women as the inspiration for chivalrous deeds, Charny's *Livre de chevalerie* exemplifies the interaction with Arthurian romance, particularly in the interesting light it casts on the role of women in the formation of a young knight.[6] This chapter further explores the interplay between romance and the theory and practice of knighthood in the thirteenth and fourteenth centuries. It concentrates on Charny in comparison with Froissart, particularly in the light of some of the recent explorations, by scholars such as Peter

Ainsworth, George Diller, and Michel Zink, of implied reservations or changing attitudes in the various versions of his chronicles.

Froissart describes Geoffroy de Charny as "le plus preudomme et le plus vailant de tous les autres"[7] [the most worthy and valiant of all] (translations mine unless otherwise indicated) and records his death at the battle of Poitiers. The knight who served and died for his king in war and the professional man of letters and tonsured cleric who wrote for more than one patron are linked by both parallels and contrasts in their presentations of the ideals of chivalry and kingship and of problems and temptations confronting those engaged in the practice of arms. In the case of both men, the literary context for chivalry cannot be ignored, of course, although the ways that the two handle this may be very different.

The subject of Froissart's historical writing is presented in his various prefaces as the recording of deeds of chivalry in a truthful way. Chivalry is the subject also of Geoffroy de Charny's three works: the *Demandes*, a series of questions on the finer points of the knightly practice of arms; the *Livre Charny* in verse; and the prose *Livre de chevalerie*, the last two dealing with the theory and practice of chivalry.[8]

The literary connections with the chivalric ideals are to be expected in an author such as Froissart, poet, writer of a romance (*Meliador*), as well as recorder of great deeds (and, of course, of other matters) in the *Chroniques*. In contrast, Geoffroy de Charny's career was based not on letters but on arms. He first saw service in Gascony in 1337, took part in the defense of Tournai against the English (1340), and in 1341 served in Brittany under Jean, future king of France. He went on an unsuccessful crusade, returned to France, made a fruitless attempt to recapture Calais, and consequently spent a year in prison in England. Jean paid his ransom and made him a member of the King's Council; he was named the bearer of the Oriflamme in 1355 and was killed defending the banner in the battle of Poitiers. But, as is only to be expected in a knight of his standing who undertook to set out the principles and practice of chivalry, he seems to be familiar with some of the treatises on chivalry such as the *Ordene de chevalerie*[9] and Ramon Llull's *Libre del orde de cavalleria*, probably in the Middle French translation[10] (both important sources for his book) and with the great Arthurian prose romances such as the *Lancelot-Grail* cycle and the *Roman de Perceforest*, knowledge of both being apparent in his work. The interplay between Geoffroy de Charny's treatise on chivalry and these other works is, not surprisingly, less subtle than that in Froissart's historical writing, his poetry, and his verse Arthurian romance *Meliador* and in their relation to a wider range of literature, an interplay explored by scholars such as Peter Ainsworth and Michel Zink.[11]

It was at Jean's request that Charny composed the *Demandes*, questions for the joust (first part), the tournament (second part), and war (third part), which seem to have been intended to be the subject of a debate among the knights of the Company of the Star. Jonathan Boulton thinks it probable that his other two works, the verse *Livre Charny* and the prose *Livre de chevalerie*, in which Charny examines the nature and duties of knighthood, may well have been written to serve as handbooks for the knights of the company.[12] This connection with an Order of Chivalry provides a link connecting Charny, the Prose *Lancelot*, and Froissart.

Froissart declares that his book sets down in writing "otant de grans fais d'armes, de mervilleuses avenues, de durs rencontres, de grandes bataillez et de touttes autres coses sus cel estat qui se dependent de membres d'armes et de proeche que de nulle histoire dont on puist lire, tant soit vielle ne nouvelle"[13] [as many great deeds of arms and marvelous events, testing encounters, great battles, and all other things of the kind which relate to matters of arms and prowess as can be found in any history to be read, no matter how old or how new]. In the Prose *Lancelot*, every knight who left Arthur's court on a quest had to swear an oath to give on his return a true account of his adventures, whether to his honor or to his shame. Gauvain swears such an oath as he sets out on the quest for the Red Knight (Lancelot): "Et li sain[t] furent aporté, si com il estoit a costume, que nus chevaliers ne movoit de la maison lo roi por aventure querre qui avant ne jurast sor sainz que il verité diroit au revenir de totes les choses qui li avandroient a son escient."[14] [And the holy relics were brought as was the custom, for no knight left the royal court to seek adventure who did not first swear on holy relics that he would on his return tell the truth as far as he knew it concerning everything that happened to him.] Later it is stated specifically, in relation to a similar oath sworn by Hector, that he must not lie "ne por sa honte covrir, ne por s'anor avancier" (*LK*, p. 406) [neither to conceal his shame nor to advance his honor]. These reports were set down in writing by four of Arthur's learned clerks in a great book that was drawn upon for the "conte Lancelot," (*LK*, p. 571) [the tale of Lancelot], and we are given the clerks' names and their city of origin. The rules to be observed by knights of the Company of the Star, as reported by Jean le Bel, echo the wording of the oath in the Prose *Lancelot*:

> Et y (at the Maison de l'Etoile) debvoit le roy, chascun an, tenir court plainiere de tous les compaignons au mains, et y debvoit chascun raconter toutes ses aventures, aussy bien les honteuses que les glorieuses qui avenues luy seroient des le temps qu'il n'avroit esté a

la noble court, et le roy debvroit ordonner .ii. ou .iii. clercs qui escouteroient toutes ces aventures, et en ung livre mettroient affin qu'elles fussent chascun an raportees en place par devant les compaignons, par quoy on poeut sçavoir les plus proeux et honnourer ceulx qui mielx le deserviroient.[15]

[And there each year, at least, the king was to hold full court with the companions. And there each of the companions was to recount all the adventures, the shameful as well as the glorious, which had come to him in the time since he had been in the noble court. And the king was to establish two or three clerks who were to listen to all these adventures and put them in a book, so that they might be reported there every year before the companions, by which one could know the most valorous (preux) and honour those who best deserved it.]

Scholars such as Boulton and Juliet Vale[16] have of course drawn attention to the general links between the monarchical orders of chivalry, particularly in relation to the Order of the Garter, and Arthur's international company of the Knights of the Round Table, links that had been made by Jean le Bel and Froissart. For example, Froissart refers to Arthur in his account of Edward III's plan to found the Order of the Garter and build a new hall at Windsor to house it:

En ce temps vint en pourpos et en volenté au roi d'Engleterre de faire redefiier le grant chastiel de Windesore, lequel li rois Artus fist jadis faire et fonder, et la ou premierement la Table Reonde fu conmenchie, dont tant de bons et vaillans chevaliers issirent et travillierent en armes et en proeces par le monde; et feroit li dis rois une ordenance de chevaliers de li et de ses enfans et des plus preus et renonmés d'Engleterre et d'autres pais aussi, qui estoient en son service, et seroient en sonme jusques a quarante et seroient nonmé li chevalier dou Bleu Gertier.[17]

[At this time the king conceived the plan to have rebuilt the great castle of Windsor, founded long ago by King Arthur. That was the place where the Round Table was first set up, from which so many good and valiant knights set forth and exerted themselves in deeds of arms and of prowess throughout the world. The above mentioned King Edward would establish an order of knights which would include himself, his sons, and those of the greatest valor and prowess from England and other countries who were in his service; there would be up to forty members of the order and they would be called the Knights of the Blue Garter.]

A little further on Froissart refers to: "le dongnon de Windesore et les cambres et le grande sale ou li rois Artus faisoit au temps de son resgne son tinel et tenoit son estat de chevaliers aventureus, de dames et de damoiselles" (*Chroniques,* Rome version, p. 596) [the great keep of Windsor and the rooms and great hall where Arthur used to hold court and maintain his household of adventurous knights, of ladies, and of damsels].

This emphasis on the knights' obligation to give full and accurate reports of their activities and on the recording in writing of these accounts in both Arthurian romance and in the statutes of the Company of the Star, the order with which Geoffroy de Charny was so closely associated, provides a particularly interesting literary background to Froissart's work, to the importance he gives to the recording of the deeds of prowess and to his references to his search for supplementary information concerning such deeds from knights who had been active participants in the activities recorded. As George Diller shows in chapter 3 of this book, Froissart presents himself as undertaking an arduous journey to reach his own informants, a journey that reminds us of the quests of knights seeking adventure and that represents a reversal of the situation in the Prose *Lancelot,* where knights return to court from perilous journeys to provide an account of their adventures for the clerks to record. The clerks of Arthur's court are in a sense the ancestors of the fourteenth-century heralds whose duty it was to have set down in writing a complete account of the knights' deeds of arms when they were away from court, and they prepare the way for Froissart's interesting variation on the Three Orders:

> Or se debrise et disfere li mondes en pluisseurs manieres. Premierement, li vaillant honme travellent lors corps en armes pour conquerir la glore et renonmee de che monde; li peuples parole recorde, et devise de lors estas; auquns clers escripsent et registrent lors oevres et baceleries, par quoi elles soient mises et couchies en memores perpetueles. Car par les escriptures puet on avoir la congnissance de toutes coses, et sont registré li bien et li mal, les prosperités et les fortunes des anciiens. (*Chroniques,* Rome version, p. 37)

> [The world can be divided up in various ways. First the men of valor strive physically with feats of arms to win the glory and renown of this world; then the people give an account through word of mouth of their activities; finally, some clerks set down in writing

their achievements and deeds of prowess so that they will never be forgotten but remembered forever. For written records can preserve knowledge of everything, of the good and the bad, of the prosperity and ill fortune of men of past times.]

Peter Ainsworth suggests that Froissart's condition as a tonsured cleric rendered him more than suitable for the Office of Secretary to the court of European Chivalry (p. 8). The tale in the Prose *Lancelot*, according to a number of formulae used to justify the inclusion or exclusion of material, presents a careful choice of the adventures relevant to the particular story being told, that is to the tale of Lancelot and of the fate of the Arthurian kingdom. Within a different historical and literary context, Froissart, too, makes his particular choices from the reports of participants in relation to events he narrates.

The links between Geoffroy de Charny's book on the theory and practice of knighthood, which is not a narrative work, and Arthurian prose romance and historical chronicle will of course be of a somewhat different nature. Let us look first briefly at the theory and practice of chivalry as it is to be found in the Prose *Lancelot*.

It is the Lady of the Lake who explains the theory of chivalry to Lancelot before she takes him as a young squire to Arthur's court to be knighted. She links the origin of knights with the situation after the Fall of Man, when all men were still equal in rank, but the strong and wicked robbed and oppressed the weak, widows, and orphans. This is, of course, in accordance with the usual medieval political theory concerning the origin of all human forms of government after the Fall, but here kings are replaced by knights. To provide protection against the strong and the wicked, the Lady of the Lake says that they established those who were most worthy in the opinion of the common people, that is, those who were full of the qualities of heart and body. The moral qualities required are as follows:

> Au commencement, qant li ordres de chevalerie commança, fu devisé a celui qui voloit estre chevaliers et qui lo don en avoit par droiture d'eslection, qu'il fust cortois sanz vilenies, deboenneires sanz felenie, piteus vers les soffraiteus, et larges et appareilliez de secorre les besoigneus, prelz et appareilliez de confondre les robeors et les ocianz, droiz jugierres sanz amor et sanz haïne, et sanz amor d'aidier au tort por lo droit grever, et sanz haïne de nuire au droit por traire lo tort avant. (*LK*, p. 142)

[Originally, when the order of knighthood began, a man who wished to be a knight, and who was accorded that privilege by right of election, was told he should be courteous without baseness, gracious without cruelty, compassionate towards the poor, generous and prepared to help those in need, and ready and prepared to confound robbers and killers; he should be a fair judge, without love or hate, without love to help wrong against right, without hate to hinder right in order to further wrong.]

She then describes the knight's function within the system of the Three Orders, as symbolized by his two-edged sword: to protect the Church, which looks after the souls of men, and the people, whose task it is to provide earthly sustenance. The knight must therefore, above all, defend the Church and be a champion of justice, and the qualities he requires are the same as those which characterize a good king.

The theory of chivalry, as presented by the Lady of the Lake, is, therefore, set firmly within the context of the Three Orders. There is no mention of duty to one's lord; nor does she draw Lancelot's attention at this point to the importance of the right kind of love for a woman in the motivation for great deeds, although she does so later when she sends a damsel to tell him that he must choose the kind of love that will inspire him to perform great exploits (*LK*, pp. 205-6). However, the tasks that the knights setting out from Arthur's court must perform make it clear that their duty to maintain justice is placed firmly within a feudal context. As I point out elsewhere, in the account of events leading up to Lancelot's installation as a knight of the Round Table, all the people whose causes he and knights such as Gauvain and Hector have to defend are *vassals* of King Arthur.[18] Lancelot himself, the greatest of knights until he is temporarily supplanted by Galahad in the allegory of the *Queste*, is a *povre chevalier*; he has been dispossessed as a baby because Arthur was unable to protect his vassal Ban, father of Lancelot, whose lands had been taken by Claudas. However, early in the romance we hear that there is a knight, brave, skillful and of good counsel, who has to make difficult decisions as he attempts to cope with his conflicting loyalties to two lords; this is Pharien, who is presented as an example of the wise knight struggling to remain a loyal vassal. Elsewhere in the romance it is the king who is told that, with the help of his great vassals and his *bas gentil homme*, it is his duty to maintain good governance and to protect the weak against the unrighteous strong (for example, *LK*, pp. 283–89, in an episode when a *preu-*

domme lectures Arthur on his duties as a king and on the way to win back the hearts of his men).

In the Prose *Lancelot*, therefore, particularly in the earliest branch of the work, we have a *theory* of chivalry based on the function of the knight to maintain justice within the world as a whole, but a *practice* that is linked closely to the duty of a king, as represented by his own knights, to maintain justice within a feudal system of land tenure.

In the *Livre de chevalerie* of Charny, the situation is somewhat different, but there are also some interesting parallels and interactions with the Prose *Lancelot* tradition of romance. The detailed account of the knighting ceremony owes more to the thirteenth-century *Ordene de chevalerie* than to the Lady of the Lake's explanation of the deeper significance of the various items of a knight's equipment in the Prose *Lancelot*, and there are variations in the symbolism attributed to these items in all three works. However, the links with the Prose *Lancelot* come out particularly clearly in Charny's account of the origin of kings, princes, and great lords, in which there is no mention of knights, but for which he seems to go back both to the Prose *Lancelot* and to Ramon Llull's treatise on chivalry. Before Charny, Beaumanoir used the romance's account of the origin of chivalry, of which there are many close verbal echoes in his work, but he transfers it to the origin of kings. However, Beaumanoir also reserves a place in it not for knights but for *gentilhommes*. It should be noted that, as might be expected in the conditions of the fourteenth century, not all good *gens d'armes* have necessarily been knighted, nor is there the same emphasis on feudal obligations. As Philippe Contamine has made clear, the seignoriovassalic relationship was no longer the main basis for military recruitment, but special contracts were used, and the men brought in by general summons were paid.[19]

What sharply distinguishes Charny from his thirteenth-century knightly predecessors who draw on the Prose *Lancelot* in their presentation of the qualities required in knights (and kings) in relation to their function in society is the importance this fourteenth-century knight gives to the role of women in the creation of good young knights or men-at-arms. None of the three knights mentioned earlier, Philippe de Novare, Philippe de Beaumanoir, and Ramon Llull, attributes any importance to women in this area, but Geoffroy de Charny makes a very practical use of the literary conventions of the inspiration of love, of *fin'amor*, to spur on his young man-at-arms. He describes how a lady can give practical advice to a young knight or man-at-arms as to what tournaments he should attend and what feats of arms he should undertake in order to increase his honor and be worthy of her love. Charny states that true and honorable love for a lady is the right frame of mind for those who desire to achieve honor (*LC*, p. 118). He also emphasizes the traditional need for secrecy in relation to love by pouring scorn on those who insist on boasting openly and sometimes falsely about their love, even declaring that they would not want to have the love of Queen Guinevere herself if they could not declare it openly. However, Charny points out that where the circumstances are such that the love can be made public (presumably in cases when the lady can be or is married to the knight), the lady's honor will be enhanced in the eyes of all the world by the achievements of the man who loves her (*LC*, p. 118).

Froissart, too, brings in an Arthurian reference in relation to the honor a lady can receive, but not with regard to secret or public love, when he compares Queen Philippa to Guinevere:

> Car depuis le temps de la roine Genoivre qui fu fenme au roi Artus et roine d'Engleterre que on nonmoit adont la Grant Bretagne, si bonne roine n'i entra, ne qui tant d'onnour reçuist, ne qui si belle generation euist, car elle eut dou roi Edouwart son mari, en son temps, sept fils et .v. filles. (*Chroniques*, Rome version, p. 159)

> [For since the time of Queen Guinevere, wife of King Arthur and queen of England, then called Great Britain, such a good queen never landed there (in England) nor was so honored, nor produced so many fine offspring, for she gave King Edward her husband seven sons and five daughters.]

But of course Guinevere had no *belle generation*, no sons or daughters to leave behind her, in the Prose *Lancelot*.

There is a strong contrast between the exalted symbolism of the knighting ceremony described by Charny and his down-to-earth descriptions of the physical discomforts of war, of the need to put up with extremes of heat and cold, to take food when it is available and to fast when it is not. He is equally forthright on matters of dress; he criticizes those who adorn themselves too much, and in particular condemns those whose attire impedes their use of arms: "Si se varainglent et se estraingnent par le ventre tant et si fort que le ventre que Dieu leur avoit donné il veulent mettre a ny qu'il n'en ont point" (*LC*, p. 188). [They girth themselves up and so rein themselves in round the middle of their bodies that they seek to deny the existence of the stomachs which God has given them.] They are then so constricted that they cannot fight properly.

A clear hierarchy in relation to events at which deeds of arms may be performed is explicit in Charny; it is rather less explicit in the Prose

Lancelot. Of the four *assemblees* linked together in that work by magic predictions from damsels from the lake, the first two are tournaments in which the fate of the kingdom is not at stake, whereas in the last two Galehot comes with an army and *filets de fer*, determined to add Arthur's kingdom to the others he has already conquered, and Arthur is prepared to die defending the land of Logres to the last. The same term, *assemblee*, is used for all four battles, and the war against Galehot shares some of the characteristics of a tournament. When Galehot declares a truce, so that Arthur can return with a bigger army and Galehot can therefore gain greater honor in defeating him, the renewal of hostilities is set for a particular day. Only the war against the Saxons does not follow the rules of chivalry. For Charny, although honor can be won in a joust, greater honor can be won at a tournament and even greater at battle in war.

There is a grading of types of knights in Charny and a hierarchy of values, although he tries always to give honor to deeds of prowess, even if performed at a lower level. For example, he looks at those who have courage and skill but are thoughtless: They spur forward in a disorderly way and do not consider the benefit or advantage for their friends or the harm done to their enemies. His verdict is that for their fine contribution in terms of physical exploits, they should indeed be called worthy, although as for being worthy in the truest sense, they could do better (*LC*, p. 150). Next he turns to those who perform great deeds in an honorable way but do not lead or advise, whom he judges to be worthy, although in relation to such a standard of prowess they might do better (*LC*, pp. 150–52). He then examines the true men of worth, brave and of good counsel. They have risked their lives gladly when young, without thought of death or of expense; with experience they acquire wisdom, while still performing valiant deeds; finally they are entrusted with command. To them he awards the highest grade, to be prized and honored above all the men of prowess mentioned before (*LC*, pp. 152–54). He also considers that men of high rank can make a greater contribution as true men of worth than can those of humbler rank, no matter how great their personal qualities and merit; he explains that those of lesser rank have not, like the great princes and lords, the means to support and encourage other men-at-arms and hence lack their influence (*LC*, pp. 106-8).

The gap between the theory of chivalry as enunciated by Charny and the practice of lesser knights is clear in his condemnation of certain types of men-at-arms (*LC*, pp. 176–78): first, those who are guilty of robbery on the highway, of treacherously stealing, for no good reason (which seems to imply that a certain amount of pillage had to be tolerated); second, those who murder others in a bad cause; third, those who commit a treacherous deed by seizing, plundering, and robbing others without any challenge and without any wrongdoing on the part of the persons attacked; fourth, those who take from the churches the wealth through which Our Lord is served and who harm those persons ordained to the noble office of serving God, as by such evil deeds this noble service will not be carried out.

Nevertheless for Charny, a very devout Christian (apparently the first named knight to be associated with the Turin shroud), the order of knighthood at its highest level is of no less value than, and has as noble a function as, the order of priesthood, and indeed for him it demands greater sacrifice (*LC*, pp. 182–84). There are perhaps echoes here of the attitude found in a Grail romance such as the Vulgate *Queste del Saint Graal*, a branch of the *Lancelot-Grail* cycle, in which it is a knight who is the supreme Grail hero and a type of Christ, although, as explained to Galahad himself, his coming should be compared to that of Christ not on the same level, but "de semblance, ne mie de hautece" (*Queste*, p. 38). There is also in Charny the association between knights and Old Testament heroes made so frequently in the ritual of knighting, in the books on the theory of chivalry, in romances such as the Prose *Lancelot*, and in the *Perceforest*, the fourteenth-century romance also drawn on by Charny in his account of the death of Julius Caesar (*LC*, pp. 160–62). There is in Charny, however, no suggestion of any need for celibacy at the top of the knightly hierarchy, and thus no conflict between ideas of *fin'amor* and heavenly chivalry, as there is in the Vulgate *Queste*; there the adventures of the Grail are not earthly adventures but have their true significance only within the context of the allegory of the Quest.

Although there is some reference to the importance of studying tactics, higher military strategy receives little attention in Charny. (Nor does it feature prominently in Froissart's work, as often pointed out.) There is a good deal on sieges in Charny, in Froissart, and indeed even in the Prose *Lancelot*, although with less practical detail in the romance than in Charny or Froissart. However, it would seem that giving advice to military leaders was not the main purpose of Charny's book, and it might well be that the *Livre de chevalerie* and the chivalric order to which it was linked were designed instead to inspire a body of young men to train in arms and to serve their king with greater dedication. It is tempting to wonder whether more attention by Charny to the occasional need to make a strategic withdrawal, rather than to seek glory in the final sacrifice of one's life, might have helped his king's cause better.

As for the possible gap between the chivalric ideal and practice, as noted, Charny condemns certain types of men-at-arms as totally unworthy but is prepared to describe as *preux* some men-at-arms who choose to achieve feats of arms at a lower level and without the same degree of selflessness as those who are prepared to lay down their lives for their king or their cause. However, the hierarchy between the different levels is made clear, and he does not seem to question the ideal or its relevance for real war, even if concessions must be made in relation to the less than perfect exponents of knightly practice.

In the Prose *Lancelot*, a knight may be described as *preu* or *bon chevalier* but also treacherous. For example, King Claudas, a brave but flawed knight who dispossessed Lancelot's father, is first introduced as "mout bons chevaliers et mout saiges et mout traïtres" (*LK*, p. 1); he is the only character other than Lancelot of whom a complete physical and moral portrait is given (*LK*, pp. 30–31). He was miserly (as opposed to the generosity always required of a good king and knight); he appreciated good knights who were landless but not those who had land and power; he did not willingly break his word, once given, but often used deception and cheating to get himself out of awkward situations. He went regularly to mass, but did little for the poor (Charny condemns those who are publicly devout and givers of alms but privately greedy [*LC*, p. 148]). Some of Gauvain's brothers are described in rather similar terms in a series of brief portraits in the Prose *Lancelot*. For example, Agravain is said to be skilled at arms and courageous but arrogant, speaking ill of others, full of envy, without pity. Mordred is characterized as brave and full of prowess but envious and *fel*, killer of many knights, someone who began well but ended badly. Gauvain, on the other hand, is presented as good at arms and brave, kind and generous to the poor, never speaking ill of others, free from envy, courteous, modest, wise, and restrained, second as a knight only to Lancelot (*LM*, vol. 2, pp. 408–11).

However, there is perhaps a hint of a more fundamental questioning of chivalric achievement in the episodes that lead up to the *Queste* and that are therefore not on the allegorical level of the *aventures del Graal*, whose true *senefiance*, we are told, concerns not deeds of arms on an earthly level but a search for the Vision of God. In the part of the romance often called the *Agravain*, even knights such as Gauvain and Lancelot, who in earlier branches—except in the thick of battle against enemies such as the Saxons—always tried to avoid killing their opponents, no longer seem to experience the same regret when their deeds of arms cause death, and the tone of the narrative becomes increasingly violent. This should be compared with Gauvain's puzzled comment in the *Queste* on the number of knights he has found himself killing, that is, ten, without having a single adventure (*Queste*, p. 147); Gauvain is here out of his depth in a quest that has nothing to do with earthly chivalry, being a search on an allegorical level for a vision of the secrets of God. Then, in the *Mort Artu,* Gauvain has to admit to his failure on the Grail Quest. He confesses that he has killed eighteen knights, not because he was a better knight than the others, "mes la mescheance se torna plus vers moi que vers nul de mes compaignons. Et si sachiez bien que ce n'a pas esté par ma chevalerie, mes par mon pechié; si m'avez fet dire ma honte" (*Mort Artu* §3, p. 2) [but *mescheance* (mischance, ill fate, sometimes associated in the text with sin)[20] turned more against me than against any of my companions. And I assure you that this was not through my quality as a knight but through my sin (*pechié*, sometimes associated with misfortune), and you have made me confess to my shame]. As the story moves in the *Mort Artu* toward its tragic end, the theme of dissension and violence associated with great deeds of arms is explored further. The adultery of Lancelot and Guinevere, exploited by Gauvain's two brave but nasty brothers, and Gauvain's excessive and unrestrained reaction to Lancelot's accidental killing of his beloved brother Gaheriet, who was only trying to intervene on the side of peace, suggest a discrepancy between the actions of even the best of the knights and the theory of chivalry as presented earlier in the text. Scholars such as Emmanuèle Baumgartner and Colette-Anne Van Coolput have suggested that in the Prose *Tristan* the gap between the ideal and the practice is widening and that doubt is being cast on the very ideal itself as it has been presented in parts at least of the *Lancelot-Grail* cycle.[21]

This brief survey of discrepancies between chivalric theory and the actions of even some of the better knights, as presented in thirteenth-century romance and in Charny's fourteenth-century treatise on chivalry, may be of some interest in the light of the very important work done recently on Froissart. I am thinking in particular of the evolution of his attitudes to be seen in the Rome manuscript, as studied by scholars such as Diller and Ainsworth and Zink. For example, Diller suggests that this version betrays the presence of "un idéal chevaleresque, et par conséquent romanesque et moral, qui se heurte constamment à sa quête inlassable de la vérité historique" (*Chroniques,* Rome version, introduction, p. 31). Ainsworth, in *Jean Froissart and the Fabric of History,* writes of a mixture of voices, perspectives, echoes, and parallels that often results in the creation of shadow areas similar to those written about by Philippe Ménard in relation to Marie de France, those necessary for art, propitious for poetry. I find such shadow areas in the *Lancelot-Grail* cycle in the contrasting ways in which great kings and great knights are presented in the light of their reputation and of their actions within the story, shadow areas that might well evoke contemporary political and social tensions. Ainsworth says: "At the heart of all the textual developments examined in this study is what I have described as the moral tension expressing the contrast between the reality and the ideal of chivalry and kingship, as they were understood by Froissart and at least some of his contemporaries" (p. 304). I think that the same moral tension is to be found in the prose romances.

As for Charny, whatever the vicissitudes of his earlier career, including an unsuccessful crusade, he would seem in the end to have put into practice what he considered to be the ultimate form of the chivalric ideal. He declared: "Ne nulz ne s'en puet ne doit excuser de soy armer et justement ou pour son seigneur ou pour son lignage ou pour soy meismes ou pour Sainte Eglise ou pour la foy deffendre et soustenir ou pour pitié d'ommes et de fammes qui ne peuent leur droit deffendre. Et en tel cas doivent il mettre baudemant, hardiement et liement leurs corps en telx faiz d'armes et en teles aventures sanz y redoubter rienz" (*LC*, p. 176). [No one can and should excuse himself from bearing arms in a just cause, whether for his lord or for his lineage or for himself or for the Holy Church or to defend and uphold the faith or out of pity for men or women who cannot defend their own rights. In such cases they should commit themselves eagerly, boldly, and gladly to such deeds of arms and adventures, fearing nothing.] In the end, Charny gave his life in the cause of his king when he died defending the royal standard at the battle of Poitiers. Despite this splendid example of a deed of chivalry, worthy to be recorded by Froissart, the battle was lost, and the Company of the Star, unlike the Order of the Garter, disappeared in the fourteenth century.

Notes

1. Richard W. Kaeuper and Elspeth Kennedy, *The Book of Chivalry of Geoffroi de Charny: Text, Context, and Translation* (Philadelphia: University of Pennsylvania Press, 1996); hereafter *LC*. The *Livre de chevalerie* was first published by Kervyn de Lettenhove as a kind of appendix to his edition of Froissart, *Oeuvres complètes de Froissart*, 11 vols. (Brussels: Académie Royale de Belgique, 1867–77), vol. 1, part iii, pp. 463–533.

2. Elspeth Kennedy, "The Knight as Reader of Arthurian Romance," in *Culture and the King: The Social Implications of the Arthurian Legend*, ed. Martin B. Shichtman and James P. Carley (Albany: State University of New York Press, 1994), 70–89. See also Kennedy, "Social and Political Ideas in the French Prose *Lancelot*," *Medium Aevum* 26 (1957): 90–106.

3. Philippe de Novare, *Les Quatre âges de l'homme: Traité moral de Philippe de Navarre*, ed. Marcel de Fréville (Paris: Firmin Didot, 1888), pp. 23–24.

4. Philippe de Beaumanoir, *Les coutumes de Beauvaisis*, ed. A. Salmon, 2 vol. (Paris: Picard, 1899–1900), para. 1453; *The Coutumes de Beauvaisis of Philippe de Beaumanoir*, trans. F. R. P. Akehurst (Philadelphia: University of Pennsylvania Press, 1992), pp. 518–19.

5. Ramon Llull, *Libre del orde de cavalleria*, vol. 1 of *Obres de Ramon Llull*, ed. A. M. Alcover, M. Obrador, and B. Bennassar, 20 vols. (Palma de Mallorca: Comission Editoria Llulliana, 1906).

6. Elspeth Kennedy, "Geoffroi de Charny's *Livre de Chevalerie* and the Knights of the Round Table," in *Medieval Knighthood*, vol. 5, eds. S. Church and R. Harvey (Cambridge: D. S. Brewer, 1995), 221–42.

7. Froissart, *Oeuvres*, ed. Kervyn de Lettenhove (see n.1), vol. 5, p. 412. (All translations in this chapter are by Elspeth Kennedy unless otherwise indicated.)

8. *A Critical Edition of Geoffroy de Charny's "Livre Charny" and the "Demandes pour la joute, les tournois et la guerre,"* ed. Michael Anthony Taylor, unpublished Ph.D. diss., University of North Carolina, Chapel Hill, 1977; for the edition of the *Livre de chevalerie* cited here, see n.1.

9. *Le Roman des eles, by Raoul de Hodenc and L'Ordene de chevalerie*, ed. K. Busby (Amsterdam and Philadelphia: Benjamins, 1983).

10. *Livre de l'ordre de chevallerie* in *Obres de Ramon Llull*, vol. 1, pp. 249–91.

11. See, for example, Peter F. Ainsworth, *Jean Froissart and the Fabric of History: Truth, Myth, and Fiction in the Chroniques* (Oxford: Clarendon Press, 1990); Michel Zink, "Froissart et la nuit du chasseur," *Poétique*, 2 (1980): 60–77.

12. D'Arcy Jonathan Dacre Boulton, *The Knights of the Crown: The Monarchical Orders of Knighthood in Later Medieval Europe 1325–1520* (Cambridge: D. S. Brewer, 1987), p. 186.

13. Jean Froissart, *Chroniques Livre I, Le manuscrit d'Amiens*, ed. George T. Diller, 4 vols. (Geneva: Droz, 1991), vol. 1, p. 1.

14. *Lancelot do Lac: The Non-Cyclic Old French Prose Romance*, ed. E. Kennedy (Oxford: Clarendon Press, 1980), p. 298; hereafter *LK*. For the edition of the cyclic version, see *Lancelot: Roman en prose du XIIIe siècle*, ed. Alexandre Micha, 9 vols. (Geneva: Droz, 1978–83); hereafter, *LM*. *La queste del saint Graal*, ed. Albert Pauphilet (Paris: Champion, 1923); hereafter, *Queste*. *La mort le roi Artu: Roman du XIIIe siècle*, ed. Jean Frappier (Geneva: Droz, 1964); hereafter, *Mort Artu*.

15. *Chronique de Jean le Bel*, ed. J. Viard and E. Deprez, 2 vols (Paris: 1904), vol. 2, pp. 204–6. The translation is from Boulton, pp. 180–81.

16. *Edward III and Chivalry: Chivalric Society and Its Context, 1270–1350* (Cambridge: D. S. Brewer, 1982).

17. Froissart, *Chroniques. Dernière rédaction du premier livre. Edition du manuscrit de Rome Reg. lat. 869*, ed. George T. Diller (Geneva: Droz, 1972), p. 595.

18. See, for example, Elspeth Kennedy, *Lancelot and the Grail: A Study of the Prose Lancelot* (Oxford: Clarendon Press, 1986), chap. 4.

19. See Boulton, pp. 170–71, and Philippe Contamine, *Guerre, état et société à la fin du moyen âge: Etudes sur les armées des rois de France 1337–1494* (Paris: Mouton, 1972), especially pp. 26–64.

20. See Elspeth Kennedy, "'Lancelot li mescheans': Mischance and Individual Responsibility in the *Lancelot-Grail*," in *De ongevalliche Lanceloet: Studies over de Lancelotcompilatie*, ed. Bart Besamusca and Frank Brandsma (Hilversum: Verloren, 1992), 134–35.

21. Emmanuèle Baumgartner, *Le Tristan en prose: Essai d'interprétation d'un roman médiéval* (Geneva: Droz, 1975), chaps. 4 and 5; Colette-Anne Van Coolput, *Aventures querant et le sens du monde: Aspects de la réception productive des premiers romans du Graal cycliques dans le Tristan en prose* (Leuven: Leuven University Press, 1986), p. 220.

10

Froissart and Chaucer

JOHN M. FYLER

Froissart was born perhaps six years before Chaucer, and he lived for probably four or five, possibly ten years after Chaucer's death. The six years' difference in age between them is significant when they are in their twenties: Chaucer's first major poem copies Froissart's, instead of the other way around. But later on, and certainly from the distance of our perspective, they seem exactly contemporary, and they offer to us an exceptionally interesting comparison, as we think about their literary responses to their time. The conspicuous points of contact between them are early: Chaucer's father-in-law was a knight from the County of Hainaut, also the birthplace of Queen Philippa and of Froissart, who entered her service when he arrived at the English court in 1362.[1] The two young courtier-poets certainly became acquainted, at least, in the years between 1362 and Philippa's death in 1369. Chaucer may have been in Milan shortly after the wedding of Lionel, duke of Clarence, to Violante Visconti in 1368, a wedding at which Froissart was in attendance.[2] But their acquaintance ended shortly thereafter. When Queen Philippa died in the following year, Froissart evidently saw no future for himself in England, and he was not to return until his final visit in 1395. He does not name Chaucer as one of the old friends he saw on that final visit; indeed, he mentions Chaucer only once in the *Chroniques*, for his part in a diplomatic mission of 1377; and Chaucer himself never mentions Froissart.

Of course, Chaucer never mentions Boccaccio either, nor does Froissart name Machaut. The most important poetic influence is the one either taken for granted or suppressed in the struggle to establish an independent poetic authority. But whatever the extent of their personal acquaintance, and despite the fact that their acquaintance certainly came to an end in 1369, Froissart and Chaucer offer us an exceedingly interesting comparison throughout their literary careers. In the 1360s and perhaps the early 1370s, there are direct points of contact between their poetic works. Later on, as we follow them into their works of maturity, the lines of attachment are more attenuated; but we may, even so, profitably compare their mature, nuanced, and darkening responses to their age.

The evidence of influence in the 1360s is in one direction, from the older poet to the younger. In the opening lines of his first major work, the *Book of the Duchess*, Chaucer echoes the opening of the *Paradis d'amour*:

> I have gret wonder, be this lyght,
> How that I lyve, for day ne nyght
> I may nat slepe wel nygh noght;
> I have so many an ydel thoght
> Purely for defaute of slep
> That, by my trouthe, I take no kep
> Of nothing, how hyt cometh or gooth,
> Ne me nys nothyng leef nor looth.
> Al is ylyche good to me—
> Joye or sorwe, wherso hyt be—
> For I have felyng in nothyng,
> But as yt were a mased thyng,
> Alway in poynt to falle a-doun;
> For sorwful ymagynacioun
> Ys alway hooly in my mynde.[3] (*Book of the Duchess*, 1–15)

The first two verses are a nearly exact translation of Froissart's first two verses, the rest of the passage a close adaptation of Froissart's phrasing. Chaucer's detailed attention to Froissart here has led James Wimsatt to argue that "in making his opening passage of the *Duchess* a near-verbatim translation of Froissart's first lines, Chaucer ostentatiously announces that he is following the compositional procedure of Froissart in the *Paradis*";[4] that is to say, Froissart's use of a dream frame from one Machaut poem (the *Fonteinne amoureuse*) and dream substance from another (the *Remede de Fortune*) provides the model for Chaucer's procedure. Chaucer uses the *Paradis d'amour* to frame his dream—at the end of the *Book of the Duchess* he returns to Froissart's poem, closely adapting its concluding lines just as he had its opening ones[5]—but he uses Machaut's *Jugement dou roy de Behaigne* as the central model for the dream itself.

This much is inarguable. But I think that Wimsatt is almost certainly wrong in the inferences he draws from Chaucer's procedure, that is to say, his overall view that "Chaucer seems to have reacted with unfailing serenity to the genius of Jean Froissart, the literary older brother who most nearly matched his powers as court writer in London" (p. 174). The best way to get at the significance of Chaucer's translation, I believe, is to compare it with a later instance of similarly exact quotation. At the beginning of *The Prelude*, Wordsworth celebrates the freedom of a summer vacation by proclaiming:

> The earth is all before me. With a heart
> Joyous, nor scared at its own liberty,
> I look about; and should the chosen guide
> Be nothing better than a wandering cloud,
> I cannot miss my way. (*The Prelude* 1.14–18)

At the end of book 12 of *Paradise Lost*, Milton had dispatched the fallen first couple into the wilderness:

> Some natural tears they dropped, but wiped them soon;
> The world was all before them, where to choose
> Their place of rest, and Providence their guide.
> They, hand in hand, with wandering steps and slow,
> Through Eden took their solitary way. (12.645–49)

Wordsworth's use of Miltonic blank verse by itself signals that he intends *The Prelude* to be an epic, a heroic poem about the "Growth of a Poet's Mind." But his direct quotation of Milton, in a very different and at first sight even parodic context, in fact shows both his taking his place within Milton's gigantic shadow as a poet, and his declaring independence and new direction at the very moment of direct quotation. The point at which Milton ended, in melancholy though hopeful expectation, is the point at which Wordsworth begins, in the exhilarated optimism of youth; the "pillar of a cloud," which leads the Israelites in their wanderings (Exodus 13.21) and suggests the inner Providence available to Adam and Eve, becomes the "wandering cloud" of a summer sky.

We would be foolhardy to seek a straightforward "anxiety of influence" in a fourteenth-century context, when very different notions of literary appropriation and allusion obviously obtain. Chaucer, notably, distinguishes between "poets" and "makers," the first worthy of being named, the second available for silent appropriation; Dante and Petrarch are the only moderns to whom he gives the poetic authority of the ancients, and he feels free to make use of other fourteenth-century poets (and at times, Dante and Petrarch too) without acknowledgment.[6] (The exception to Chaucer's habitual silence, Oton de Grandson, is evidently mentioned as much for his apparent friendship with Chaucer as for his poetic skill as the "flour of hem that make in Fraunce" [*Complaint of Venus*,

82].) Nonetheless, Chaucer's appropriation of Froissart is less a serene response to a "literary older brother" than what we might call a sibling rivalry, particularly since these opening lines of their first major works both owe a large filial debt to Machaut's *Fonteinne amoureuse*.[7] Chaucer also stands in relation to Froissart as Wordsworth does to Milton, with two significant differences. There is at least the possibility that he could have influenced Froissart in return; and at the start of the *Book of the Duchess* he mimics the beginning of Froissart's poem, not its end.

Wimsatt's view of the "serenity" in their relationship certainly derives in part from his belief that Froissart is indebted in turn to Chaucer, that the *Book of the Duchess* preceded, and in fact influenced, Froissart's *Dit dou bleu chevalier*. For him, these mutual borrowings evidently mark "their mutual respect and good will" (pp. 178–79).[8] I am myself more persuaded by Susan Crane's argument that the *Bleu chevalier* predates the *Book of the Duchess* and may have influenced it,[9] and by William Calin's provocative but I think compelling assertion that "we have no data in *Les Chroniques* or the poetic corpus to indicate that Froissart learned to speak and read English."[10] It is quite likely that some of Chaucer's earliest poetry was written in French (as Wimsatt and others have argued), and plausible that Froissart and Chaucer might, in French, have felt "mutual respect and good will." But if in every other respect the influence is in fact one-way, like Milton's on Wordsworth, the picture of serenity and mutuality must be replaced by something more sharp-edged but at least as interesting. That is to say, from his first major poem, Chaucer—writing in English—signals his self-confident insertion of himself into the French poetic tradition.

For if Chaucer does appropriate details, large and small, from the *Paradis d'amour*—the name Eclympasteyr (*BD* 167), the underlying themes that dreams bring comfort to true lovers, and that jealousy without hope allows the heart to listen to nothing but its own melancholy[11]—the most conspicuous fact of his opening lines is their exact quotation and then quick departure from Froissart.[12] The effect of beginning a poem with a nearly exact translation of the opening of another poem, written only a few years earlier and certainly familiar to Chaucer's courtly audience, is startling, and it is particularly startling if we imagine the first reading of the *Book of the Duchess* to have been at a ceremonial commemoration of Blanche's death. Like Froissart, Chaucer prays to Morpheus and Juno for a comforting dream, with the story of Ceyx and Alcyone inserted as the pretext for his doing so. His dream then echoes the conundrum of Machaut's *Jugement* poems: whether an unrequited or betrayed lover is better or worse off than one whose lover has died. But instead of imitating

Machaut's narrator, a love poet inexperienced in the actualities of love and chivalry,[13] Chaucer keeps Froissart's, the love poet who is himself the amorous hero of his dream. The effect is something like the reverse of having the Ancient Mariner show up at the wedding feast. The obsessive self-regarding ruminations of a sleepless lover-poet threaten to be strikingly inappropriate, even offensive at a scene of mourning; and much of the poem is taken up by the dreamer's failure to realize that the Man in Black is not his alter ego—another somewhat embittered unrequited lover.[14] The narrator's befuddlement may in part excuse him. He claims—after thirty lines of dazed self-pity—not to know why he is sleepless, though he goes on to say that he has had this "sicknesse" for eight years and suspects that "there is phisicien but oon" who can heal him (36–39); Froissart, by contrast, quickly tells us that he cannot dispel the "Pensees et merancolies" [thoughts and melancholy ideas] in his heart because he doesn't wish to forget "la belle" for whose love he suffers and wakes (7–12). By adopting the pose of the obtuse and self-obsessed lover, Chaucer is poking fun not only at his own position (in order to set up the consolation that his elegy will provide) but also—inevitably—at Froissart's characteristic pose in his early *dits*.

What we find here, in sum, is a complex revision and amalgamation of the poetic subjectivities in his sources: Chaucer begins with the model of the *Paradis d'amour* (the self-obsessed lover as hero); as the poem progresses, it in part shifts to the model of the *Bleu chevalier* or the *Fonteinne amoureuse* (an eavesdropping narrator who comforts a knight-lover), grafted onto the scene of the *Jugement* (the conundrum of who's worse off), but with the added complexity of having the Froissartian self-obsessed lover as one of the disputants.[15] Chaucer's first poem, then, notably displays the paradox that Larry Benson described in a talk some years ago: that the earlier poems are at once the most derivative and the most original of his works. The *Book of the Duchess* is a pastiche of allusions and quotations from Machaut and Froissart, but it recombines, cuts and pastes, its materials in an entirely original collage. In all of his poems—perhaps most tellingly in *Troilus and Criseyde*—the most interesting points are often those when Chaucer departs from a source that he has been following closely; we may thus see this technique developing from the beginning of his career, when he conspicuously marks an identical starting point with Froissart's dit of love and then heads off immediately in a sharply different direction.

We may also find, in the comparison of these two first poems, the source of the salient points of contact and distinction between Froissart and Chaucer in their mature works, after they have lost whatever personal acquaintance they once had. These have to do with a few complex, related issues. Both writers continue to finesse the difficulties of courtly patronage and of being in an aristocratic world but not of it, but with very different ways of inserting themselves into their works. Both writers respond to the courtly world and the chivalric ideal, but there are significant differences in their responses. Both writers are masters of impersonation. Just as the *Chroniques* is notable for its enlivening of events by means of dialogue,[16] so Chaucer in *Troilus and Criseyde* radically revises his source so as to turn it into a series of extended, crucially important conversations, and in the *Canterbury Tales*, he withdraws behind his impersonations of the various voices telling the tales. Both writers, finally, are steeped in the Ovidian tradition, and both depend on their audiences' having a more than passing acquaintance with Ovid's works.

These differences are all worth further exploration, and I am in fact forced to omit a discussion on the relation of the two writers to memory, personal and historical, and to the past: the chronicler as recorder of events, the poet as the holder of the "key of remembrance" and his duty as the revivifier of the illustrious dead. There is a fascinating difference in their attitudes toward their own poetic corpus, in their retrospective views of their poetic careers. Froissart's careful construction of his poetic anthology, in which he copies the example of Machaut (Huot, pp. 238–41, 303–5), and his nostalgic gathering together and presentation of his twenty-year-old poems on love to Richard II are vividly opposed to Chaucer's pose of ironic carelessness. Instead of *chroniques*, Chaucer leaves us the quotidian scraps of a civil servant's legal documents, the most laconic of poetic references to current events, and a list of his poetic works only as they are put into the mouths of an inept reader and critic (the Man of Law), a diffident defense attorney (Alceste in the *Prologue* to the *Legend of Good Women*), or *in propria persona*, in a list of vanities the dying poet hopes will not be held against him at the Day of Doom.

This contrast, and others, would be well worth pursuing; but I find myself pulled, like many before me and like others at the Amherst conference, to the complex, vivid, and mysterious "Voyage en Béarn," and to the relevance it has to an account of the two writers' Ovidian inclinations. This section of the *Chroniques* offers a very interesting comparison to fragment 5 of the *Canterbury Tales*, the tales of the Squire and the Franklin; although these works are entirely independent of each other,[17] they have some striking points of contact as the mature responses of Froissart and Chaucer to questions of romance and chivalry. I have written elsewhere about both of Chaucer's tales (as have many others),[18] and need hardly give a full account of them here, but I should recall a couple of points that will make their relevance to Froissart evident. The Squire, in the "General Prologue," is presented as very much the opposite of his father, the austere Crusader. The Squire is young, accomplished, elegantly dressed, fighting "to stonden in his lady grace" (I. 88), with the military experience of campaigns in Picardy and Flanders rather than at the outer boundaries of Christian Europe. There is in this portrait a hint, much developed in his tale, that he acutely senses his own belatedness, the impossibility of recapturing the significance and scope of his father's military accomplishment. The result, in his tale, is a debunking skepticism about the chivalric past. He does not search for the chivalric in ancient Athens (where the Knight's Tale finds it) or Arthurian Britain; Gawain "with his olde curteisye," he tells us, is in Fairyland (V. 95–96), and Lancelot "is deed" (287). Instead, he finds it in the nearly contemporary, exotic otherness of Cambyuskan's Tartar court, a place of magic, exoticism, youth, and innocence (though an innocence hedged in and threatened by experience in the form of treachery, political or amatory). The Squire also, in his account of the various marvels he finds—a magical flying brass horse, a mirror, a ring, and a sword—worries out loud about the risk of explaining magic away, of puncturing it, of trying to touch it only to see it disappear—in effect, of dispelling the exotic by domesticating it.

The Franklin, by contrast, sets his tale—centrally about the attempt to keep love alive within the framework of marriage—in a Brittany within a pagan past, in which "a mature innocent wisdom"[19] fights against the illusion and self-delusion of adulterous love; his is a lesson, less narrowly aristocratic than the Squire's, about the infectious power of *gentillesse* and the delusions of a self-enclosed and self-regarding *fin amor*. The threat of death in the rocks on the Breton coast is set against a May garden of love poetry and fantasy; its reality, when Aurelius's brother learns that all his old friends in Orléans are dead (V. 1181), offsets the magician who tells him so, who knows why they have come (1176), and who offers Aurelius, in his book-lined study, a magical vision of hunting and falconry, jousting, and the apparition of "his lady on a daunce, / On which hymself he daunced, as hym thoughte" (1200–1201). The framing of this fantasy by a sharp reminder of mortality makes Aurelius's long self-indulgence seem all the more self-destructive and pointless; and the Franklin couples together the clerk's magic and the lover's obsessive fantasy, the one a heathen illusion of a sort that Holy Church now protects us from (1133–34), the other a marker of the unrequited love, and threats to true love, that characterize the fallen world. In this tale, which recalls an amorous ideal associated with the Golden Age, Chaucer strikingly makes use of several names that recall that goldenness: Dorigen, Aurelius, Orléans; he also makes use of a garden, a *plaisance* that investigates but finally belies its paradisal associations.

The "Voyage en Béarn" is in effect a fusion of these two tales. It shares their concern with the chivalric, the exotic, belatedness, the mysterious and the magical, the Golden Age, and the threats to it of contingency and death. In ways that combine the serendipitous and the purposive, this section of Froissart's *Chroniques* also has an eery appositeness to another of Chaucer's works. The House of Fame in Chaucer's poem of that name, as in his source in Ovid's *Metamorphoses,* is set "Ryght even in myddes of the weye / Betwixen hevene and erthe and see" (714–15), in a central location to which all sound, significant or not, true or merely fabulous, comes. It is the wellspring of stories, true and false, and of stories in which true and false together become one tiding ("oo tydynge") (2109). For Froissart, the court of the comte de Foix at Orthez is a chivalric House of Fame, a place where fact is fictionalized, in particular, set against a subtext of Ovidian myth; and given the literariness of his approach to Béarn (as George Diller remarks in chapter 3 of this book, Froissart presents his voyage there as a chivalric quest), it is likely enough that he has Ovid's House of Fame on his mind. "Je ne pourroie mieulx ou monde escheoir pour estre justement infourmé de toutes nouvelles" (11.2–3) [I could not choose a better place in the world to be truly informed of all news],[20] he says, because of the great number of knights and squires who travel to Béarn, its neutrality, and its geographically central position as a gathering point for tidings:

> On veoit, en la salle et parmy les chambres et en sa court, chevalliers et escuiers d'honneur aler et venir, devisans d'armes et d'amours; et d'autres propos n'y oioit-on parler, et à la vérité tout honneur estoit en celle court trouvée. Nouvelles de quelque pays, ne de quelque roiaulme que ce fuist, en celle court on y apprendoit; car de tous pays pour la vaillance du seigneur elles y applouvoient et venoient. (11.88)

> [One saw knights and squires coming and going in the hall and the rooms and the courtyard, and one heard them talking of arms and love. Every subject of honour was discussed. Reports from every country and kingdom were to be heard, for, because of the reputation of the master of the house, they were brought there in great abundance. (Brereton, p. 266)]

The news comes, Froissart adds, from Spain, Portugal, Navarre, Aragon, England, Scotland, and Languedoc (11.88–89), and this role of Orthez as a focal point is later underlined by the story of Orton the familiar spirit, who conveys news from far away almost instantaneously—in effect, a fourteenth-century wire service. Chivalric tidings in Béarn are evidently very broadly disseminated. In Froissart's ninth *Pastourelle*, set on the banks of the Gave de Pau, shepherds discuss European heraldry, with particulars about arms from a large number of lands.[21] And its location, Froissart says, now that the North is in a peaceful period, allows him the opportunity to record feats of arms and chivalry in the South (11.2).[22]

The court of the comte de Foix, like the House of Fame, is the home of tidings; and Froissart hears from his informants, and recounts, many tales, and many tall tales. In the *House of Fame*, heralds, trumpeters, jugglers, and magicians (notably "Colle tregetour" [1277]) inhabit the same world as the poets and historians, and at least partly contaminate their dignified integrity (the historians themselves turn to squabbling, later in the poem). Chaucer points out his own potentially self-interested position when he is asked his name: "Artow come hider to han fame?" (1872); he replies that he does not care about his own fame but has come "Somme newe tydynges for to lere" (1886). Froissart's situation at Orthez is even more self-consciously ambiguous, since he and Gaston undertake so conspicuous a mutual flattery, the reward for Froissart being the invitation to read *Meliador* to the court night after night, and for Gaston the promise of immortality in the *Chroniques*, which he observes will be "more famous" ["plus recommandée," 11.3] than any other such work.[23] In other chapters of this book, George Diller remarks on the paradox of Froissart's "reading at night to his daytime informants," and Peter Ainsworth on the unseemly effort of brigands to buy their way into the *Chroniques*.[24] Gaston's court is a place that brings to the foreground the complex relationship of history, fame, and mere puffery.

Orthez is also, for Froissart, the equivalent of the Squire's Tartar court—set apart from the disenchanted context of the all too real world outside (including the middle-aged duc de Berry's unseemly eagerness to marry a youthful heiress and her inheritance). It is, in Froissart's words in the *Dit dou florin*,[25] a "paradys terrestre" (364) of chivalry, filled with talk of arms and love, and a world—however close to home—that is also filled with the marvelous and the exotic, in which even the everyday is conspicuous for its mysterious qualities. Its ruler, Gaston III, thought of himself by his surname Fébus, omnipresent in his battle cry "Febus avan" and the inscriptions on some of his castles "Febus me fe."[26] He gave himself this surname in 1358, after his *reise* with the Teutonic Knights and at the time of his delivering French noblewomen at Meaux from the Jacquerie (Tucoo-Chala 1991, p. 71), when he first used the battle cry. He evidently named himself after the god of the sun because of his shoulder-length golden hair, but certainly as well with a view to the broader mythological implications of the name: Phoebus as solar symbol, Apollo as the brother of Diana the goddess of the hunt (Tucoo-Chala 1991, p. 90).[27]

Given the singular self-consciousness in Gaston's choice of his own name, Froissart's flattery of this larger-than-life figure has one notable oddity: that Froissart never refers to him by his surname of choice, the sole name by which he signs himself: "Fébus."[28] Nonetheless, Froissart's narrative continually plays on this unuttered surname, in the texture of quotidian life in Béarn and in the mythological resonances of the events he describes as occurring there. As Michel Zink has said, "ce prince au surnom solaire menait une vie nocturne" [this prince with a solar surname led a nocturnal life],[29] dining at midnight and, one might add, attended, shortly before and after the winter solstice, by Froissart, who arrives in Orthez "sur le point de soleil esconsant" [at the moment of sunset], and "descends" ("je descendi") to the "ostellerie à la Lune" [hostelry of the Moon, 11.84] where he stays for the several months of his visit (largely because Gaston's castle is not large enough to house many visitors):

> Messire Espang de Lyon, en laquelle compaignie j'estoie venu, monta amont ou chastel, et parla au conte de ses besoingnes et le trouva en ses galleries; car à celle heure ung petit devant avoit-il disné, car l'usage du conte de Fois est telle ou estoit alors, et l'avoit tousjours d'enfance tenu, que il se descouchoit à haulte nonne et soupoit à my-nuit.
>
> Le chevallier luy dist que j'estoie là venu. Je fus tantost envoié querre en mon hostel, car c'estoit ou est, s'il vit, le seigneur du monde qui le plus voulentiers veoit estrangiers pour ouïr des nouvelles. (11.84–85)

> [Sir Espan de Lyon, in whose company I had traveled, presently went up to the castle to discuss his affairs with the Count. He found him in his gallery, having just had supper, for it had been the Count of Foix's custom since boyhood to arise at high noon and to sup at midnight. The knight told him of my arrival. He immediately sent down to the hostelry to fetch me, for he was—and is now, if he is still alive—particularly interested in meeting strangers and in hearing their news. (Brereton, p. 263)]

The count loves minstrelsy, the singing of "chansons, rondeaulx et virelais," and the performance of exotic interludes ["estranges entremets,"

11.88]; he is also given particularity, and singularity, by the individual coloring of his ideal chivalric features. "Les chiens sur toutes bestes il amoit, et aux champs, esté et yver, aux chasses voulentiers estoit. D'armes et d'amours voulentiers se déduisoit" (11.86) [He loved dogs more than all other animals and was very fond of hunting, both in summer and winter. He took great pleasure in arms and love. (Brereton, p. 264)]. He has strong opinions and oddities of behavior.[30] He also presides over a realm in which somnambulism, accidental death, second sight, and familiar spirits have their place.

This is a world in which we are soon aware of the blurring of fact and fiction, the symbiotic interchange between the real world of Béarn, the fiction of *Meliador,* and Froissart's romance of chivalry in the *Chroniques.* Meliador's name appears in a list of famous lovers in the *Paradis d'amour:* "Et chils a che biel Solel d'Or / On l'appelle Melyador" (985–86) [and the one with the splendid Golden Sun they call Meliador]. It may be that Froissart had begun his long romance in the 1360s before this first of his public poems; but it is more likely the case that, when he assembled his retrospective anthology in 1393–94, he inserted his hero's name after the fact.[31] He evidently, in return, uses the somnambulism of Gaston's brother in a later revision of *Meliador* (Zink, pp. 62, 66),[32] just as he had earlier inserted lyrics by his patron Wenceslas (as he reports in the *Dit dou florin* 300–306). Likewise, although Froissart's emphasis on "arms and love" in Béarn is nothing new in the *Chroniques*—there are several earlier points where the talk of knights (sometimes with, sometimes without ladies) turns to "arms and love"—it is also very much of a piece with Gaston's own charming "Prologue" to his *Livre de chasse,* which he evidently was revising about the time of Froissart's visit. In that prologue Gaston reports his lifelong devotion to three things, arms, love, and hunting, confessing that there are others who know or have succeeded more in the first two, but that in the third he admits to having no master.[33]

Froissart's romance and his "Voyage en Béarn" also share an allusive nostalgia for a fast-disappearing Golden Age. The poem describes the *enfances* of Arthur's court, its adventures taking place nine or ten years before the appearance of the familiar Arthurian heroes, (*Meliador,* 28)[34] and long before their familiar fallen predicaments;[35] and this Golden Age is recounted in the "terrestrial paradise" of Foix, where Froissart reads his romance to the sanguine namesake of the sun god, his romance of Meliador, the "chevalier au soleil d'or" (*Meliador,* 4470; also *Dit dou florin,* 379–80). Orthez, which derives its name from the Latin *orthesium,* is a *hortus,* a paradisal garden.[36] And like the Brittany of the Franklin's Tale, Béarn is a world whose goldenness is hinted at in its names, from *Meliador,* the "chevalier au soleil d'or" himself, to Orthez the town to Horton the familiar spirit, even to Orion, the village where the comte de Foix dies. The *Dit dou florin* enacts a comically poignant account of the Golden Age, its diminution and loss. Froissart is rewarded for his reading of *Meliador*, he tells us, by being given nightly whatever wine remained ("le demorant de son vin") in Gaston's golden cup ("vaissiel d'or fin") (*Florin*, 371–72) and, when he leaves Orthez, eighty gold florins (383). But he observes that "Change est paradys a l'argent" (38) [Exchange, or change, is paradise to money];[37] and he outlines the process by which the eighty florins he receives from Gaston are reduced to sixty, then exchanged for forty francs, all of which disappear overnight, lost or stolen, in Avignon (381–409).[38] He is left with only one remaining, talking florin, hidden in a corner of his purse, and the fellow traveler on his long journey to and away from Béarn—abandoned by its fellows, Froissart decides, because diminished by excessive trimming (126–34). After threatening the florin with further injury (119–25, 139–42), he promises to keep it for its apt moralizations on the transitory nature of money and helpful advice on how to replenish his purse (475–78).

This poem is in part a comic variant on Froissart's last nostalgic visit to England, in which he laments the death of his friends and the loss of the chivalric Golden Age of Edward III and Philippa (Brereton, pp. 402–8). Professors Zink and Ainsworth have taught us to think about bears in Béarn;[39] I would add the aura of *or*, and its inevitable loss, to the ursine. There is also here, conspicuously, the aura of Ovid. Douglas Kelly and others have shown that Froissart is, like Chaucer, a poet steeped in Ovid: he makes many allusions to the *Metamorphoses*, and invents notable pseudo-Ovidian narratives of his own.[40] Both poets, I would maintain, show a direct and detailed knowledge of Ovid, not merely one gained—as is often argued—by way of the *Ovide moralisé*. As Sylvia Huot says, "In his later dits Froissart treats the *Metamorphoses* in somewhat the same way that he treats the works of Machaut: he takes the collection of stories as a whole and pieces together composite narratives that draw on several different tales" (pp. 304–5). Agreeing with Kelly and Zink, Huot sees "deliberate artistry in Froissart's modifications of Ovidian material rather than, as some would have it, numerous errors resulting from an imperfect knowledge of Ovid" (p. 309n). My argument here is an extension of hers; for Froissart, very interestingly, follows this procedure not only in the fictional dits but in the *Chroniques* as well. Like Chaucer, Froissart expects us, I think, to pick up allusions, the original contexts of those allusions, and his purposeful misprisions of Ovidian material. Froissart may be in some respects even more Ovidian than Chaucer; for although Chaucer engages in some Ovidian mythmaking in the *Prologue* to the *Legend of Good Women*, where he says that Alceste, who saved her husband's life by offering to die in his place, was metamorphosed into a daisy,[41] he offers nothing quite like Froissart's complex layering of Ovidian mythic material.

There are three myths in particular that Froissart, in this section of the *Chroniques* and in earlier poems, has in mind and conflates in various combinations; earlier critical discussions have focused on those of Actaeon and of Cephalus and Procris, the first of which Froissart explicitly mentions, the second evidently on his mind because he confuses Actaeon with Cephalus. In this section of the *Chroniques*, so much concerned with bears, I think we must add a third Ovidian story of hunting, about the bear who was once Callisto. Indeed, just as the unspoken name Phoebus underlies the story of the comte de Foix (and just as Ovid's extended account of Phaethon [*Metamorphoses* 1.747–2.332] offers parallels to the accidental death of Gaston's only legitimate son, and the ascent necessary to reach the court of the solar father, who sits in solitary nighttime splendor),[42] so the unnamed story of Callisto—which immediately follows the story of Phaethon in the *Metamorphoses* (2.401ff.)—pulls together the Ovidian threads of the other two myths. All three are stories about hunting mishaps, or near mishaps. Callisto is one of Diana's warriors, a huntress who, to escape the hot sun, rests in a shady grove, where she is raped by Jupiter (who first appears to her disguised as Diana and pretends to be interested in hearing of her hunting exploits). When her pregnancy is visible, Diana banishes her; and Juno, to punish her for bearing Jupiter's child, turns her into a bear. "Many a time," Ovid says, "barking hounds drove her through rocky places, and the huntress fled, terrified of the hunters. Often she forgot what she was, and hid when she saw wild beasts; though a bear herself, she shuddered at the sight of bears in their mountain haunts" (tr. Innes, p. 63).[43] When she sees her son, now fifteen, out hunting and tries to approach him, he is about to kill her with his spear when Jupiter prevents this crime by turning them both into constellations. Juno has the last word, by keeping poor Callisto away from water. Diana had forbidden her a bath: "'I procul hinc' dixit 'nec sacros pollue fontis'" (*Met.* 2.464) ["Off with you! Do not defile this sacred spring!" (Innes, p. 62)]. Juno now asks Tethys and Oceanus to "prevent the Bear from entering your dark blue waters"; "do not let my rival bathe in your pure tide" (Innes, p. 64).[44]

When Procris is reunited with Cephalus after a period of estrangement, she gives him two presents that she has received from Diana: a dog and a spear (*Met.* 7.753–57). The dog later turns to stone, in the middle of a chase it cannot end; the spear kills her. When Cephalus is out hunting alone, he rests in the cool shade and calls on "Aura," the breeze (7.813), to relieve "the burning heat that scorches me" (Innes, p. 177).[45] Procris, thinking that "Aura" is the name of a nymph, secretly follows him; and he accidentally kills her when, resting after a successful hunt, he hears a rustling and, "thinking it was some wild creature, hurled my javelin" (Innes, p. 178) ("Sum ratus esse feram telumque uolatile misi" [*Met.* 7.841]). Actaeon, in the most often repeated of these stories, escapes the midday heat after a successful hunt by entering a shady valley where he accidentally sees Diana bathing (*Met.* 3.141ff.). She throws a handful of water in his face, turning him into a stag; and he is pursued and killed by his own dogs.[46]

Béarn is a world that has many odd points of contact with these Ovidian tales. It is ruled by a master of the hunt, a great lover of dogs (*Chron.* 11:86; Brereton, p. 264; Tucoo-Chala 1991, p. 280) who has sixteen hundred of them, plus the four additional heroic canine hunters, "Tristran, Hector, Brun et Rollant," which Froissart reports are being given to him as a present (eighth *Pastourelle*, v. 25). Gaston Fébus, estranged from his wife, accidentally kills his own, his only legitimate son with the point of his penknife. His bastard brother, Peter, is afflicted by somnambulism, in which he arises, arms himself, and fights with shadows—an affliction that began the very night after he hunted and killed a huge bear. Peter's wife, expecting evil to come, leaves him because her father once hunted the same bear "et en chaçant une voix luy dist (et si ne vit riens): 'Tu me chaces, et si ne te vueil nul dommaige; mais tu mourras de male mort'" (11:104) [and while hunting a voice said to him (and yet he saw nothing): 'You hunt me and yet I mean you no harm. But you will die a bad death']. Froissart tells the squire from whom he hears this story that he believes it,

> "car nous trouvons en l'escripture que anchiennement les dieux et les déesses à leur plaisance muoient les hommes en bestes et aussi en oiseaux, et aussi bien faisoient les femmes et par espécial quant ils les troubloient. Aussi puet estre que cest ours avoit esté ung chevallier chassant ès forests de Bisquaie. Si courroucha ou dieu ou déesse en son temps, pour quoy il fut mué en fourme de ours, et faisoit en ces désers sa pénitance, sicomme Actéon fut mué en cherf." (11:104–5)

[for we find in ancient books that in the old days the gods and goddesses at their pleasure changed men into beasts and also into birds, and likewise women, and especially when they annoyed them. So it may be that this bear had been a knight hunting in the forests of Biscay. He may have angered some god or goddess in his time, for which he was changed into the form of a bear, and was doing his penance in these desert places, just as Actaeon was changed into a stag.]

When the squire asks about Actaeon, Froissart gladly tells the story, but with some significant alterations. Actaeon, in his version, "aymoit le déduit des chiens sur toute riens" (11:105) [loved the divertissement of dogs above all others], is so absorbed in hunting a stag that he loses sight of his men and dogs, and comes to a meadow with a fountain, where he sees Diana by accident. She tells him: "'Actéon, qui cy t'envoia, si ne t'ayma guères'" (11:105) [Actaeon, whoever sent you here was no friend of yours (Brereton, p. 279)]; and she gives him his punishment ("pénitance") by changing him, she exults, "'en la fourme que le cherf que tu as huy chacié, est' [into the form of the stag which you have been hunting today]. Tantost Actéon fut mué en cherf, qui de sa nature ayme les chiens. Ainsi puet-il advenir de l'ours duquel vous m'avés fait vostre compte, et que la dame dessus nommée y scet autre chose ou sçavoit que elle ne dist pour l'eure. Si la doit-on tenir pour excusée" (11:106). [Actaeon was immediately changed into a stag, who by his nature loves dogs. A similar thing may have happened to the bear you told me about, and possibly the lady knows more about it, or knew more than she said at the time. If so, she ought not to be blamed (Brereton, p. 279).][47] Froissart's version of the Actaeon myth is quintessentially Ovidian; Actaeon keeps his human mind within his new form, just as Ovid describes the metamorphosed Callisto: "Mens antiqua manet (facta quoque mansit in ursa)" (*Met.* 2.485) [she had become a bear, but even so her mind remained unchanged (Innes, p. 63)]. Actaeon, in this version, still loves dogs even as a stag; but for anyone who knows Ovid's version of the story, Froissart's blandness here hides a grim joke.

We also hear of Orton, or Horton, the familiar spirit, who brings news as fast as the wind from all over Europe to the lord of Corresse, Gaston's friend and fellow in having second sight (11:192; Brereton, p. 296); in a new outcome to an old literary debate, Orton decides that he's better off serving a *chevallier* than his former master, a *clerc* (11:194). When the lord asks to see Horton (at Gaston's suggestion), the spirit's first response points out the risks of unnecessary curiosity: "'souffisse-vous, quant vous me oyés et je vous rapporte certaines nouvelles des loingtaines contrées'" (11:197) [let it suffice that you hear me and I bring you certain news from distant lands]. When the lord persists, Horton appears first, unrecognized, in the guise of "deux longs festus sur le planchier, qui tournoioient et se jouoient ensemble" (11:198) [two long straws twirling and twisting about on the floor (Brereton, p. 301)]. The lord insists again, and Horton warns him that "'vous me requérés trop avant'" [you are asking too much of me], and then promises: "'vous me verrés demain au matin, et prenés garde que la première chose que vous verrés quant vous serés yssu hors de vostre chambre, ce seray-je sans doubte nulle'" (11:199) [you will see me tomorrow morning, and remember that the first thing you see when you come out of your room, that will be me without any doubt]. The next morning, the lord looks down into his courtyard,

> et la première chose que il vyt, c'estoit que en sa court avoit une truye, la plus grande que il avoit oncques veue; mais elle estoit tant maigre que par samblant on n'y veoit que la pel et les os, et avoit les oreilles grandes et longues et pendantes et toutes deschirées, et avoit ung musel long et agu et tout affamé. (11:199)

> [and the first thing he saw was the most enormous sow he had ever seen, but it was so thin that it seemed to be nothing but skin and bones, and it had great long teats [sic] dangling under it and a long hungry-looking snout. (Brereton, p. 301)]

The lord orders his men to let out the dogs: "'je vueil que celle truie soit pilliée et devourée'" (11.199) [I want that sow to be savaged]. "Adont la truie jetta ung grant brait et regarda contremont sur le seigneur de Corasse qui s'appuioit devant sa chambre à une estaye. L'on ne la vit oncques puis, car elle s'esvanouy, ne l'on ne sceut penser qu'elle devint" (11:200) [The sow uttered a loud cry and looked straight up at the lord of Corresse as he leaned out of the gallery. It was not seen again, for it disappeared, and no one knew where it went to (Brereton, p. 301)]. The lord realizes that he has seen Horton and lost him forever: "car oncques depuis Horton ne repaira en l'ostel du seigneur de Corasse, et morut le bon chevallier dedens l'an enssieuvant" (11:200) [for Orton never again returned to the castle of the lord of Corresse, and the good knight died in the ensuing year]. What connects the stories of Peter of Béarn and Horton the spirit? In both cases, there's a parallel to Chaucer's Squire's Tale, specifically the Squire's anxiety at dispelling the magical, or to the disappearing vision in the Wife of Bath's Tale. The bear is killed and takes revenge; Horton, attacked by dogs when he has taken on the guise of a sow, never returns again. Both stories have an underlying link with the story of

Actaeon. All three concern the consequences of seeing and disturbing a mystery, whether on purpose or by accident.

Our reading of this section of the *Chroniques* owes much to the work of Zink and Ainsworth: Ainsworth's disentanglement of "myth, fiction, and history," and Zink's deft homage to Charles Laughton's *Night of the Hunter*, in the title of his exceedingly interesting essay. (I've been trying to find an excuse to call this essay "La Nuit de Chaucer.") Even closer in spirit to this intertextual, allusive olio, I think, is Nabokov, who in *Lolita* asks us to negotiate our way among "The Enchanted Hunters," the "Hunted Enchanters," and "Ted Hunter, Cane, NH." Froissart's odd reading of the Actaeon story in his conversation with the Squire is particularly notable because he in fact knows the story quite well, and tells it in full in the *Joli buisson de Jonece* (2233–88). (He also makes use of it in his account of Camel de Camois the somnambulist at the beginning of *Meliador*.) He knows it better than James Wimsatt does, as a matter of fact. Wimsatt presents Melampus, named as Actaeon's dog in the *Paradis d'amour* (1137–38), as an example of the sort of pseudo-Ovidian name that Froissart invents;[48] Melampus is in fact prominent in Ovid's mock-epic catalogue of Actaeon's dogs, who chase their metamorphosed master (in both *Met.* 3.208 and the *Ovide moralisé*). Froissart, significantly, conflates Actaeon with Cephalus in *L'espinette amoureuse* (2807–20), saying that Actaeon killed his beloved by accident while hunting.

This all becomes of particular interest because Froissart's account of the death of Gaston Fébus (14:325–27) in the Hôpital-d'Orion (a real place, but evidently not where the archival evidence says that Gaston actually died)[49] is at its heart nothing other than one more, final rewriting of the Actaeon story. Froissart reports that the count stopped for lunch, after hunting a bear all day and after the dogs were given their portion (*la curée*, 14:325) of the kill.[50] He goes into a room that is as close as a room can be to the shady retreat of Actaeon, or Cephalus, or Callisto: "verdure fresce et nouvelle" (14:326) [greenery fresh and new] is scattered on the floor, and festooned on the walls; and the room offers relief from the heat of the August day. Gaston talks about his dogs with Espan du Lyon, his friend and Froissart's former traveling companion. The tables are set; Gaston asks for water to wash himself.

> Il se leva du siége et tendi les mains avant pour laver. Si trestost que l'eaue descendi froide sur ses dois que il avoit beaulx, longs et drois, le vyaire luy paly, le cuer luy tressailly, les piés luy faillirent, et chéy là sur le siége tourné en disant: 'Je suis mort! Sire, vray Dieu, mer-

chy!' Oncques plus ne parla, mais il ne dévia pas si trestost et entra en paynnes et transses. (14:326)

[The Count rose from his seat and stretched out his hands to be washed. As soon as the cold water fell on his fingers, which were well-shaped, long and straight, his face turned white, his heart throbbed violently, his legs failed him, and he fell back on to the chair, exclaiming: 'I am dying. Lord God have mercy!' These were the last words he spoke, though he did not die at once, but fell into a state of pain and shivering. (Brereton, pp. 386–87)]

(The two squires who poured the water rush to try it themselves, in order to prove that there has been no foul play; and the count dies within half an hour.) This is, as others have noted, the perfect hunter's death—sudden, after the triumph of doing what he loves best to do, and talking about what he most loves to talk about.[51] We may also, indeed must, think of the mythic resonances of this scene: perhaps that Orion was killed or metamorphosed by Diana (Tucoo-Chala 1991, pp. 339–40); that Phoebus is Diana's male counterpart (Ainsworth, *Jean Froissart*, p. 155); certainly, that Diana transforms Actaeon—who also is finished hunting and escaping the heat of the day—by sprinkling water on him. Michel Zink notes that hunting the bear is an archetypal *rite de passage*, and that the bear is a totem of the subterranean world (pp. 67 and 76; also see Ainsworth, *Jean Froissart*, pp. 166–67).

However, I want to end with a more general comment on romance, mythical allusion, and the marvelous themselves. Chaucer's Squire worries that explaining his marvels—by the science of optics or by bringing to bear the precedent of *olde stories* (the Trojan Horse, or Pegasus, as a context for the magic horse)—is to explain them away, to destroy their magic. The gap that romance must maintain between us and the Other is a large reason for its most notable generic quality: its perpetual deferring of an ending. It may be that explaining Peter of Béarn by referring to Actaeon risks explaining him away, "of temporarily dampening down any potential" the story "might have had to disturb, in so far as the reassuring voice of an *auctoritas* (Ovid/Froissart) offers his audience both a precedent and an 'explanation' for the events recounted" (Ainsworth, *Jean Froissart*, p. 164).[52] But in the death of Gaston Fébus, the myth itself, in its final variant, is what is disturbing: Diana is absent; whatever may have annoyed her (if anything did) is left unspoken; and this lover of dogs is not changed to anything we can see, hunt, or be haunted by. If Froissart's *Meliador* is the quintessence of what Patricia Parker has called "inescapable romance"[53] ("interminable" is the word of choice for the poem's critics), the end of Gaston Fébus is terminal, but fittingly inconclusive.

Notes

1. See Anthime Fourrier's introduction to his edition of Froissart's *"Dits" et "Débats"* (Geneva: Droz, 1979), pp. 7–8, which corrects Froissart's error in remembering 1361 as the date of his arrival in England.

2. See *Chaucer Life-Records*, ed. Martin M. Crow and Clair C. Olson (Oxford: Clarendon Press, 1966), p. 30.

3. All quotations from Chaucer are from *The Riverside Chaucer*, 3rd ed., general ed. Larry D. Benson (Boston: Houghton Mifflin, 1987).

4. James Wimsatt, *Chaucer and His French Contemporaries: Natural Music in the Fourteenth Century* (Toronto: University of Toronto Press, 1991), p. 178.

5. See Colin Wilcockson's note, in the *Riverside Chaucer*, to ll. 1324–34 of the *Book of the Duchess*.

6. Cf. Kevin Brownlee, *Poetic Identity in Guillaume de Machaut* (Madison: University of Wisconsin Press, 1984), p. 7: "It is only in the fourteenth century that the semantic field of the very term 'poète' in French is expanded to include vernacular, contemporary poets," its earliest examples being Deschamps's elegiac praise of Machaut in two *ballades*; likewise, Deschamps's ballade to Chaucer addresses him as "poete."

7. Both Chaucer and Froissart are copying the lover's complaint at ll. 699ff. of the *Fonteinne amoureuse*. Froissart's primary debt in the *Paradis d'amour* is to Machaut's poem; Machaut's poem was probably written in 1360–61, and Froissart's between the beginning of 1361 and the end of 1362. See Peter F. Dembowski's edition of *Le paradis d'amour; L'orloge amoureus* (Geneva: Droz, 1986), p. 13.

I would qualify Dembowski's assertion that, at the beginning of the *Book of the Duchess*, "Nous sommes . . . dans le domaine de l'art conventionnel et par conséquent, imitatif" (p. 115), a remark that describes more accurately the relation of the *Paradis*, Froissart's first poem, to its antecedents in Machaut. See Sylvia Huot, *From Song to Book* (Ithaca and London: Cornell University Press, 1987), pp. 303-5, for a stimulating discussion of the *Paradis d'amour* as the first piece in Froissart's poetic anthology, itself constructed (in 1393–94) on the pattern of Machaut's, and on the poem as "an initial statement of the themes and the poetics of the whole." Froissart, that is to say, was conspicuously imitating Machaut, both when he composed the poem and when he, much later, collected his poems: "These textual reminiscences underscore the prefatory function of the *Paradis* as the opening piece in a collection portraying the poetic career of an individual" (Huot, p. 304). Chaucer, by contrast, quickly diverges from the path set out by his source and never undertakes an equivalent task of assembling his oeuvre.

8. For Wimsatt's argument at greater length, see his article "The *Dit dou Bleu Chevalier*: Froissart's Imitation of Chaucer," *Mediaeval Studies* 34 (1972): 388–400. For a fuller treatment of this poem, see Rupert Pickens's essay, chap. 7 of this book.

9. Susan Crane, "Froissart's *Dit dou Bleu Chevalier* as a Source for Chaucer's *Book of the Duchess*," *Medium Aevum* 61 (1992): 59–74.

10. William Calin, *The French Tradition and the Literature of Medieval England* (Toronto: University of Toronto Press, 1994), p. 523.

11. A central point, perhaps the moral, of Froissart's poem is Esperance's injunction not to let jealousy, of which a little is necessary for every true lover (663–67), take over the lover's heart: "Car jalous a le coer si tendre / Que il ne voet a riens entendre / Fors seul a sa merancolie" (699–701) [For the jealous man has so tender a heart that he does not wish to attend to anything except solely his melancholy]. If the lover's fate is as much in suspense at the end of the poem as it is at the beginning, he at least can recognize that Plaisance and Esperance have done their work, that Morpheus has given him a dream, "tel songe / Ou nulle riens n'a de mençonge" (1710–11) [the kind of dream where there's nothing at all of falsehood], that Orpheus has shown him the art of singing, and that Iris, Morpheus's messenger, has with the god of sleep granted that "tout li vrai amant / Sont conforté, et c'est raisons, / En songes et en visions" (1719–21) [all true lovers are comforted, and rightly so, in dreams and in visions].

12. Chaucer, interestingly, makes a similar quick departure from a notable opening in his next major poem. In the *House of Fame* the dreamer sees the first line of the *Aeneid* inscribed on a table of brass: "'I wol now synge, yif I kan,/ The armes and also the man" (*HF* 143–44), adding an un-Vergilian tentativeness to Vergil, as the dreamer then retells the story of Aeneas's wanderings, but with an Ovidian coloring, at one point inventing a speech for Dido on his own poetic authority.

13. As Huot notes (p. 306), "In the *Fonteinne* Machaut separates the roles of writer, performer, and lover." (Also see Brownlee, p. 157.)

14. I have made this argument at greater length in "Irony and the Age of Gold in the *Book of the Duchess*," *Speculum* 52 (1977): 314–28; reprinted in *Chaucer and Ovid* (New Haven and London: Yale University Press, 1979), pp. 65–81.

15. Brownlee notes (p. 159) that in the *Jugement dou roy de Behaingne* itself we expect Machaut to be the amorous hero of his poem; after "a radical shift in perspective," he "ceases to function as a character and takes on the role of witness, becoming, as it were, a kind of narrative device."

16. See Peter F. Ainsworth's essay "Style direct et peinture des personnages chez Froissart," *Romania* 93 (1972): 498–522.

17. See, however, William Askins's essay "The Historical Setting of *The Manciple's Tale*," *Studies in the Age of Chaucer* 7 (1985): 87–105, which argues that the story of Phoebus shows Chaucer's knowledge of Froissart's "Voyage en Béarn."

18. See my essays "Domesticating the Exotic in the *Squire's Tale*," *ELH* 55 (1988): 1–26; and "Love and Degree in the *Franklin's Tale*," *Chaucer Review* 21 (1987): 321–37.

19. The phrase is Northrop Frye's: *Anatomy of Criticism* (Princeton: Princeton University Press, 1957), p. 202.

20. All quotations from Froissart's *Chroniques* are from the edition of Kervyn de Lettenhove, *Oeuvres de Froissart*, vol. 11 (Brussels: Victor Devaux, 1870), and vol. 24 (1872). The translations are, when possible, from Froissart, *Chronicles*, tr. Geoffrey Brereton (Harmondsworth: Penguin, 1968), but at times mine or with my emendations.

21. *The Lyric Poems of Jehan Froissart: A Critical Edition*, ed. Rob Roy McGregor Jr., North Carolina Studies in the Romance Languages and Literatures 143 (Chapel Hill: University of North Carolina Press, 1975), pp. 167–69.

22. Pierre Tucoo-Chala has outlined Froissart's intention in "Froissart dans le Midi Pyrénéen," in *Froissart: Historian*, ed. J. J. N. Palmer (Woodbridge, England: Boydell Press, 1981), p. 118.

23. Tucoo-Chala has outlined this exercise in mutual flattery for mutual benefit (*Froissart: Historian*, pp. 128–29).

24. Also see J. J. N. Palmer (*Froissart: Historian*, p. 1): "The roll-call of his noble patrons and of those members of the higher nobility known to have possessed copies of the *Chronicles*, serves to highlight their fame during Froissart's lifetime, as does the evident alacrity with which many of his contemporaries sought to ensure their personal immortality by regaling their author with accounts of events and feats of arms in which they had participated. As Froissart wryly remarks of one such encounter, his would-be informant seemed prepared to recount his entire life history and would no doubt have done so had he not been inopportunely summoned to the dinner table of the count of Foix, a summons which cheated him of immortality by half-an-hour."

25. "Le dit dou florin," in Jean Froissart, *"Dits" et "Débats,"* ed. Fourrier, pp. 175–90.

26. Pierre Tucoo-Chala, *Gaston Fébus: Prince des Pyrénées (1331–91)* (Pau: Editions Deucalion, 1991), p. 10.

27. Tucoo-Chala (1991), p. 19: "Par ce geste d'orgueil et de puissance, rare au Moyen Age, il signifiait à tous que sa vie serait un rêve de gloire."

28. "Au total Fébus—et curieusement on ne trouve aucune allusion à ce surnom choisi pourtant par le comte lui-même—est en quelque sorte le modèle de la chevalerie" (Tucoo-Chala, *Froissart: Historian*, p. 128).

29. Michel Zink, "Froissart et la nuit du chasseur," *Poétique* 11 (1980), p. 61.

30. He calls his servants, not by name, but as "mau me sert," expatiates on the healthful effects of hunting, eats poultry (mainly legs and wings) and drinks very little wine, is devoutly Christian, and asks his guest Froissart to read from *Meliador* as a nightly entertainment (ll.85–88).

31. See Peter Dembowski's note to ll. 985–88 of the *Paradys d'amours*: "Ces couplets, qui contiennent les noms des héros de *Meliador* (roman que Froissart a achevé longtemps après *P*) ont été sûrement interpolés ici après la composition du roman." Also see his *Jean Froissart and His "Méliador": Context, Craft, and Sense*

(Lexington, Ky.: French Forum, 1983), pp. 57–59; and B. J. Whiting, "Froissart as Poet," *Mediaeval Studies* 8 (1946):pp. 214–15.

32. Also see Laurence Harf-Lancner, "Chronique et roman: les contes fantastiques de Froissart," p. 60, in *Autour du roman: Études présentées à Nicole Cazauran* (Paris: Presses de l'École Normale Superieure, 1990): "Où commence le roman? où finit l'histoire? . . . Y contait-il déjà les malheurs de Camel de Camois (devant Pierre de Béarn) ou le motif du somnambulisme serait-il une interpolation ajoutée après le voyage en Béarn? Le somnambulisme de Pierre de Béarn serait-il au contraire calqué sur celui du personnage romanesque? En tout cas, chronique et roman se nourrissent ici l'un de l'autre et si le roman ne franchit pas sur ce point la frontière de l'étrange, la chronique s'enfonce peu à peu dans le merveilleux."

33. ." . . je Gaston, par la grace de Dieu, surnommé Febus, comte de Foys, seigneur de Bearn, qui tout mon temps me suis delité par espicial en trois choses, l'une est en armes, l'autre est en amours, et l'autre si est en chasce, et, quar des deux offices il y ha heü de meilleurs maistres trop que je ne suy, quar trop de meilleurs chevaliers on esté que je ne suy et aussi moult de meilleures cheances d'amours ont eu trop de genz que je n'ay, pour ce seroit grant niceté se je en parloye. . . . mes du tiers office, de qui je ne doubte que j'aye nul maistre, combien que ce soit vantance, de celuy vouldray je parler, c'est de chasce": "Prologue" to Gaston Phébus, *Livre de chasse*, ed. Gunnar Tilander (Karlshamn: E. G. Johansson, 1971), p. 51.

Tucoo-Chala [1991], p. 302, points out that the comte de Foix was singular in his dislike of tournaments: "il n'aime pas et n'organise aucun tournoi. . . . Fébus estimait que la guerre était affaire trop sérieuse pour être singée par des exercises qui risquaient d'inculquer des comportements peu conformes aux exigences d'un combat réel. Pour lui la meilleure propédeutique de la guerre était la chasse."

34. *Méliador*, ed. Auguste Longnon, Société des Anciens Textes Français, 3 vols. (Paris: Firmin Didot, 1895–99), 1:2.

35. For discussion see Dembowski, *Jean Froissart and His Méliador*, pp. 73–75.

36. See Tucoo-Chala (1991), p. 255. Daniel Poirion's comment on Froissart's poetry is interestingly apposite here: "Ce besoin d'un espace concret pour élaborer le monde imaginaire se confirme dans les dits de Froissart: c'est dans un *paradis* ou un *temple*, autour d'une *espinette* ou d'un *buisson* que le poète place ses personnages." See *Le poète et le prince* (Paris: Presses Universitaires de France, 1965), p. 488. The *paradis* or garden is often in fourteenth-century poetry, as it is in the *Paradis d'amour* (912ff.), the setting for "l'amoureuse cache" (945) [the amorous hunt]. This point of connection with hunting in Béarn and, as we shall see, in Ovid's *Metamorphoses* is connected to another. The *locus amoenus*, in Ernst Robert Curtius's classic description, characterizes both the lover's garden and the hunter's shady retreat from the midday sun. "It is . . . a beautiful, shaded natural site. Its minimum ingredients comprise a tree (or several trees), a meadow, and a spring or brook. Birdsong and flowers may be added. The most elaborate examples also add a breeze"; see *European Literature and the Latin Middle Ages*, trans. Willard R. Trask (Princeton: Princeton University Press, 1953), p. 195.

37. The passage reads:
   Argens trop volentiers se change:
   Pour ce ont leur droit nom li change,
   Pas ne le scevent toute gent.
   Change est paradys a l'argent
   Car il a la tous ses deduis,
   Ses bons jours et ses bonne nuis:
   La se dort il, la se repose,
   La le grate on, c'est vraie chose,
   La est frotés et estrillés,
   Lavés et bien appareilliés. (*Dit dou florin*, 35–44)
38. Froissart says that upon his arrival in Avignon,
   Et voloie, voir je te di,
   Mettre tous ces florins au change.
   Mes pourpos, qui se mue et change,
   Se mua en moi sans sejour. (*Florin*, 392–95)
39. Zink, "Froissart et la nuit du chasseur"; Peter F. Ainsworth, "Knife, Key, Bear and Book: Poisoned Metonymies and the Problem of *Translatio* in Froissart's Later *Chroniques*," *Medium Aevum* 59 (1990): 91–113; and more generally, his *Jean Froissart and the Fabric of History: Truth, Myth, and Fiction in the Chroniques* (Oxford: Clarendon Press, 1990).
40. See Douglas Kelly, "Les Inventions ovidiennes de Froissart: Réflexions intertextuelles comme imagination," *Littérature* 41 (1981): 82–92.
41. Cf. Froissart's invention of the myth of Hero and Cepheus to explain the origin of the daisy in *Le joli buisson de Jonece*, ed. Anthime Fourrier (Geneva: Droz, 1975), ll. 3216–41.
42. Pynoteus, Froissart's pseudo-Ovidian character, tells the story of Phaethon in the *Prison amoureuse*, ll. 1767–1876.
43. I have used Mary M. Innes's translation of the *Metamorphoses* (Harmondsworth: Penguin, 1955). The Latin reads:
   A! quotiens per saxa canum latratibus acta est
   Venatrixque metu uenantum territa fugit!
   Saepe feris latuit uisis, oblita quid esset,
   Vrsaque conspectos in montibus horruit ursos. (2.491–94)
I have used the edition of Ovid's poem by Georges Lafaye (1928; rpt. Paris: "Les Belles Lettres," 1966).
44. "At uos si laesae tangit contemptus alumnae,
   Gurgite caeruleo Septem prohibete triones
   Sideraque in caelo stupri mercede recepta
   Pellite, ne puro tingatur in aequore paelex." (*Met.* 2.527–30)
45. "Aura," (recordor enim) "uenias" cantare solebam
   "Meque iuues intresque sinus, gratissima, nostros,
       Vtque facis, releuare uelis, quibus urimur, aestus." (*Met.* 7.813–15)
46. The common elements of these three myths—a hunter seeking relief from

the heat of the day in a shady grove, often near water—also appear in the story of Narcissus (see *Met.* 3.407–14), which Froissart retells in the *Joli buisson de Jonece*, 3252ff.; Froissart, very interestingly, makes Narcissus a version of Actaeon, as a stag-hunter and employer of hunting dogs.

47. The metamorphosis of a human being into a bear, with its precedent in the story of Callisto, also relies for its credibility on the ways in which bears may seem nearly human. As Zink notes (pp. 64–65), Gaston's *Livre de chasse* echoes the claim by Aristotle and Pliny that bears have sex in a human fashion: "Et, quant l'ours fet sa besoigne aveques la ourse, ilz font a guise d'omme et de femme, touz estenduz l'un sur l'autre" (ed. Tilander, p. 85).

48. "In the poem [the *Paradis d'amour*] he refers to Morpheus, Iris, and Juno, Achilles and Polyxena, Leander and Hero, and many such. He associates with these figures names that have an authentic ring but are found in no classical dictionary: Leucothea, an alleged inamorata of Neptune; Melampus, a wailing dog attributed to Actaeon; and Enclimpostair, messenger of the God of Sleep. . . . In his evident invention of such names Froissart's main predecessor was Jean de le Mote" (*Chaucer and His French Contemporaries*, p. 190).

49. Pierre Tucoo-Chala, *Gaston Fébus: Un Grand prince d'Occident au XIVe siècle* (Pau: Éditions Marrimpouey Jeune, 1976), pp. 205-6, constructs a plausible hypothesis to argue that Gaston's corpse was moved from l'Hôpital-d'Orion to Sauveterre-de-Béarn, where the notarial records situate his death; also see Tucoo-Chala, in *Froissart: Historian*, p. 180 n.3.

50. See Tucoo-Chala (1976), p. 205: "Tout au plus peut-on s'étonner un peu de noter la présence, au début d'août, d'ours dans cette forêt, à une époque où ces plantigrades pouvaient trouver à se nourrir facilement dans la haute montagne. Peut-être Froissart a-t-il jugé plus pittoresque pour ses lecteurs de substituer un ours à quelque sanglier?" In his 1991 biography of Gaston, Tucoo-Chala notes another discordant detail: "le texte précise 'après avoir vu la capture de l'ours, la curée faite'"; but, "comme Fébus l'enseigne à ses veneurs, il n'y a pas de curée après la prise de l'ours, que la *curée* ne se dit que du cerf" (pp. 338–39).

51. See Ainsworth, *Jean Froissart*, pp. 164–65, and Tucoo-Chala (1991), p. 339.

52. Zink makes an analogous observation, that "il est remarquable que Froissart fasse immédiatement appel à la mythologie et qu'il ne fasse pas la moindre allusion aux histoires de loup-garou qui circulaient au Moyen Age et que la littérature avait exploitées." Part of the reason, he argues, is the prestige of Antiquity and Latin. The other is the domestication of the classical pantheon, even thought of as demons triumphed over by Christianity. "Il est donc plus satisfaisant scientifiquement et plus orthodoxe du point de vue religieux d'admettre qu'Actéon a pu être changé en cerf par Artémis que de croire aux histoires brumeuses et inquiétantes de loups-garous celtiques ou germaniques" (pp. 68–69).

53. Patricia Parker, *Inescapable Romance* (Princeton: Princeton University Press, 1979).

V

Image and Reception

11.1. Miniature, four scenes from the opening of the *Chroniques*. Paris, B.N. fr. 2663, f. 6. Reproduced by permission of the Bibliothèque Nationale, Paris.

11

Image and Propaganda

The Illustration of Book 1 of Froissart's *Chroniques*

Laurence Harf-Lancner

In a recent article, Alberto Varvaro considerably enhances our knowledge of the manuscripts of book 1 of Froissart's *Chroniques* through an iconographic analysis.[1] His point of departure is the mention, in the *Journal* of Jean Le Fèvre, chancellor of Louis d'Anjou (the uncle of Charles VI), under the date of December 12, 1381, of a seizure, carried out at the duke's order, of fifty-six quires of the text of the *Chroniques*, which Froissart had had illuminated in order to offer them to the king of England, Richard II.[2] This troubling occurrence is related to an enigmatic image. In several illuminated manuscripts of the first book of the *Chroniques*, an initial miniature offers, in four scenes, an iconographic summary of the opening of book 1 (fig. 11.1):

1. Froissart offers a book to a king of England, who can be identified as Richard II.
2. Isabelle, queen of England, who with her son fled her husband, Edward II, is welcomed in France by her brother Charles IV in 1325.
3. Isabelle and the future Edward III disembark in England at Saint Edmond's Abbey, at the head of an expedition.
4. They lay siege to Bristol.

These four scenes read, as is customary with such imaged tables of contents, from left to right and from top to bottom. The frontispiece refers clearly to the opening of book 1: the flight of Isabelle and her reconquest of power (with an armed force led by Jean of Hainaut), which was to lead to the deposing of Edward II and the coronation of Edward III in 1327.[3] But if the three last scenes present no difficulty of interpretation, the first poses an apparently insoluble problem: Froissart's offering of a book to the king of England does not correspond to any episode in book 1. Froissart never offered a book to Edward III. As for Richard II, he ascended the throne in 1377, and Froissart did not meet him until 1395, on the occasion of the pilgrimage-voyage to England that he recounts in book 4; what he offers the king then is not a book of the *Chroniques* but a book that treats of love—"traite d'amours"—a book of poems that has been identified with the manuscript B.N. 830–831.[4] The first scene of the frontispiece of book 1, however, could hardly refer to an episode occurring almost seventy years after the three others.

Varvaro develops a hypothesis of Kervyn de Lettenhove that this image echoes Froissart's project, in 1381, to offer a book of the *Chroniques* to the English king (Kervyn, I, 2, p. 83). In the manuscript he had illuminated for Richard II, the chronicler would have had himself represented with his dedicatee. This hypothesis justifies the presence of Richard II in the illustration of a number of manuscripts of book 1. It also throws light on the existence of a family of illuminated manuscripts of book 1 that all present the same frontispiece and quite similar iconographic programs: All may derive from the manuscript that Froissart had destined for Richard II and that the duke of Anjou ordered seized in 1381. Almost all are French manuscripts, most of them Parisian, of the beginning of the fifteenth century. The manuscript confiscated by Louis I of Anjou would have served as model in Parisian ateliers in the years 1410–20, in the circle of the Master of Rohan, through the intermediary of Louis II of Anjou and Yolande of Aragon.[5]

Here is the list of manuscripts that present as frontispiece an iconographic summary of the beginning of book 1 of the *Chroniques*:[6]

- Besançon, B.M. 864–865 (books 1–3). Parisian manuscript whose paintings are attributed to the Master of the Apocalypse of the duc de Berry, active from 1407 to 1420 (Meiss, p. 370; Varvaro, fig. 1).
- Brussels, B.R. II 88 (fragments). Manuscript from the years 1410–15 bearing the arms of the family of Coucy.[7]
- Brussels, B.R. IV 251 (book 1). Miniatures completed between 1405 and 1415 in a Parisian atelier in which worked the Master of Bedford and the Master of Rohan.[8]
- The Hague, B.R. 72 A 25 (book 1). All paintings executed by the Master of Virgil, in the service of the duc de Berry and active in Paris in the first fifteen years of the fifteenth century (Meiss, p. 409; Varvaro, fig. 4).
- New York, Pierpont Morgan, M 804 (books 1 and 2). Created in Paris

for Pierre de Fontenay, painted by the Master of Boèce ca. 1412.[9] Pierre de Fontenay, lord of Rances (b. between 1360 and 1365, d. 1427), served the dukes of Burgundy Philippe le Hardi and Jean Sans Peur before entering the king's service. In 1408 and 1409, he was counselor concerning aides in France, then governor of the royal finances. After the Treaty of Troyes in 1420, he passed to the service of Henry V and of Bedford.

- Paris, B.N. fr. 2642 (book 1). In the opinion of François Avril, "the origin of this manuscript is definitely Parisian and the style of the decoration and the paintings allows us to date it ca. 1410–1415 and to connect it with the atelier of the Master of Boucicaut."[10]
- Paris, B.N. fr. 2649 (book 1). Parisian manuscript of 1415–17 whose paintings are related to those of the Master of the Apocalypse of Berry (Meiss, p. 371).
- Paris, B.N. fr. 2662 (book 1). Probably from the atelier of the Master of Rohan, ca. 1405.[11]
- Paris, B.N. fr. 2663–2664 (books 1–2). The painter is close to the Master of the Apocalypse of Berry (Meiss, p. 371). At the bottom of folio 405v. we read: "Ce livre donna messire Tangui du Chastel à Jehan sire de Derval." Tanguy II de Chatel (ca. 1425–ca. 1477), a Breton lord, son of Tanguy I (one of the heads of the Armagnac party, compromised in the murder of Jean Sans Peur in 1419, later in the service of Charles VII), had himself been in the service of Charles VII and then of Louis XI. Jean de Derval, also Breton, a great bibliophile, was the chief chamberlain of the duc de Bretagne (d. 1482).
- Paris, B.N. fr. 2675 (book 1). Parisian manuscript of the 1430s related to the Master of the Cité des Dames (Meiss, p. 382).
- Paris, B.N. fr. 6474–6475 (books 1, 3). As M. H. Tesnière has shown, Raoul Tainguy completed the copying of this manuscript at Jagny (Val d'Oise) on July 4, 1413, at Arnaud de Corbie's.[12] In the opinion of François Avril, the paintings are to be attributed to the atelier of the Master of Boucicaut.
- Paris, B.N. n.a. fr. 9604–9606 (books 1–3): a later manuscript painted after 1453 for René d'Anjou; the painter has been compared to the Master of the Missal of Bishop Jean Michel, composed in Angers ca. 1440.[13] As Tesnière pointed out, B.N. fr. 6474 is clearly the model.
- Stonyhurst, Bibl. des RR. PP. de la Compagnie de Jésus (book 1). Parisian manuscript from the beginning of the fifteenth century, probably from the atelier of the Master of Rohan.[14]

- Toulouse, B.M. 511 (book 1). Manuscript ca. 1415 whose painter is close to the Master of Rohan.[15]

Here we find an ensemble that is remarkably coherent in space and in time, manuscripts from the same Parisian ateliers of the beginning of the fifteenth century (with the exception of B.N. n.a. 9604), and from the same model, which was perhaps the manuscript illuminated in 1381 following the directions of Froissart himself.

One can, moreover, compare these manuscripts with the contemporary Parisian manuscripts of the *Grandes chroniques de France*. A. D. Hedeman, with regard to the *Grandes chroniques*, in fact underlines the passage in the reign of Charles VI from royal history to national history; this passage is evident, in the Parisian production of the early fifteenth century, in fewer luxurious manuscripts, less illustrated (thirty to fifty paintings) than those destined for Charles V or Charles VI, and destined for French lords.[16] All these manuscripts seem to come from the same ateliers. A miniature introducing the life of Louis the Pious in two Parisian manuscripts of the *Grandes chroniques* from the beginning of the century presents a curious structural resemblance to scene 2 of the frontispiece of Froissart's book 1 in the contemporary Parisian manuscripts, the presentation by Isabelle of her son Edward to Charles IV. In the *Grandes chroniques*, Charlemagne, at the left of the image, presents the young Louis to a bishop, who occupies a place at the right of the image, symmetrical with that of the king, and who blesses the child. Behind the king are two nobles; behind the bishop, one or three monks, according to the manuscript. In the frontispiece of Froissart's *Chroniques*, Isabelle, followed by ladies, replaces king Louis, and Charles IV, followed by nobles, replaces the bishop; the child occupies the same place. Might there be a common model?[17]

Since M. L. Le Guay's study of the illustration of book 4 of the *Chroniques*, we are familiar with another, equally coherent ensemble of manuscripts: the Flemish manuscripts of the end of the fifteenth century composed for the court of Burgundy in the ateliers of Bruges, for which a specific iconographic tradition exists.[18] It is also noteworthy that all the illuminated manuscripts containing the four books of the *Chroniques* are of Flemish provenance.

- Anvers, Musée Plantin Moret, fr. 5. Contains the first three books of the *Chroniques*, each illustrated with a frontispiece. It bears the arms of Philippe de Montmorency, count of Hornes (1522–68).[19]
- Staatsbibliothek, Berlin, Dépôt Breslau, fonds Rhediger I, 1–4. Often designated the Breslau Froissart (Le Guay, pp. 47–50, 365–67). The

manuscript belonged to Thomas Rhediger in the sixteenth century and was left to the city of Breslau (Wroclaw), where it remained until World War II, when it was transferred to Berlin. The four volumes correspond to the four books of the *Chroniques*. The colophon indicates that the text was copied in Bruges in 1468 by David Aubert for Antoine, the Grand Bâtard of Bourgogne (1421–1504), half-brother of Charles the Bold, whose arms figure in the margins with, at the end of the volume, the signature and *devise*: "Nul ne s'y frotte. A. de Bourgogne." The four volumes contain 117, 45, 38, and 23 miniatures, respectively; for books 1, 2, and 4 they are in grisaille with colored elements and for book 3 are paintings. For the painters, the names of Loyset Liédet, Philippe de Mazerolles, and Liévin van Lathem have been proposed.

- Paris, Arsenal 5187–5190. The Arsenal manuscript, executed between 1467 (date of an inventory of the library of the dukes of Burgundy in which it does not figure) and 1487 (date at which it appears in the inventory) (Le Guay, pp. 50–52, 369–70). The four books are illustrated with 33, 39, 24, and 11 miniatures, respectively, in grisaille with elements of color. Their style, close to that of the atelier of Loyset Liédet, relates this manuscript to that of Breslau, with which it has several points in common.

- London, B.L. Add. 38658. Contains the four books in two volumes. Made in the first half of the fifteenth century for Jean de Roubaix (d. 1449), knight of the Golden Fleece, chamberlain of the duc de Bourgogne.[20]

- London, B.L. Royal 14 D 2–6. Manuscript in the style of Bruges containing the whole of the *Chroniques* in five volumes. Commissioned by Thomas Thwaytes, familiar of Lord Hastings (royal lieutenant of Calais, 1471–83) (Le Guay, pp. 40–43, 377–78).

- Paris, B.N. fr. 86 (book 1). For F. Avril, "a Bruges production of 1470–1480, judging from the writing and the style of the paintings, which one may attribute to the artist designated as the Master of Louis of Bruges or the Master of Marguerite of York."

- Paris, B.N. fr. 2643–2646. The Froissart of Louis de Bruges, lord of la Gruuthuse (1422–92), knight of the Golden Fleece, chamberlain of Philippe le Bon in 1461, and great bibliophile (Le Guay, pp. 43–47, 370–71). The arms of Louis de Bruges have been replaced by those of Louis XII in the lower margin of the frontispiece. The four books include 47, 13, 22, and 28 paintings respectively; books 1 and 2 were illustrated by Loyset Liédet, books 3 and 4 by Philippe de Mazerolles and the Master of Dresden.

Most of the manuscripts of the first book of the *Chroniques* seem, then, to have come from a Parisian atelier of the beginning of the fifteenth century or a Flemish atelier of the end of that century. Two among them, however, both of which present an initial miniature, occupy a special place:

- The famous Amiens manuscript (B.M. 486), of the first half of the fifteenth century, offers perhaps the oldest redaction of book 1. It contains a unique initial miniature, with the arms of Jean de Croy, count of Chimay, elected knight of the Golden Fleece in 1431, later grand-bailli of Hainaut.[21]
- The Chantilly manuscripts (Musée Condé 501), MSS 501 and 478, give an abridged version of books 1 and 2. Volume 1 has five miniatures. The frontispiece includes the arms of Antoine de Chourses and of his wife, Catherine de Coëtivy, and the date 1472. Antoine de Chourses (d. 1487), favorite of Louis XI, was an enlightened bibliophile.[22]

As Varvaro noted, the classification of the manuscripts of book 1 according to iconographical analysis confirms that of Siméon Luce based on textual analysis, according to which our manuscripts belong to the "first redaction properly so-called" of book 1.[23] Among the manuscripts that derive from this redaction, Luce further distinguishes two classes: the manuscripts of the first class, whose text is complete, and those of the second class, whose text is more or less abridged. The two ensembles of illustrated manuscripts that we have distinguished, on the basis of origin, correspond in large part to these two classes established on the basis of textual analysis:

1. To the first class: the manuscripts of Besançon, The Hague, and B.N. 2642, 2649, 2662, 2663, 2675, 6474.
2. To the second class: the manuscripts London B.L. Royal 14 D 2, Paris Arsenal 5187, B.N. 86 and 2643, Breslau, and Toulouse.

The manuscripts belonging to the first of these classes are French, the others Flemish, with the exception of the manuscript of Toulouse.

It is interesting to conduct a parallel analysis of the frontispieces of the Parisian and Flemish manuscripts and to determine whether they present a specificity. Such a finding would corroborate, with iconographic evidence, the existence of two families of manuscripts of the *Chroniques*. Furthermore, the Flemish manuscripts, like the Parisian ones, coming from the same ateliers and sometimes illustrated by the same painters, are very close to each other. Confronted with these two ensembles, each clearly anchored in a very different space and time, one is tempted to seek in the illustration the traces of ideology. The seizure by the duke of Anjou proves that in 1381 Froissart was considered to be pro-English and his text to be dangerous for the French cause. Parisian ateliers of the beginning of the fifteenth century, working for French lords, and Flemish ateliers of the end of the century, working for the Burgundian court, may well give a different interpretation of the text. What then is the part of propaganda in these manuscripts?

The Frontispieces of Book 1 of the *Chroniques*

The miniature placed at the head of a manuscript plays the role of an overture. It is more carefully executed than the others and, when the illustration is reduced to a painting, the latter is generally found in the initial position. Most often of large size, it has an important function: to guide the reader toward a certain interpretation of the text.[24] The typology of the frontispieces may be summarized in three forms:

1. The representation of the writer at work or offering his work to the dedicatee.
2. A single scene representing an episode of the opening of the narrative.
3. An imaged table of contents that summarizes the beginning or the entirety of the narrative, often in four tableaux. This iconographical summary can include a representation of the author, writing or offering his book to the recipient. The juxtaposition, in the image, of the activity of writing and the narrative subject matter thus makes visible the connection between the writer and his creation, showing the text in the course of its writing.

The illustrated manuscripts of book 1 of the *Chroniques* (like those of the other books) conform to this typology. But the distribution of the types of frontispieces varies from one family of manuscripts to the other, confirming the existence of two distinct iconographic traditions.[25] The frontispieces of the Parisian manuscripts of the beginning of the fifteenth century present, as we have seen, an iconographic summary in four or in two tableaux.[26] In the manuscripts of Besançon, Brussels (II 88 and IV 251), London Add. 38658, Paris B.N. 2649 and 2663, and Stonyhurst, we find from left to right and from top to bottom, Froissart's offering to Richard II and the three scenes connected with the conquest of England by queen Isabelle (Isabelle and Charles IV, the return to England, the siege of Bristol). The painter of MS B.N. 2675 contributes a small modification: The masculine dedicatee is replaced by a woman, a queen of England, who wears the same robe vertically divided ("mi-partie") (the arms of England are represented in quarterly fashion, "ecartelees," to the arms of France) and has the same face as the queen Isabelle of the three other tableaux. As it could not be Isabelle, however, the explication is perhaps to be found in the painter's knowledge (or that of the maître d'oeuvre) of Froissart's text. Often the painters, far from limiting themselves to the illustration of the rubrics, attest their knowledge of the text they illustrate by the inclusion of details not found in the rubric. Carrying out a critical reading of both Froissart's text and the iconographic model, the painter may have replaced Richard II with a queen of England who would then be Philippa of Hainaut, referring effectively to an episode in book 1 in which Froissart, at the time of his first voyage to England in 1361, offers a book to Queen Philippa.[27]

The Hague manuscript is probably inspired by the same model, but the painter has chosen to highlight four sovereigns through the following four scenes: the king of France receives a letter borne by an English herald (the challenge of Edward III?); the king of Castille mounts his horse; the king of England embarks on a ship; a prince on a throne addresses his troops. The identification of this prince has been proposed, from his arms, as the count of Holland (Varvaro, fig. 4 and p. 18). But as he is wearing a crown, is he not instead the king of Scotland, who bears very similar arms in B.N. 2642?[28] The painter seems to have sought to underline the European character of the conflict and to represent the four nations mentioned in the rubric: "Cy commencent les croniques que fist maistre Jehan Froyssart, qui parlent des nouvelles guerres de France et d'Angleterre, d'Escoce, d'Espaigne et de Bretaigne, lesquelles sont divisees en .IIII. parties." [Here begin the Chronicles of master John Froissart, which tell of the new wars of France, England, Scotland, Spain and Britain, divided into four parts.]

The manuscripts of New York, Paris B.N. 2662, and Toulouse present only the first two scenes of the iconographic summary: Froissart's offering and the encounter of Isabelle and Charles IV. But B.N. 2642 does not follow the same model; it presents, in two symmetrical scenes, the confrontation of the king of France and the king of England to the left, and that of the king of England and the king of Scotland to the right. The sovereigns are easily identifiable by their emblazoned shields and their banners. As in the Hague manuscript, the painter seems to want to illustrate the rubric that enumerates the countries at war. Finally, the frontispiece of the Chantilly manuscript, painted in 1472, presents Froissart's offering of his book to a queen who cannot be identified; it is improbable that the influence of the earlier manuscripts is still felt (Meurgey, plate lxxxv).

The Flemish manuscripts, on the other hand, never present an iconographic summary in four tableaux. They privilege either the single scene or the representation of the writing of the text. Unlike the French manuscripts, they often contain the four books of the *Chroniques* and in that case offer four parallel initial paintings.[29] The frontispieces with a single scene lose their specificity and differ from the other miniatures only in their size. It is, however, interesting to determine which episode is chosen to be placed at the head of the book. In B.N. 2643 (the Froissart of Louis de la Gruuthuse), it is the arrival of Isabelle in Paris. The queen of England, mounted on a horse on whose cover the arms of both England and France are depicted, is welcomed at the gates of Paris by her brother Charles IV, on a horse whose cover is decorated with fleurs-de-lis. There is a similarity in the construction of the scene between this painting and the frontispiece of book 4 of the Breslau manuscript, which presents the entry into Paris of another Isabelle, Isabeau de Bavière, on the occasion of her *entrée solennelle* of 1389: the movement of the two processions is the same, from outside Paris toward the Porte Saint-Denis, as is the representation of Paris. The two manuscripts are connected with the Bruges atelier of Loyset Liédet (as is the Arsenal manuscript). In the Anvers manuscript, a large miniature shows the confrontation of English and Scottish knights and foot-soldiers.

The other manuscripts adopt the first type of frontispiece, the scene of writing, which is favored, too, by the text of the prologue, in which the author presents himself in his activity as writer. The Amiens manuscript, which occupies a special place in the manuscript tradition of the *Chroniques*, offers a single initial miniature, the width of a column, showing the writer at work. In the other manuscripts, the representation of the writer is accompanied by an illustration of the content of the work, as if the book, seen in the process of creation or as the object of a gift, were opening before the reader.

The frontispiece of the Breslau Froissart (fig. 11.2) is divided into two tableaux. The painter has depicted the writer in the process of writing at his worktable. To the right is a king of France enthroned, almost full-face, seated beneath a blue canopy decorated with fleurs-de-lis and holding a scepter in his left hand. The king is surrounded to the left by nobles, to the right by a cleric and a religious. Unlike the quadripartite miniatures of the French manuscripts, the two scenes are here disjoined; Froissart does not offer his book to the king, whose image incarnates the central matter of the *Chroniques:* the French-English war and the conflict between the Valois and Edward III for the throne of France. The frontispiece of the Arsenal manuscript (fig. 11.3) has two tableaux similar to those of the Breslau

11.2. Frontispiece, Breslau Froissart manuscript: Froissart at worktable (left panel); King Richard II of England, seated (right panel). Berlin, Staatsbibliothek, Dépôt Breslau, fonds Rhediger I, I, f. 1. Reproduced by permission of the Berlin Staatsbibliothek.

Cy commence le premier volume des cronicques compillees par iehan froissart contenant les guerres et les occasions dicelles qui durerent longuement entre le roy de france phelipe et le roy edouart dangleterre et plusieurs aultres leurs successeurs.

ffin que honnorables aueue et nobles auentures faitz darmes par les guerres de france et dangleterre soient notablement et moult honnorablement registres et mis en memoire perpetuele par quoy les preux hommes et vaillans aient exemple de eulx vigoureusement encouraigner. En bien faisant le vueil traictier et recorder hystoire et matiere de

grant louenge. Mais auant que ie la commence ie requier au sauueur de tout le monde qui de neant cra toutes choses quil vueille arer et mettre en moy sens et entendement si vertueux que ce liure que iaycommence ie puisse continuer et perseuerer en tele maniere que tous ceulx et toutes celles qui le liront verront et orront y puissent prendre bonne consolacion et esbatement deduit et plaisance. et moy encheoir en leur grace. On dit et vray est que tous edifices sont maconnes et ouures lune pierre apres laultre et toutes grosses riuieres sont faictes et rassemblees de diuers lieux et de pluseurs ruisseaulx et sources. tout pareillement les sciences sont extraictes

11.3. Frontispiece, Arsenal manuscript: Froissart in prayer before God (left panel); anonymous king on throne, and nobles (right panel). Paris, Arsenal 5187, f. 1. Reproduced by permission of the Bibliothèque de l'Arsenal.

manuscript: the writer at work and a king in his court. But the writer is not seated at his worktable; he is kneeling, eyes raised to heaven, praying to God with hands clasped. A book is open at his feet. The *clerc* is only the scribe of God, who is represented in the upper left of the image as a bearded king, crowned and holding a globe in his left hand. The painter here adopts a religious model, that of the sacred text dictated by God to the evangelist (see Toubert, p. 100). The scene on the right is in complete opposition to that on the left. The heavenly king is replaced by an anonymous terrestrial king, whom the painter did not choose to identify. The solitude of the clerc contrasts with the crowd of nobles at the royal court. The clerc, larger than the king and the other personages, turns his back to them; he is kneeling, not before the earthly king but before the heavenly king. Finally, the frontispiece of the London manuscript (Royal 14 D 2), like the two preceding ones, includes a representation of the writer in a double tableau (Varvaro, p. 20).

These manuscripts derive from a single iconographic tradition, one different from that of the French manuscripts. Le Guay demonstrated this for book 4, in terms of recurrent images such as that of the *bal des ardents* (pp. 152–59). The division into chapters and the rubrics are identical. Furthermore, we can ascertain precise connections between certain manuscripts. Thus, the Breslau and Arsenal manuscripts probably derive from the same atelier; for four illustrations of book 4, the construction of the tableau is the same: the *bal des ardents*, the delivery of Isabelle de France to Richard II, the battle of Nicopolis and the coronation of Henry of Lancaster (Le Guay, p. 164). Do we find here a common model, or an influence of the Breslau manuscript on the Arsenal manuscript? The two manuscripts were illustrated at Bruges by painters connected with the atelier of Loyset Liédet.

In book 1, two miniatures of the two manuscripts present similarities.[30] Both are in grisaille with colored elements. In the foreground of the first scene (figs. 11.4, 11.5), a lord and a lady wearing a crown embrace: probably the farewell of Isabelle to the count and countess of Hainaut. In the background, behind the count, a group of ladies (one of them at her side in the Arsenal manuscript); behind the queen, we find her son in the Arsenal manuscript, three lords in that of Breslau. Not only the structure of the image but the costumes are identical.

In the two images illustrating the departure of Edward III for Scotland, the king is on horseback, wearing the crown, having the same hairstyle and the scepter in his right hand (Breslau, f. 15; Arsenal 5187, f. 15; Olivier, figs. 6, 7). The banner bearer precedes him on horseback, as is customary. He is seen turning away from the viewer and entering the road that en-

11.4. Miniature, Breslau manuscript: the farewell of Queen Isabelle of England (foreground) to the count of Hainaut, with ladies and lords (background). Berlin, Staatsbibliothek, Dépôt Breslau, fonds Rhediger I, I, f. 6v. Reproduced by permission of the Berlin Staatsbibliothek.

11.5. Miniature, Arsenal manuscript: the farewell of Queen Isabelle (right) to the count and countess of Hainaut; her son, the future King Edward III, stands behind her. Paris, Arsenal 5187, f. 6. Reproduced by permission of the Bibliothèque de l'Arsenal.

circles the hill. The standard bearer, on the other hand, is behind the king. In the Breslau manuscript, the banner carries only the arms of England (gueules with three gold leopards passant); in that of the Arsenal, it carries the vertically divided arms (*miparties*) of England and of France, which Edward III adopted only in 1340. From their composition, style, and repetition of motifs, it is evident that the images were constructed according to a common schema.

There are, then, two iconographic traditions of book 1 of the *Chroniques*. Do they reflect two opposing ideologies?

Iconography and the Weight of Ideology

Philippe Contamine examined the place of the *Chroniques* in the princely libraries at the end of the Middle Ages.[31] He notes the absence of Froissart in the libraries of Charles V, Charles VI,[32] and Charles d'Orléans (who did possess a *Meliador*) and his brothers, Jean d'Angoulême and Dunois. But Guillaume de Boisratier offers a Froissart to the duc de Berry in 1407 (B.N. fr. 2641; Kervyn, I/2, p. 201). The abstention of the French princes is probably due to political reasons: Froissart is considered pro-English. On the other hand, Philippe le Bon has his Froissart bound in 1419. The French reticence seems to end toward the middle of the century, but Froissart remains more popular in Burgundy, where the ducal library contains five volumes of Froissart in 1467, seven in 1487 (Le Guay, pp. 200-202). In 1481 Louis XI arranges for binding a Froissart that will be transmitted to Charles VIII, but the book is not illustrated, just the opposite of the famous exemplar of the *Grandes chroniques de France* that Charles VII had painted by Jean Fouquet ca. 1459 (B.N. fr. 6465).[33] However, if Froissart is hardly popular among the French princes, he is more so among the counts; he was not the historian of kings but of the counts, among whom he sought his patrons and whose political decline he deplores at the end of the fourteenth century, such as Guy, count of Blois, constrained to sell his comté to the duc d'Orléans.[34] To this may be due the abundance, at the beginning of the fifteenth century, of French manuscripts less sumptuously illustrated than the Burgundian manuscripts of the end of the century.

In the manuscripts composed in Paris for French lords before the English occupation, we may expect to find traces of a pro-French ideology. On the other hand, the situation is very different in Burgundy in the second half of the century. Hainaut is Burgundian territory from 1428, and the glorification of Hainaut that is at work in book 1 of the *Chroniques* thus spills over onto Burgundy. In addition, the period is marked by the alliance between Edward IV and Burgundy. In 1466 Edward IV concluded an alliance with the count of Charolais, which led in 1468 (the very year in which David Aubert copied the Breslau manuscript) to the marriage of Charles the Bold with Marguerite of York, sister of the English king. During the War of the Roses, Edward IV, overthrown, found refuge in Flanders before reconquering his kingdom. The Flemish manuscripts were, then, created during a period of close relations between Burgundy and England.

The weight of ideology can clarify certain images. For example, two manuscripts offer a frontispiece that seems to betray a political second thought. These are manuscripts B.N. 6474 and B.N. n.a. 9604, the first serving as model for the second.[35] In the first scene of this diptych frontispiece, on the left (fig. 11.6), Froissart kneels before a king of France to whom he offers his book. The king is enthroned in majesty, in three-quarters profile, surrounded by his uncles and counselors, wearing a robe with fleurs-de-lis and ermine and bearing the scepter in his right hand, under a canopy decorated with fleurs-de-lis. This king is Charles VI, for the canopy bears his *devise:* "Jamès." However Bertrand Du Guesclin is also represented in this painting, standing behind Froissart, dressed as constable with his arms (a black eagle with red claws and beak and a red bend). On the right, the king of England is enthroned, crowned, beneath the arms of England; he too is surrounded by nobles, body facing forward, head in three-quarters profile; at his feet there is a man in a blue robe, in whom Kervyn sees a messenger, the kitchen servant sent by Charles V to challenge Edward III.[36] The frontispiece of manuscript 6474, taken up by manuscript 9604, clearly bears a political message, but the essential element is the presence of Du Guesclin in the image, which evokes the reconquests of the reign of Charles V. Even if the devise is that of Charles VI, the presence of Du Guesclin encourages us to see in the scene on the right the challenge addressed by Charles V to Edward III. Now Tesnière notes, in manuscript 6474, "new lessons which, from the point of view of history, are particularly interesting . . . [they] valorize Brittany and the Bretons" and "seem due to Froissart . . . the illustration accords perfectly with this text of the *Chroniques,* which features the constable and his Breton knights. We have to do here, beyond any possible doubt, with a 'French' version of Froissart's *Chroniques*" (pp. 301-8). It is significant that this scene is placed at the opening of book 1; the result is to erase the terrible French defeats that marked the reigns of Philippe VI and Jean le Bon, to accentuate, with Du Guesclin, the restorative reign of Charles V.

Pro-French ideology seems also to show through the surface in the frontispiece of B.N. 86, which is nonetheless Flemish (fig. 11.7). Here we

11.6. Frontispiece, Paris, B.N. n.a.f. 9604, f. 1.: Froissart kneeling before King Charles VI of France, with Du Guescin at far right (left panel); messenger kneeling before King Edward III of England (right panel). Reproduced by permission of the Bibliothèque Nationale, Paris.

see a vast, very confused battle scene with confrontation of knights. In the lower left corner of the painting, Froissart writes at his worktable; through this *mise en abyme*, the image of the battle appears to arise directly from the book. But we notice above all, in the foreground to the right, a banner on the ground, its staff broken, in the midst of fragments of armor and severed human limbs; it is an English banner, the English leopards being juxtaposed in four quarters with the arms of France. This symbol is of frequent use in iconography to emphasize the outcome of a battle by indicating the vanquished, whose banner has fallen in the dust and is trampled underfoot. The procedure is constant in the Breslau manuscript, for example, for the battles of Crécy and Poitiers.[37] But the frontispiece of manuscript 86 is its unique illustration; hence the painter would seem to seek to give to the French-English war an orientation favorable to the French cause, which raises questions, given the Bruges origin of the manuscript whose patron is unknown.

Pro-English ideology is equally evident. The frontispiece of book 1 of the Breslau manuscript (fig. 11.2) in effect presents a problem of interpretation. In this diptych, Froissart, at his writing table, occupies the left part; to the right, a king of France enthroned (identifiable by a canopy with fleurs-de-lis), almost full-face, scepter in his left hand. We cannot suspect in this Burgundian manuscript a desire to "Frenchify" Froissart; the king of France would appear here rather as simply one of the two principal protagonists of the French-English war. But a few pages later, we find a curious illustration of the coronation of Edward III: the same canopy with fleurs-de-lis above the young king who is being blessed by two bishops, with the following rubric below the image: "Comment par la deliberation et conseil des nobles et communaulté d'Angleterre Edouard fut couronné roy du vivant son pere" (folio 10v) [How through the deliberation and counsel of the nobles and commoners of England Edward was crowned king during his father's lifetime]. There is nothing of the kind in the corresponding scene of the Arsenal manuscript, from the same atelier (folio 10). The painter of the Breslau manuscript has deliberately represented Edward III as king of France (with the same canopy as Jean le Bon on the occasion of his sacring), thus supporting his pretensions to the crown of France. Does the image of the frontispiece have the same signification? It is not impossible.

The political ideology in the images is not limited to the frontispieces. The iconographic representation of the battles of Crécy and Poitiers is also revealing. Froissart's narrative, which for Crécy takes up and develops that of Jean le Bel, anchors Crécy and Poitiers in the medieval *imaginaire* of battle, making of it a judgment of God, in a duel of princes accompanied

11.7. Frontispiece, Flemish manuscript, Paris, B.N. fr. 86, f. 11: French defeat; Froissart describing the battle at his writing table (inset). Reproduced by permission of the Bibliothèque Nationale, Paris.

by their full armies.[38] The account of the Battle of Crécy is built upon a play of oppositions that turns constantly to the advantage of the English (and that will be found again in book 4, in the account of the battle of Nicopolis, now to the benefit of Bajazet). The English are calm and disciplined, the French undisciplined and disordered. The slowness of the Genoese crossbows cannot withstand the English longbows. And especially, God is on the English side and abandons the French: Rain and thunderbolts fall upon the French camp, accompanied by a flight of crows, in which the wisest see a dire presage. When the sun once again shines, it is to the French detriment, for it strikes them in the face and blinds them. At the outcome of the two battles, one could hardly underline more than Froissart does the extent of the French disasters of Crécy and Poitiers: the flight of Philippe VI and the toll of French casualties, and the capture of Jean le Bon by the Black Prince.

In the illustrations, however, the French defeats are more or less accentuated from one manuscript to the other. Two miniatures illustrate the Battle of Crécy in the Breslau manuscript. The first (folio 144v) shows the preparations for the battle and scrupulously follows the text of Froissart. The two scenes read from right to left: Edward III dines with his men on the eve of the battle and receives communion the following morning at dawn.[39] The battle itself (folio 146v) is presented as an infantry engagement, from which the kings are absent. The French are to the left of the image, the English to the right; the banner with the fleurs-de-lis is on the ground in the left foreground, beside a dead soldier, while the English banner is still brandished. This procedure is constantly utilized, as noted above, to indicate the outcome of combats. For the battle of Poitiers, the painter has represented three successive episodes in three miniatures, with the preliminaries of the battle followed by two confrontations. Thus we see a combat of infantry, with the English now to the left, banner waving, while two French soldiers lie on the ground to the right beside their trampled banner; then a man-to-man struggle in which the French once again occupy the left of the image, in whose midst we see the banner bearing the fleurs-de-lis on the grass. In the Arsenal manuscript (folio 135v), the two armies are face to face at Crécy, French to the left, English to the right, identifiable by their banners and, for the English, by the Cross of Saint George on the coats of arms. Crossbowmen to the left, against archers to the right. A dead crossbowman pierced by an arrow, in the foreground on the French side, reveals the outcome of the battle. In manuscript 2643 (folio 165v), the French are again at the left at Crécy: to the English banners are opposed the banner with fleurs-de-lis and the oriflamme. Genoese crossbowmen and English archers are equally opposed, and it is once again a dead crossbowman, to the left, who represents the French defeat; in the background, French knights flee before the English knights. For Poitiers, the English are to the left, the French to the right; in the foreground, the French knights flee before the English archers.

The paintings of the three Flemish manuscripts are constructed on the same model and do not include the intervention of the princes. On the other hand, in the representation of Crécy in MS B.N. 2642 (folio 159v), in which we easily identify the French to the left and the English to the right, the two kings confront each other, beneath their banners and surrounded by their knights; in the foreground, archers against crossbowmen. In the French camp a man lies on the grass in the center of the image, signifying the French defeat.

But certain Parisian manuscripts give a different vision of the battle. The painter of B.N. 2662 utilizes the symbolic value of the oriflamme to magnify the French side (fig. 11.8). In the fourteenth century the king of France would indeed take the oriflamme from Saint-Denis when enemies, even Christian enemies, threatened the kingdom; Philippe VI and Jean II in fact did so in 1346 and 1356, before the battles of Crécy and of Poitiers.[40] In manuscript 2662 we see once again the two armies in confrontation, the French to the left and the English to the right, infantry in the foreground, cavalry in the background. Three French banners to the left oppose three English banners to the right, bearing the arms of the princes mentioned by Froissart: those of the king of France, Philippe VI; the king of Bohemia, Jean of Luxembourg; and Charles, count of Alençon (the king's brother). The three English banners and the coats of arms of the three princes bear leopards. But the dominant element of the image is the gigantic oriflamme that flies well above the banners, extending even beyond the frame. In the foreground, in the middle of the image, we see also a heap of bleeding dead from one or the other side; the outcome of the battle is still uncertain and the disproportionately large oriflamme dominates the scene, as if the painter had refused to depict the French defeat. It is quite different, however, for the battle of Poitiers in the same manuscript (folio 196v). The combatants are all on foot, with the French this time to the right. In the first rank of the two armies are the two princes, Jean II and the Black Prince, the first followed by the duc de Bourbon and the count of the Marche, the second by the captal de Buch and the count of Suffolk, all six identifiable by their banners and coats of arms. This time the bodies on the ground are distinctly placed to the right, on the French side, clearly signifying the defeat. But the painter again depicts the oriflamme, immense, above the other banners and the frame of the image. He is the only one to

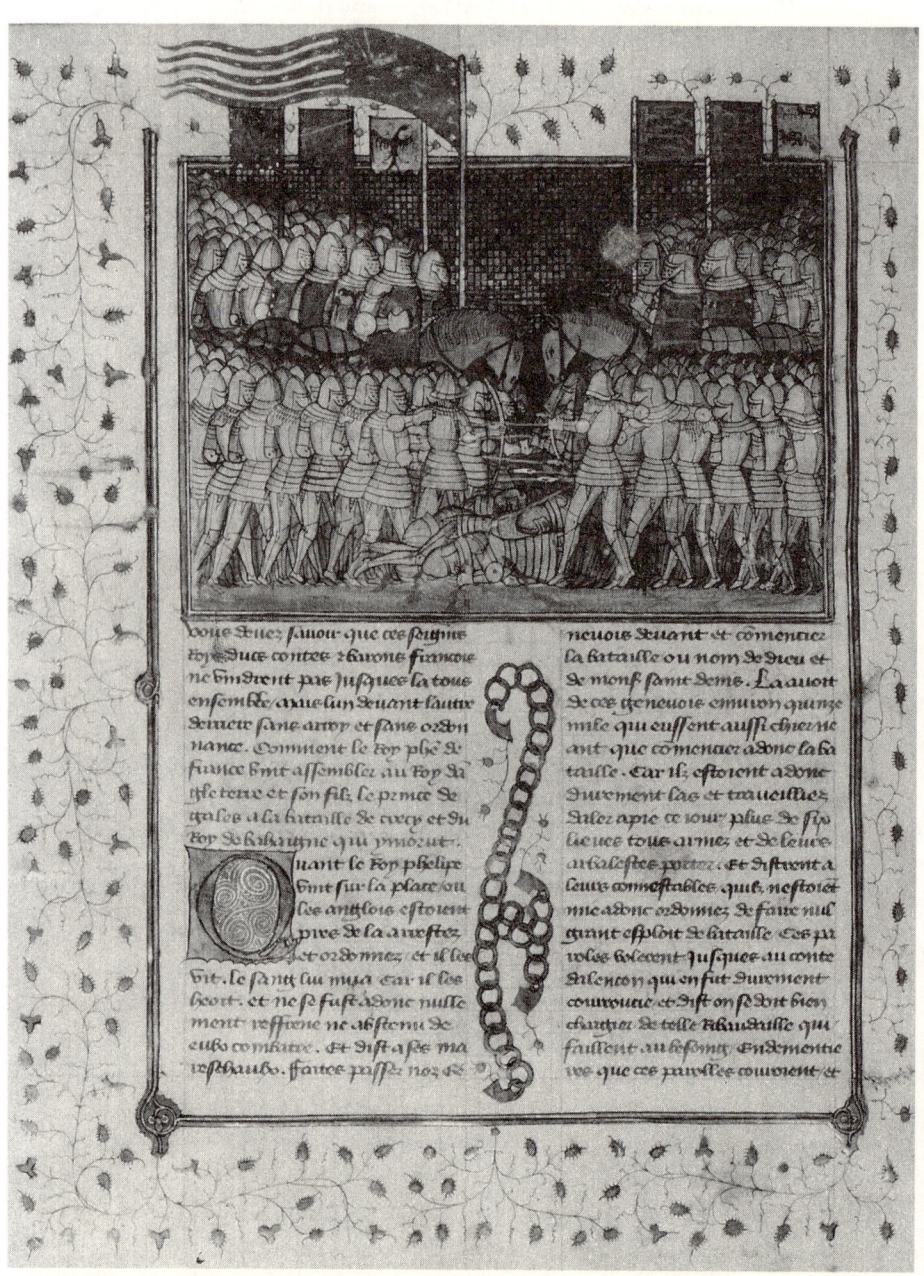

11.8. Miniature, Paris, B.N. fr. 2662, f. 150v.: the Battle of Crécy. Reproduced by permission of the Bibliothèque Nationale, Paris.

give it this gigantic size, unlike, for example, the painter of B.N. 2643, who also shows it at the battle of Poitiers.

We note that from one manuscript to the other, the French and the English are placed now to the left, now to the right of the image. Is this placement significant? In the fourteenth and fifteenth centuries, the right half of the image (for the viewer) comes to be negatively connoted, and the left half receives a positive connotation.[41] Here the French, defeated, are most often placed in the left half of the image, and the English victors in the right, whether the manuscript be French or Flemish; in addition, in the Breslau manuscripts B.N. 2643 and 2662, the French are placed sometimes at left, sometimes at right: Spatial symbolism seems to have no role here.

Thus certain French manuscripts play the illustration against the text, in an attempt to attenuate the weight of the disasters of 1346 and 1356. On the other hand, in the almost uniformly laudatory portrait that Froissart sketches of the king of England Edward III who, for him, embodies the chivalric ideal, certain details clash; from one manuscript to another, these details will be retained or omitted by the illustrators. The first of these concerns the famous burghers of Calais. In 1348, after long months of siege and despairing of aid from the king, Philippe VI, the inhabitants of Calais decide to surrender to Edward III. The latter demands that the keys of the city be presented to him by six of its burghers, *en chemise* and with ropes about their necks. Six of the leading citizens consent to make the sacrifice. In spite of all supplications, the king is intractable concerning their fate and yields only upon the intervention of Queen Philippa, in an advanced state of pregnancy, who casts herself at his feet to obtain the pardon of the six burghers.[42] This episode, which Froissart takes from Jean le Bel and which Michelet takes from Froissart, is all to the glory of good Queen Philippa and much less to that of King Edward, who in this instance shows cruelty and obstinacy. Froissart also adds to the text of Jean le Bel the names of the six burghers, not mentioned by his predecessor. The Flemish manuscripts (Breslau, B.N. 2643) illustrate the siege of Calais but not the episode of the burghers, which is found, on the other hand, in two Parisian manuscripts, B.N. 2642 (fig. 11.9) and B.N. 2663 (folio 164). In both paintings the six men, kneeling and half-naked in their white *chemises* with ropes around their necks, appear as martyrs before an all-powerful English king surrounded by his men, with the following rubric in MS 2642: "Comment les .VI. bourgois partirent de Calais tous nudz en leurs chemises, la hart ou col et les clefz de la ville en leurs mains, et comment la royne d'Angleterre leur sauva les vies."[43] [How the six burghers left Calais naked in their *chemises*, with ropes about their necks

11.9. Miniature, Paris, B.N. fr. 2642, f. 179: the siege of Calais. The Calais burghers (left) beg for mercy before King Edward III of England. Reproduced by permission of the Bibliothèque Nationale, Paris.

and the keys to the city in their hands, and how the queen of England saved their lives.] In this manuscript, the king orders the executioner, standing at his side, to decapitate the burghers, whereas there is no question, in the text, of anything but calling the "cope teste" (*Chroniques*, vol. 4, p. 62). The presence of the king beside the executioner cannot fail to devalorize the royal image.

In the same way, another image of MS 2663 (fig. 11.10) contrasts with the usual iconographic representation of Edward III as prestigious *chef de guerre*. It illustrates the English disembarkation in Normandy in 1346. On that occasion, Edward III makes a false step in setting foot on the French soil and falls, injuring himself: "Quant la navie dou roy d'Engleterre eut pris terre en la Hoge et elle fu toute arestee et ancree sus le sablon, li dis rois issi de son vaissiel; et dou premier piet qu'il mist sus terre, il cheï si roidement que li sans li vola hors dou nés" (*Chroniques*, vol. 3, p. 133). [When the navy of the king of England had made landfall at the Hague

11.10. Miniature, Paris, B.N. 2663, f. 133: King Edward III of England falls while disembarking in Normandy. Reproduced by permission of the Bibliothèque Nationale, Paris.

and was still and anchored on the sand, the aforesaid king went out of his vessel; and with the first step he took on land, he fell so violently that blood spurted from his nose.] The king is quick to give a favorable interpretation of his fall, in saying that the land of France has thus shown how much it desired him, but clearly this minute detail is not to the advantage of the English king, and it is probably for that reason that it, like the episode of the burghers of Calais, is integrated into the iconographic program of MS 2663: Edward III is represented in ridiculous posture, scarcely regal, with frightened face and in complete disequilibrium.[44]

Iconographic analysis, in summary, confirms the existence of two families of manuscripts of the first book of the *Chroniques*. The first comprises the French manuscripts, most of them executed in Paris in the first years of the fifteenth century for French lords; the second, the Flemish manuscripts, more luxurious, produced in the second half of the century in the sphere of influence of the court of Burgundy. In each of the two series the manuscripts are closely related: in provenance of Parisian ateliers dominated by the Master of Rohan in one case, in the other of Bruges ateliers whose most prominent figure was Loyset Liédet. Although all the painters are scrupulously faithful to Froissart's text, political ideology nonetheless shows through, in the choice of scenes to illustrate and in different interpretations of the same episode.

Evident above all is the complexity of the problem of the reception of the *Chroniques*. Froissart very probably appeared pro-English at the beginning of the fifteenth century, and the kings of France refused him a place in their libraries—but not the French lords, who commissioned the manuscripts from the Parisian ateliers. He is particularly appreciated in Burgundy at the end of the fifteenth century, in a period of Anglo-Burgundian *rapprochement;* but why not earlier in the century? Perhaps the political ideology of the *Chroniques* is sufficiently vague to satisfy all publics and malleable enough to lend itself, under the illustrator's brush, to divergent interpretations.

Translated by Sara Sturm-Maddox

Notes

1. A. Varvaro, "Il libro I delle *Chroniques* di Jean Froissart. Per una filologia integrata dei testi e delle immagini," *Medioevo Romanzo* 19 (1994): 3–36, and "Due note sui manoscritti delle *Chroniques* di Jean Froissart," ibid., 293–300. The first of these gives the list of the manuscripts of book 1.

2. Cf. Froissart, *Oeuvres*, ed. Kervyn de Lettenhove (Brussels: Devaux and Closson, 1867–77), I (1) p. 286, and I (2) pp. 81–82.

3. *Chroniques*, Livre I, ed. S. Luce (Paris: Renouard, Société de l'Histoire de France, 1869), I, para. 6, 11, 12.

4. *Chroniques*, Livre IV, ed. Kervyn, p. 167; Varvaro, p. 31.

5. Varvaro, pp. 28–31. On the Master of Rohan see Millard Meiss, *Les Heures de Rohan* (Paris: Draeger, 1973), and *French Painting in the Time of Jean de Berry*, vol. 3 (New York: Pierpont Morgan Library, 1974), p. 369.

6. In addition to the list established by Varvaro, see, for the illuminated manuscripts of the *Chroniques*, the *Catalogue des expositions organisées par la ville de Valenciennes en l'honneur de Jehan Froissart du 11 septembre au 10 octobre 1937*.

7. See C. Gaspar and F. Lyna, *Les principaux manuscrits à peintures de la Bibliothèque Royale de Belgique*, 3 vols. (Brussels, 1937–89), vol. 2, pp. 11–13: "The style of these miniatures very closely recalls those of the paintings decorating three other illustrated copies of the *Chroniques*, B.N. 2622, MS 511 of Toulouse, and one of the four manuscripts formerly belonging to the Duke of Newcastle (sold at Sothebys in 1937)." See also F. L. Ganshof, "Jean Froissart," *Annales de la Société Royale d'Archéologie de Bruxelles* 42 (1938): 256–72, pl. 4; Varvaro, fig. 3 (figs. 2 and 3 seem to be reversed).

8. *Bibliothèque royale de Bruxelles, quinze années d'acquisitions: 1954–1968* (Brussels, 1969), pp. 52–55.

9. Meiss, p. 371; Varvaro, fig. 6. In this manuscript, as in B.N. 2662 and the Toulouse manuscript, the iconographic summary is reduced to the first two scenes: Froissart offering his book to Richard II, and Isabelle and her son before Charles IV.

10. I thank François Avril for his invaluable assistance.

11. J. Porcher, *Les manuscrits à peintures en France du XIIIe au XVIe siècle*, exposition at the Bibliothèque Nationale, Paris (B.N., 1955), pp. 106–7.

12. M. H. Tesnière, "Les manuscrits copiés par Raoul Tainguy," *Romania* 107 (1986): 282–368. Raoul Tainguy was the official copyist of Arnaud of Corbie, chancellor of France from 1388 to 1413. The latter possessed five volumes of Froissart's *Chroniques*: B.N. fr. 2640, B.N. fr. 6474–6475, Brussels B.R. IV 1102 (the book 2 that completes the preceding MS); Leyden B.U. Vossius Germ. Gall. 9 I.

13. C. Sterling, *La peinture médiévale à Paris (1300–1500)* (Paris: Bibliothèque des arts, Fondation Wildenstein, 1987 and 1991), II, p. 120; F. Avril and N. Reynaud, *Les Manuscrits à peintures en France, 1440–1520* (Paris: Flammarion, 1995), p. 105.

14. J. Porcher; Meiss, p. 404; Varvaro, fig. 2 (figs. 2 and 3 seem to be reversed).

15. Meiss, p. 404; Varvaro, fig. 5. Varvaro adds to this list MS X, formerly at Clumber Park, now in an unknown private collection (p. 19).

16. A. D. Hedeman, *The Royal Image: Illustrations of the Grandes Chroniques de France* (Berkeley and Los Angeles: University of California Press, 1991), pp. 139, 145.

17. Hedeman, figs. 94 and 95; the manuscripts in question are Valenciennes, B.M. 637, f. 134, and Paris, B.N. fr. 2604, f. 145.

18. L. Harf-Lancner and M. L. Le Guay, "L'illustration du livre IV des *Chroniques* de Froissart: les rapports entre texte et image," *Le Moyen Age* 96 (1990): 93–112; M. L. Le Guay, *Les manuscrits enluminés du livre IV des Chroniques de Froissart: les rapports entre le texte et l'illustration*, thèse de Paris IV, 1992.

19. J. Denucé, *Museum Plantin-Moretus, Catalogue des manuscrits* (Anvers, 1927), pp. 13–16.

20. *Catalogue of Additions to the Manuscripts in the British Museum in the Years 1911–1915* (London, 1925), p. 188.

21. See Kervyn, I/2, pp. 190–93, and George Diller, ed., Froissart, *Chroniques, le manuscrit d'Amiens*, livre I, vol. 1 (Geneva: Droz, 1991), introduction.

22. See J. Meurgey, *Les principaux manuscrits à peintures du musée Condé*, Publications de la Société française de reproduction des manuscrits à peintures, 14 (1930), pp. 124–25.

23. Varvaro, p. 22; *Chroniques*, ed. S. Luce, I, pp. xxxiv–xxxviii.

24. See E. Baumgartner, "La première page du *Tristan en prose*," *Littérales* 2 (1987): 51–63; M. Dauzier, "L'image porche ou la première page enluminée dans les romans médiévaux," in *From Sign to Text*, ed. Y. Tobin (Amsterdam: J. Benjamins, 1989), 509–18; L. Harf-Lancner, "L'élaboration d'un cycle romanesque antique au XIIe siècle et sa mise en images: Le *Roman de Thèbes*, le *Roman de Troie* et le *Roman d'Eneas* dans le manuscrit B.N. français 60," in *Le monde du roman grec* (Paris: PENS, 1992), 291–306; V. Roland, "Folio liminaire et réception du texte, les manuscrits parisiens du *Merlin en prose*," *Bulletin bibliographique de la Société internationale arthurienne* (1991): 257–72; E. Salter and D. Pearsall, "Pictorial Illustration of Late Medieval Poetic Texts: The Role of the Frontispiece or Prefatory Picture," in *Medieval Iconography and Narrative* (Odense: University Press, 1980), 100–123; H. Toubert, "Formes et fonctions de l'enluminure," in *Histoire de l'édition française*, vol. 1 (Paris: Promodis, 1982), 99–100; L. Walters, "The Use of Multi-Compartment Opening Miniatures," in *The Illustrated Manuscripts of Chrétien de Troyes*, vol. 1 (Amsterdam: Rodopi, 1993), 331–50.

25. On the frontispieces of book 4, see Le Guay, pp. 70–76 and 135–52.

26. Varvaro, pp. 15–22. Cf. the frontispieces of the *Grandes Chroniques de France*: see Hedeman, pp. 155ff., figs. 98–99 and pl. 7 and 8.

27. This allusion is found in the prologue of the manuscripts of the first redaction properly so called (following the classification of S. Luce), to which the manuscript B.N. 2675 belongs: "Et ce nonobstant si emprins je assez hardiement, moy yssu de l'escolle, a dittier et a rimer les guerres dessus dites et porter en Angleterre le livre tout compilé, si comme je le fis. Et le presentay adont a tres haulte et tres

noble dame, dame Phelippe de Haynault, royne d'Angleterre, qui doulcement et lieement le receut de moy et me fist grant proffit" (*Chroniques*, ed. Luce, I, p. 210). [And despite this I began boldly, having had my schooling, to write and to make poems of the aforesaid wars and to take the completed book to England, as in fact I did. And I presented it then to the most exalted and noble lady, my lady Philippa of Hainaut, queen of England, who accepted it from me sweetly and gladly and gave me great profit of it.]

28. The king of Scotland: "gold with a red lion enclosed in a double tressure flory and counter-flory the same"; see J. B. Rietstap, *Armorial général*, 2 vols. (Gouda: Van Goor Zonen, 1884–87). Cf. the frontispiece of B.N. 2642 (f. 1), which presents the confrontation of the king of England and the king of Scotland.

29. These are the manuscripts of Breslau, London Royal 14 D 2–6, Arsenal, and B.N. 2643–2646.

30. P. Olivier, *Les rapports entre texte et image dans le livre I des Chroniques de Froissart*, Mémoire de Maîtrise at Paris III (1995), pp. 56–59.

31. Seminar, Paris X, 1987–88.

32. The inventory of 1422, however, mentions two titles: *Les guerres d'Angleterre et d'Ecosse* and *La guerre du roi de France et d'Angleterre*.

33. *Les Grandes chroniques de France*, facsimile of the Fouquet miniatures, presented by F. Avril, M. T. Gousset, B. Guenée (Paris: P. Lebaud, 1987).

34. F. Autrand, seminar, Ecole normale supérieure, 1987–88.

35. Porcher, p. 139; Tesnière, p. 306; C. De Mérindol, *Le roi René et la seconde maison d'Anjou* (Paris: Le Léopard d'Or, 1987), pp. 182, 305, and 310, fig. 156.

36. *Chroniques*, SHF vol. 7, p. 107, para. 609–610: "Et porta uns de ses valés de cuisine, breton, les dittes deffiances et passa la mer si a point que il trouva a Douvres les dessus dis, le conte de Salubruce et messire Guillaume de Dormans . . . ." [And one of his kitchen servants, a Breton, carried the aforesaid challenges and crossed the sea until he found the above-named men, the count of Salisbury and my lord Guillaume de Dormans, at Dover. . . .]

37. See M. C. Mangin, *Le Froissart de Breslau*: list of the miniatures of MS Dépôt Breslau I (1, 2, 3, 4) in Berlin, Nancy, 1977; a typescript may be consulted in the Cabinet des manuscrits of the Bibliothèque nationale, pp. 6 and 7.

38. See G. Duby, *Le Dimanche de Bouvines* (Paris: Gallimard, 1973).

39. *Chroniques*, I, vol. 3, p. 168: "Si donna li dis rois a souper les contes et les barons de son host, et leur fist moult grant ciere; . . . et se leva l'endemain assés matin par raison, et oy messe, et li princes de Galles ses filz; et se acumenierent, et en tel maniere la plus grant partie de ses gens: si se confesserent et misent en bon estat." [That king offered supper to the counts and barons of his army, and showed them great cheer; . . . the next morning he arose quite early and heard Mass, along with the Prince of Wales his son; they took communion, and with them most of their men; they made confession and set themselves right.]

40. See P. Contamine, "L'oriflamme de Saint-Denis aux XIVe et XVe siècles," *Annales de l'Est* 25 (1973): 179–244.

41. M. Pastoureau, *Figures et couleurs* (Paris: Le Léopard d'or, 1986), p. 205. Cf.

F. Garnier, *Le Langage de l'image au Moyen Age*, vol. 1 (Paris: Le Léopard d'or, 1982), pp. 88–91, and C. Raynaud, *La Violence au Moyen Age* (Paris: Le Léopard d'or, 1990), p. 143.

42. *Chroniques*, I, vol. 4, pp. 53–63. See L. Chalon, "La scène des bourgeois de Calais chez Froissart et Jean le Bel," *Cahiers d'analyse textuelle* 10 (1968): 68–84.

43. B.N. 2663: "Comment Calais fut rendu au roy d'Angleterre et le meschief que ceulx de la ville souffrirent ainçois qu'ilz se rendissent." [How Calais was surrendered to the king of England and the grief that the townspeople suffered before they surrendered.]

44. On this scene and that of the bourgeois of Calais, cf. Olivier, pp. 126–27.

CONTRIBUTORS

Sara Sturm-Maddox is professor of French and Italian at the University of Massachusetts, Amherst. Her books include *Petrarch's Metamorphoses: Text and Subtext in the "Rime sparse"* (1985) and *Petrarch's Laurels* (1992).

Donald Maddox is professor of French and Italian at the University of Massachusetts, Amherst, and visiting professor, Paris III–Sorbonne Nouvelle, in 1998. Among his books are two studies on Chrétien de Troyes, *Structure and Sacring* (1978) and *The Arthurian Romances of Chrétien de Troyes: Once and Future Fictions* (1991); *Semiotics of Deceit: The Pathelin Era* (1984); and *Voix et textualités du récit eschatologique* (1995).

Peter F. Ainsworth holds a chair in medieval French studies at the University of Liverpool. He is author of *Jean Froissart and the Fabric of History: Truth, Myth and Fiction in the "Chroniques"* (1990) and numerous other studies of Froissart and the fourteenth century, and is a contributor to the forthcoming collective edition of the works of Jean Froissart.

Charles T. Wood is professor of history at Dartmouth College and translator of the *Chroniques* of Jean Froissart (Garland, forthcoming). Among his many publications are *Joan of Arc and Richard III*; he is coeditor of a collection of essays on the age of Joan of Arc.

George T. Diller is professor of French at the University of Florida, Gainesville. Editor of *Froisssart. Chroniques, Dernière redaction du premier livre, MS de Rome* (1972), and of *Froissart. Chroniques, le manuscrit d'Amiens, Livre I* (1991) and *Livre II* (1992), he is author of *Attitudes chevaleresques et realités politiques chez Froissart: Microlectures du premier livre des Chroniques* (1984).

William W. Kibler is Linward Shivers Professor of French at the University of Texas, Austin. He is the editor of the *Garland Encyclopedia of Medieval France* and of collective volumes on Eleanor of Aquitane and on the

Prose *Lancelot,* and coeditor of *Lion de Bourges;* he is the author of *Medieval French* (MLA).

Keith Busby is Wilbur Cross Professor of French and Director of the Center for Medieval Studies at the University of Oklahoma, Norman. He is the author of *Gauvain in Old French Literature,* editor of Chrétien de Troyes, *Le Conte du Graal,* and coeditor of *The Legacy of Chrétien de Troyes,* volumes 1 and 2, and of *Les manuscrits de Chrétien de Troyes.*

Douglas Kelly is Julian E. Harris Professor of French and Medieval Studies at the University of Wisconsin, Madison. Among his recent books are *The Arts of Poetry and Prose* (1991), *The Art of Medieval French Romance* (1992), *Medieval French Romance* (1993), and *Internal Difference and Meanings in the "Roman de la Rose"* (1995).

Rupert T. Pickens is professor of French at the University of Kentucky. His books include a study of Chrétien de Troyes's *Conte del Graal,* critical editions of the *Conte del Graal* and of Jaufré Rudel's songs, and a translation of the Lancelot-Grail *Merlin;* he has edited three volumes of scholarly essays.

Michel Zink has taught at the Sorbonne and now holds the chair in medieval French studies at the Collège de France. Among his numerous books are *La pastourelle; Les chansons de toile; La subjectivité littéraire: Autour du siècle de Saint Louis; Roman rose et rose rouge: Le Roman de la Rose ou de Guillaume de Dole de Jean Renart;* and *Introduction à la littérature française du Moyen Age.* He is editor of the series Lettres Gothiques and coeditor of *Dictionnaire des lettres françaises: Le Moyen Age.*

Elspeth Kennedy is professor emerita, St. Hilda's College, Oxford, and the editor of *Medium Aevum.* She is editor of *Lancelot do Lac: The Non-Cyclical Old French Prose Romance* (1980), coeditor of the *Livre de Chevalerie* by Geoffroi de Charny, and author of *Lancelot and the Grail: A Study of the Prose Lancelot* (1986).

John M. Fyler is professor of English at Tufts University. He is the author of *Chaucer and Ovid* and of numerous essays on late medieval English and Continental literature.

Laurence Harf-Lancner is professor of medieval French literature at the Université de Paris III–Sorbonne Nouvelle. Author of *Les Fées au Moyen Age: Morgane et Mélusine,* she has also published an edition and translation into modern French of the *Lais* of Marie de France and of the medieval *Roman d'Alexandre.*

Index

Ainsworth, Peter, 2, 4–5, 41, 80n.29, 119, 180, 184, 191, 192, 203, 206, 211
Allegory, 7, 95, 103, 111–13, 116n.24; allegorical interpretation, 108; allegorical invention, 110
Amherst Colloquium, "Froissart Across the Genres," 1–2, 15, 63
Andreas Capellanus, *De amore*, 115n.17
Arnald of Villanova, 130, 149n.32
Aubert, David, 225, 236
Autobiography, 4, 67, 77; pseudoautobiography, 4, 6, 10, 64, 146; quasiautobiography, 120, 138
Avicenna, 149n.31
Avril, François, 223

"Bal des Ardents," 32, 232
Ball, John, 42–46
Baumgartner, Emmanuèle, 191
Beaumanoir, Philippe de. *See Les Coutumes de Beauvaisis*
Belle dame sans merci, La, 107
Bennett, Philip E., 36n.4, 38n.21
Benson, Larry, 199
Bestiaire d'amours, 104; response to, 104–5
Biblical echoes, 70
Black Plague, 67
Bleu chevalier, Le, 3, 5, 10, 18, 82, 86–88, 99n.11, 106–7, 111, 113, 119–52, 171, 198, 199
Boccaccio, 195
Boethius, *Consolation of Philosophy*, 112, 132, 135
Bolingbroke, Henry, 24–26
Book of Job, 21
Boulton, Jonathan, 181, 182
Bradley-Cromey, Nancy, 89
Brault, Gerald J., 123, 147n.13

Brittany, wars of, 57–58
Brownlee, Kevin, 214n.15
Busby, Keith, 3, 6, 28, 38n.21

Calais, Burghers of, 243–44, 246
Calder, Angus, 33
Calin, William, 11n.1, 59n., 198
Cartier, Normand, 119, 120, 125
Cerquiglini-Toulet, Jacqueline, 22, 26, 28, 60n.14, 100n.22, 111, 161
Chançons royales et serventois, 98
Chareyron, Nicole, 24
Charny, Geoffroy de, 4, 9; *Demandes*, 180, 181; *Livre Charny*, 180; *Livre de chevalerie*, 9, 179–94
Chartier, Alain. *See La belle dame sans merci*
Chaucer, Geoffrey, 3, 9, 77, 132, 195–218—works: *Book of the Duchess*, 9, 107, 119, 196, 198–99; *Canterbury Tales*, 200–202; Franklin's Tale, 205; Squire's Tale, 210, 212; Wife of Bath's Tale, 210; *Complaint of Venus*, 197; *Legend of Good Women*, 200, 207; *Troilus and Criseyde*, 199, 200
Chevalier au papegau, Le, 158
Chevalier au Soleil d'Or. *See Meliador*
Chivalry, 179–94; Froissart's portrayal of, 3, 10, 18; inheritance of, 15; theory and practice of, 4, 9
Chrétien de Troyes, 81—works: *Chevalier au lion (Yvain)*, 37n.9, 81, 157; *Chevalier de la charrette (Lancelot)*, 81, 160; *Cligés*, 81; *Erec et Enide*, 81; *Conte du Graal (Perceval)*, 81, 160
Christine de Pizan, 22, 118n.40
Chroniques, 1–3, 8, 10, 15–35, 40–49, 63, 64, 69, 142, 155, 156, 162, 168, 170, 171, 180, 183, 195; "Voyage to Béarn" episode (book 3), 5, 9, 19, 26–27, 41, 50–60, 200, 202–5

Cizek, Alexandru, 117n.29
Cleomadés, 89
Company of the Star, 181, 183, 192
Constantinus Africanus, 126–27, 129, 131–32, 148n.26, 149nn.31, 32, 150n.34
Contamine, Philippe, 186, 235
Cour d'amour, of Mahieu le Poirier, 89
Courtly culture, Froissart's critique of, 4, 64
Courtoisie, 4, 6, 10, 65, 68–69, 75–77
Coutumes de Beauvaisis, Les, 179, 186
Covenanters, 32–33
Crane, Susan, 198
Crécy, battle of, 45, 58, 68, 238, 240, 241

Dante, 53, 101, 197
Debat dou cheval et dou levrier, Le, 88
De Looze, Laurence, 138
De Mazerolles, Philippe, 225
Dembowski, Peter, 63, 64, 79n.15, 114n.10, 115n.16, 119, 138, 156, 159, 164, 172, 173n.7, 213n.7, 215n.31
Diller, George, 3, 5, 10, 37nn.10, 14, 180, 183, 191, 202, 203
Discourse, legal, 98
Dit de la marguerite, Le, 82, 85
Dit dou florin, Le, 5, 22, 53, 54, 56, 57, 65, 96–97, 138, 203, 205–6
Diverres, Armel, 156

Edward III, king of England, 1, 3, 16, 20, 24, 42, 45–46, 67–68, 170, 206, 221–22, 229, 232, 236, 238, 240, 243–44, 246
Enclinpostair, son of Morpheus, 81, 107
Enclosure, images of, 6, 81–100
Enthymeme, 7, 37n.13, 101, 106-9, 116n.24
Escanor. See Girart d'Amiens
Espan de Lyon, Bascot de Mauléon, 27, 41, 50–51, 53, 58, 204, 211
Espinette amoureuse, L', 4, 5, 7, 8, 10, 64–68, 75, 77, 88–90, 98, 99n.13, 106, 111, 113, 133, 138–45, 162, 167, 168, 211

Fin'amor, 186, 189
Foix. *See* Gaston Fébus
Fortune, 71, 106
Fouquet, Jean, 235
Fourrier, Anthime, 64, 65, 70, 84, 114n.7, 116n.19, 119, 121, 124, 125–26, 161

Freeman, Michelle, 64
Froissart, Jean: critical reception of, 1, 9–10, 117n.25; as inspiration for Sir Walter Scott's figure of Old Mortality, 35; and ideology, 3, 10; and patronage, 3, 10, 69, 71; and subjectivity, 3, 8; and oral extemporization, 20
Frost, Robert, 17
Fyler, John M., 3, 9, 28, 37n.14

Gage, John, 124
Galen, 149n.31
Gaston Fébus, count of Foix-Béarn, 3, 5, 8, 10, 22–23, 27, 28–32, 50–52, 114n.7, 156, 171, 202–6, 208–13; *Livre de chasse*, 60n.14, 205, 218n.47
Genres, Froissart's practice of, 2, 4, 8, 10, 19, 33, 119
Geoffroy de Charny. *See* Charny, Geoffroy de
Girart d'Amiens, 169, 170
Gloss, 103–4, 109, 114n.11
God of Love, 72, 74–75, 82
Grail Castle, 55
Grandes chroniques de France, 224, 235
Gui de Châtillon, count of Blois, 22, 52, 56, 59, 65, 68–69
Guiette, Robert, 63
Guillaume de Lorris, 107
Guinevere, 187

Harf-Lancner, Laurence, 3, 10, 11n.4, 216n.32
Heaney, Shamus, 4, 16, 19
Hedeman, A. D., 224
Heraldry, 121–23, 142, 203, 235; treatises on, 7, 124, 240, 249n.28
Hildegard of Bingen, 127, 148n.24, 149n.28
Historiography, English, 11n.1
Horace, 108
Horton, in the "Voyage en Béarn," 209–10
Houghton, Adam, 43
Huizinga, Johan, 27–28
Hundred Years' War, 66
Huot, Sylvia, 206, 213n.7

Imitation, 117n.29
Interlace, in composition, 21, 28
Isabelle, queen of England, 221, 227, 228, 232

Jacquart, Danielle, 132
Jean de Condé, 163
Jean le Bel, *Chronique*, 2, 20, 40, 54, 58, 79n.15, 181, 182, 243
Joan of Boulogne, 55, 57
Joan of Kent, mother of Richard II, 5, 42–48
Johannes Afflacius, 129, 131, 149n.32, 150nn.35–38
John of Gaunt, 42–43
Joli buisson de Jonece, Le, 4, 5–6, 8, 10, 22, 26, 63–80, 93–96, 98, 107, 112–13, 114n.11, 162, 163, 167, 211
Joli mois de mai, Le, 82, 84
Jonece (Jeunesse), in *Le joli buisson de Jonece*, 72–73, 94, 95, 112–13

Kelly, Douglas, 3, 4, 36n.3, 37nn.13, 14, 75, 77, 83, 119, 133, 206
Kennedy, Elspeth, 3, 4, 9, 36n.4
Kervyn de Lettenhove, 119, 222, 236
Kibler, William W., 3, 4, 5–6, 89, 138
Kittredge, G. L., 173

Lancelot-Grail cycle, 9, 116n.21, 180, 189, 191
Lapidary tradition, 7
Last Judgment, 72
Le Fèvre, Jean, 221
Le Guay, M. L., 224, 232
Liédet, Loyset, 225, 229, 232, 246
Livre des fais du mareschal Bouciquaut, 21
Llull, Ramon, 179; *Libre del ordre de cavalleria*, 180, 186
Longnon, Auguste, 23
Louis, duke of Orleans, 23
Luce, Siméon, 226
Lyric insertion, 82, 87

Machaut, Guillaume de, 2, 11n.3, 53, 75, 85, 99n.9, 120, 121, 134, 141, 163, 195, 200, 206—works: *Confort d'ami*, 132, 133; *Dit dou lyon*, 37n.12, 39n.32, 63, 65, 66; *Fontaine amoureuse*, 125, 132, 196, 198, 199, 213n.7; *Jugement du roy de Behaigne*, 132, 196, 199; *Remede de fortune*, 77, 122, 132, 196; *Voir dit*, 68, 83, 91
Macrobius, *insomnium*, 111–12, 118n.38
Maddox, Donald, 172
Manuscript context, of Froissart's narrative poetry, 81

Manuscript illustration, of *Chroniques* Book 1, 221–50
Manuscripts, illustrated, of *Chroniques* Book 1
  Amiens, B. M. 486: 226, 229
  Anvers, Musée Plantin Moret, fr. 5: 224, 229
  Berlin, Staatsbibliothek, Dépôt Breslau (the "Breslau Froissart"): 224, 226, 229, 232, 235, 238, 240, 243
  Besançon, B.M. 864–865: 222, 226, 227
  Brussels, B.R. II 88: 222, 227; B.R. IV 251: 222, 227
  The Hague, B.R. 72A25: 222, 226, 228
  London, B.L. Add. 38658: 225, 227; B.L. Royal 14D 2–6: 225, 226, 232
  Musée Condé 501 (the "Chantilly Manuscript"): 226, 228
  New York, Pierpont Morgan, M 804: 222, 228
  Paris, Arsenal 5187–5190: 225, 226, 229, 232, 235, 238, 240; B.N. fr. 86: 225, 226, 236; B.N. fr. 2642: 223, 226, 228, 243; B.N. fr. 2643–2646: 225, 226, 229, 243; B.N. fr. 2649: 223, 226, 227; B.N. fr. 2662: 223, 226, 228, 241, 243; B.N. fr. 2663–2664: 223, 226, 227, 243–46; B.N. fr. 2675: 223, 226, 227, 248; B.N. fr. 6474–6475: 223, 226, 236; B.N. n.a. fr. 9604–9606: 223, 236; Stonyhurst, Bibl. des RR.PP. de la Compagnie de Jésus: 223, 227
  Toulouse, B.M. 511: 224, 226, 228
Manuscript tradition, of Froissart's works, 3, 23, 26; iconographic elements, 10
Marbode of Rennes, *Liber lapidum seu de gemmis*, 125
Marie de France, 191; *Bisclavret*, 37n.9
Masters of manuscript illustration: Master of the Apocalypse of Berry, 223; Master of Boèce, 223; Master of Boucicaut, 223; Master of Dresden, 225; Master of Louis of Bruges, 225; Master of Marguerite of York, 225; Master of Rohan, 222, 223, 224, 246
Matière de Bretagne, 136
McGregor, Jr., Rob Roy, 63
Medical theory, medieval: "heroic love," 7, 128–32

Meliador, 2–3, 4, 5, 8, 10, 22–23, 52–59, 63, 64, 65, 68, 82, 83, 97, 116n.22, 121, 155–76, 180, 203, 205–6, 211, 235
Ménard, Philippe, 191
Mercury, 40, 48
Metamorphosis, 6, 107–10, 113, 162
Mise en abyme, 57, 58, 93
Modus tractandi, 4, 6, 101–18
Mort Artu, 191
Morton, Henry, in *Old Mortality*, 32–33
Mythological exempla, 6, 71, 73, 79n.23, 80n.26, 95, 101–3, 108-11, 132–33, 198, 207–9, 212

Narcissus, 107–8, 110, 111, 113, 115n.11
Nature, 70
Nicholas de l'Escale, 31–32
Northumbria, 159, 160, 170

Ordene de chevalerie, 180, 186
Order of the Garter, 182, 192
Orloge amoureus, L', 84–85, 94
Oton de Grandson, 197
Ovid, 9, 89, 106, 109–10, 134—works: *House of Fame*, 9, 202–3, 214n.12; *Metamorphoses*, 207–8; *Remedia amoris*, 132, 134
Ovidian tradition, 200; Froissart's use of, 7, 79n.23, 85, 95, 107, 133, 206–9, 211–12
Ovide moralisé, 89, 93, 101, 106, 109, 114n.10, 134, 206, 211

Palmer, J. J. N., 215n.24
Pannier, Léopold, 125
Paradis d'amour, Le, 8, 55–56, 81–82, 99n.13, 101–5, 109, 161, 173n.7, 196, 198, 199, 205, 211, 213n.7
Paradise Lost, 197
Paris, Gaston, 10
Parker, Patricia, 213
Pastourelle, Froissart's ninth, 203
Peasants' Revolt, English (1381), 5, 42–48, 49n.5
Perceforest, 158, 169, 180, 189
Percock, John Ferrant, 58
Petrarch, Francesco, 197
Philippa of Hainaut, queen of England, 1, 3, 16, 42, 59, 67–69, 121, 156, 169, 187, 195, 206, 228

Philippe de Beaumanoir. *See Les coutumes de Beauvaisis*
Philippe de Novare, 186; *Les quatre âges de l'homme*, 179
Philozophie, Lady, in *Joli buisson*, 67, 69–72, 94, 112–13
Pickens, Rupert T., 3, 7–8
Plaidoirie de la rose et de la violette, La, 65, 98, 123–24, 146n.2
Poirion, Daniel, 63, 79n.22, 216n.36
Poitiers, battle of, 9, 58, 238, 240, 241, 243
Prison amoureuse, La, 3, 6, 8, 18, 19, 22, 68, 85, 90–93, 95–98, 99n.13, 102–4, 107, 108–11, 114n.10, 138, 161, 168
Prose *Lancelot*, 4, 9, 53, 106, 160, 179, 181, 183–84, 186, 187, 189; Agravain, 190
Prose *Tristan*, 109, 169, 191
Pseudoautobiography. *See* Autobiography

Quatre âges de l'homme, Les. *See* Philippe de Novare
Queste del Saint Graal, 185, 189, 190

Reconfort de la dame, in *L'espinette amoureuse*, 89
Regimen sanitatis salernitanum, 149n.30
Reverdie, 84, 85
Richard II, king of England, 5, 23–26, 41–48, 59, 99n.3, 170, 171, 200, 221–22, 227–28, 232
Richard de Fournival. *See Le Bestiaire d'amours*
Robert de Namur, 65
Romance, Arthurian, 2, 8, 52, 54–55, 68, 82, 88, 89, 155–60, 165–66, 169
Roman de la dame à la Licorne et du beau chevalier au lion, 172
Roman de la rose, 81, 89, 93, 101, 105; of Jean de Meun, 4, 112–13, 135–36

Salernitan Question, 126–27, 148n.25
Schmolke-Hasselmann, Beate, 155, 169
Scott, Sir Walter: *Old Mortality*, 5, 17–18, 32–35
Shakespeare, William, 24
Shears, F. S., 119
Sherborne, James, 41
Signs, astrological, 66

Socrates, 133–35, 137, 139
Songe du vergier, Le, 124
Sturm-Maddox, Sara, 246

Tablets, wax, 20–21, 37n.17
Tainguy, Raoul, 223, 247n.12
Temple d'honneur, Le, 82–84, 94
Tesnière, M. H., 236
Three Orders, the, 183, 185
Trachsler, Richard, 169
Tucoo-Chala, Pierre, 216n.33, 218nn.49, 50
Tuve, Rosemond, 7, 103, 108, 111
Tyler, Wat, 46–47

Vale, Juliet, 182
Van Coolput, Colette-Anne, 191
Van Latham, Liévin, 225
Varvaro, Alberto, 10, 221–22, 226
Venus, in *Joli buisson de Jonece,* 26–27, 65, 72, 94, 113

Villon, François, 21
Virgin Mary, 64, 65, 75, 76
Voeux du paon, Les, 89
"Voyage en Béarn." *See Chroniques*

Watriquet de Couvin, 163
Wenceslas of Luxembourg, duke of Brabant, 3, 8, 52, 59, 68–69, 79n.20, 91, 97, 110, 121, 138, 141, 142, 169
Whiting, B. J., 119, 147n.12, 175n.18
William, count of Hainaut, 67
Wilmotte, Maurice, 125
Wimsatt, James, 119, 121, 196, 198, 211
Wood, Charles T., 3, 5, 39n.37
Wordsworth, *The Prelude,* 197–98

Ysaÿe le Triste, 169
Yvain, son of Gaston Fébus, 28–32

Zink, Michel, 3, 4, 8, 26, 28, 60n.7, 138, 180, 191, 204, 206, 211, 212, 218n.52